UNCOMMON SENSE

UNCOMMON SENSE

Aesthetics after Marcuse

CRAIG LEONARD

FOREWORD BY NATHIFA GREENE

The MIT Press
Cambridge, Massachusetts
London, England

The MIT Press would like to thank the anonymous peer reviewers who provided comments on drafts of this book. The generous work of academic experts is essential for establishing the authority and quality of our publications. We acknowledge with gratitude the contributions of these otherwise uncredited readers.

This book was set in Adobe Garamond and Berthold Akzidenz Grotesk by Jen Jackowitz. Printed and bound in the United States of America.

Library of Congress Cataloging-in-Publication Data

Names: Leonard, Craig (Professor of art), author. | Greene, Nathifa, writer of foreword.
Title: Uncommon sense : aesthetics after Marcuse / Craig Leonard ; foreword by Nathifa Greene.
Description: Cambridge, Massachusetts : The MIT Press, [2022] | Includes bibliographical references and index.
Identifiers: LCCN 2021049850 | ISBN 9780262544467 (paperback)
Subjects: LCSH: Marcuse, Herbert, 1898–1979. | Aesthetics, Modern—20th century. | Aesthetics—Political aspects. | Philosophy, German—20th century.
Classification: LCC B945.M2984 L435 2022 | DDC 193—dc23/eng/20220423
LC record available at https://lccn.loc.gov/2021049850

10 9 8 7 6 5 4 3 2 1

Contents

Foreword

I am happy I accepted the invitation to write this foreword. There is much to consider, for readers who are primarily interested in Herbert Marcuse, as a sole figure, as well as those who are mainly interested in theories of art or the Frankfurt School. Scholars will find a historically grounded discussion of various aspects of the ideas that Marcuse developed, and implications that link to broader concerns. The interpretations of artistic movements and the meaning of art are careful engagements with Marcuse, as well as his interlocutors in dialectical historical materialism and Frankfurt School critiques of capitalism. But there are also implications that extend further, tracing the analyses of key themes.

I will mention at the outset that I am not an expert in Marcuse, and my research areas are not limited to Frankfurt School critiques of political economy and culture. I do believe that the appeal of this text to scholars whose primary areas of research are related, such as myself, is a strength. I will confess that I become very quickly bored with intense discussions of scholarly arcana, which do have their place; this is just a reference to my scholarly temperament, in William James's sense of the term (and I will leave it to those who prefer arcana more than I do to determine whether Marcuse would be tender- or tough-minded, according to James).

Reading this text, it is easy to imagine how the insights on art in Marcuse could also be helpful to scholars in many fields, and not only to specialists on Marcuse—even as there is much to consider here for those whose theoretical concerns are more narrowly defined. My appreciation for the author's insights on Marcuse in this text stem from our shared interests and many enjoyable conversations about habit, and scholarly analyses of habits in wide-ranging discussions across epistemology, existential phenomenology, and social theory. Although our institutional affiliations are very different, the treatment of habit in defamiliarization, according to Marcuse, is only one indication of the reasons that our conversations are so enjoyable—and reasons that are far less surprising than our institutional affiliations might initially suggest. The implications of these ideas will be of interest to readers whose scholarly concerns may be as narrowly technical as the existential-phenomenological structure of lived experience, or as broad as the questions of dialectical materialist historiography, as well as the more likely interlocutors in Frankfurt School critical theory.

Depending on the interests that a reader brings to this text, certain moments may stand out and create further connections to intellectual lineages, connecting Marcuse in ways that one would expect, as well as links that are more unexpected and thought provoking. *Uncommon Sense* is in the lineage of texts that are more commonly read in Western aesthetic theory, recalling poetics in Plato and Aristotle, as well as the *sensus communis* in Kant's *Critique of Judgment.* Some of these themes may also seem to be unlikely pairings, as in the discussion of habituation in Marcuse alongside Peirce and treatments of habit in American Pragmatism. The treatment of instinct also situates Marcuse in dialogue with interlocutors who may seem unlikely, at first glance, from a cursory sense of where Marcuse might fit in the trajectory of European ideas about art in the twentieth century. Scholars interested in Henri Bergson would note that Marcuse discusses instinct in ways that often recall Bergson. And, although the popularity of Bergson and the extent of the "Bergson boom" before the First World War may be lost on contemporary readers, instinct was a concept that moved from scholarly discourses into everyday language, much like concepts developed by Freud—which may also be understood in European intellectual history as a descendant of Bergsonian instinct.

Freudian interpretations of instinct also suggest how this discussion of Marcuse also links to further themes, which Marcuse did not consider. For example, it is remarkable how psychoanalytic interpretations of drives, and sexual drives in particular, became a proxy for political discussions of violence in the mid-twentieth century, after the Second World War. Leonard suggests an opening onto other ways of interpreting the myopic limitations in Marcuse, treating these as more than simple ethnocentrism. If ethnocentrism is understood as a confinement to European authors, the history of Europe, and Western intellectual traditions, then this problem would be resolved by including more authors, and attention to colonialism beyond Europe. But there is more than the mere inclusion of topics and issues that are linked to race, gender, and colonial forms of difference.

Leonard rejects the misinterpretations of defamiliarization and anti-art that attribute idealism to Marcuse—which is frequently the pathway to discussions of Eurocentric ethnocentrism in Marxist and Hegelian historiography. On this note, Sylvia Wynter—who is cited in this text—is indispensable for further reading. Wynter's essay "On How We Mistook the Map for the Territory" describes how critical analyses of capitalism are often limited, analyzing symptoms or structures instead of the actual problems that need to be addressed. Marcuse's notion of *anti-art* is an example of a critique that mistakes the map for the territory, in Wynter's sense. Marcuse is concerned with the alienating effects of capitalism, the instrumental reduction and use of human beings, and the ideological problems in societies that are formed around capitalist economies and the modern liberal state. Critiques of such concepts and social practices are certainly necessary, as maps. And it remains important to note that Marcuse fails to consider these maps. But mistaking the map for the territory, in Wynter's sense, is much more than a failure to include ideas or examples or authors that should be included.

On one conceptual map, the consolidation of Europe into a distinct geographical and historical "West" is an artifact of the Cold War. But scholars who are mindful of European colonialism would also note the Berlin Africa Conference in 1884–1885, as another significant moment of political integration that unified Europe, across national borders, and the mechanized forms of dehumanization and genocidal violence in colonies, which prefigured the outbreak of war within Europe in 1914 and 1939. The lineage that Wynter identifies as the reclassification of Man—as separate and with dominion over the natural world, and in contrast to human Others—occurred at key moments when the West institutionalized itself into a geocentric center of the universe. Leonard shows how Marcuse is situated in discussions both within and beyond the Frankfurt School, with insights on various themes, including technology, instinct, habituation, and the social dimensions of capitalist political economy. In this way, the nuanced discussions of artistic movements and intellectual lineages beyond those that Marcuse considered, such as Caribbean Surrealism, are more than mere inclusions of non-European texts or traditions. The actual and more fundamental problem is the reclassification of Man in terms that would support settler-colonial rule, to build concepts of Western civilization in terms of a subhuman Other. Therefore, in Wynter's terms, Marcuse is working with a partial and distorted reproduction of a section of the map that has been mistaken for the territory.

What stands out most, for me, is that art is a material practice that remains engaged with materials throughout—art is not a mere chimera, or a relatively unimportant proxy for another aspect of political economy, interchangeable with any other social phenomenon in a superstructure of capitalism. I am writing this introduction on unceded Piscataway land, not a mile from a market where enslaved human beings were bought and sold, and a harbor where human beings would be trafficked further south. From this perspective, the concepts and political structures under scrutiny in dialectical materialism—such as the capitalist notions of market, or property—are very clearly the result of settler colonial dispossession of land, and the flesh and anguish of the violence that is required to transform human beings into a property valuation—the whole human being first, before the later refinement of buying and selling labor, valued in terms of money as markets became more industrialized.

After reading this text, I am left with the sense that there are implications that Marcuse only suggests but could not fulfill, by retaining a sense of the material in social practices, including art, and at every stage in dialectical analyses of epistemic and political structures that situate individual and collective experience. But this is more than a mere demonstration of limits with Marcuse's frame of reference. It is also an invitation to provide more robust interpretations and conceptual tools, as in those that have been developed in radical Black critiques of racial capitalism and anti-colonial movements—as well as the intersections of these—in art and intellectual history.

Nathifa Greene
July 2021

1 ART IN THE ONE-DIMENSIONAL SOCIETY

This book argues for the contemporary relevance of the aesthetic theory of Herbert Marcuse—an original member of the Frankfurt School and outspoken advocate for the New Left[1]—while also identifying and responding to his philosophical limits. I aspire to this end by placing him in dialogue with the remarkable thinking of Sylvia Wynter, whose work formally and conceptually stretches his predominantly European and patrilineal intellectual framework—while still retaining his aesthetic theory's fundamental characteristics—toward a human dimension requiring decolonial, feminist, anti-racist, and counter-poetic perspectives.[2] Both Marcuse and Wynter were influenced by Marxism and Surrealism, placing aesthetics at the center of their sociopolitical philosophies.[3] Where Marcuse was drawn to the European Surrealism led by André Breton, Wynter's approach was informed by the Négritude movement.[4] As such, I believe Wynter's thought offers a critical perspective on Marcuse's aesthetics in a comparable yet contemporary way to what the Négritude movement provided to Surrealism and Marxism in the 1930s. As much as this book is a defense of Marcuse's aesthetics it is also a test of his claims that "art preserves and transcends its class character. And transcends it, not toward a realm of mere fiction and fantasy, but toward a universe of concrete possibilities."[5]

In the first four chapters I analyze Marcuse's primary argument that *art is political* through its refusal to operate according to the repressive rationality that establishes and maintains relationships dictated by advanced capitalism. Such an analysis focuses on several key terms. First, I consider Marcuse's various uses of *anti-art*, which functions as a window into understanding his position on the political character of artistic autonomy. Second, at the center of artistic autonomy (a problematic term that warrants scrutiny) is *defamiliarization*, which is the aesthetic technique that sparks the development of what Marcuse refers to as "radical sensibility"[6]—and what I am calling *uncommon sense*. Third, based on this argument, I reconsider the effects of the art historical category of institutional critique—defined as a range of artistic strategies that bring to light "the tension between the theoretical self-understanding of the institution of art and its actual practice of operation"[7]—by way of a Marcusean form of *instinctual critique* that demonstrates care rooted "in compassion, in our sense for the suffering of others"[8] through its reliance on the defamiliarization of habit.

When Marcuse speaks of the instincts, he implies their manipulation through *habitualization*.[9] This point is significant, since his emphasis on the instincts is the basis for his multilayered aesthetic theory that assembles psychoanalytic, philosophical, economic, and sociological perspectives into a unified critique of what he labels in *One-Dimensional Man* (1965) as *technological rationality*. Marcuse defines this concept not only in terms of its economic framework, which shapes "thought and behavior that develop in the execution of the technological project,"[10] but also with respect to *technē* (technique; skill) in its general association to all forms of human activity. As a result, Marcuse argues that resistance to technological rationality must happen on at least three interconnected fronts: (1) the reorganization of the production process away from human and environmental exploitation; (2) the reshaping of work away from alienation and competition; and (3) the transformation of individual needs away from the capitalistic "gratification that guarantees the repressive reproduction of the commodity world."[11] Broadly speaking, while all three of these requirements fall within economic and political spheres, through the subject of *needs*, the last is centered within the cultural. Nevertheless, whenever Marcuse addresses economic and political crises, he always returns to the importance of the cultural sphere as part of a total program of critical refusal. At the core of his critique of culture, it is the *aesthetic dimension*—the most profound expression of freedom—which serves both as framework and platform for "the subversion of experience and individual consciousness [and for] a radical revolution of the system of needs and gratifications."[12]

THE GREAT REFUSAL REVISITED

On March 8, 1967, Marcuse gave a public lecture at the School of Visual Arts in New York titled "Art in the One-Dimensional Society" (figure 1.1), which was reprinted in *Arts Magazine* in May of the same year.[13] In his lecture, Marcuse alludes to Theodor W. Adorno's assertion that it is impossible to write

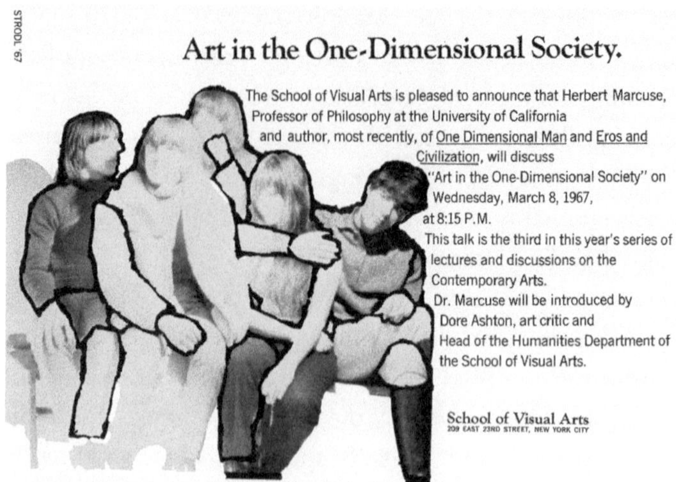

Figure 1.1
"Art in the One-Dimensional Society" (poster), March 8, 1967. Courtesy of School of Visual Arts, New York, NY. © Dan Strodl

poetry after Auschwitz. In a *dialectical* fashion (in contrast to a rhetorical one)[14] Adorno was not stating that poetry can no longer be written, but after the horrors of Auschwitz *not* writing poetry succumbs to its antithesis: barbarism.[15] Marcuse would repeat but expand on Adorno's position in an informal "Letter to the Chicago Surrealists," where he writes: "In the third chapter of *Counterrevolution and Revolt*, I implied an affirmative answer to the question whether after Auschwitz and Vietnam, art is still possible. The ideas and images of liberation still have a home in art, and they are still akin to the aesthetic form of estrangement."[16] Concisely, I replace Marcuse's descriptive phrase "the aesthetic form of estrangement" with a single word: defamiliarization.

The central role that defamiliarization plays in Marcuse's aesthetic theory has been overlooked. For Marcuse, it not only identifies artistic value (that is, art versus anti-art), but also serves as a practical technique that links the aesthetic dimension with the political transformation of the individual, which "can perhaps best be illuminated by discussing the change in the social use of instinctual energy."[17] Accordingly, it is an openness and attention to direct experiences with defamiliarization that transforms an artistic technique into a sociopolitical counter-technique through its subversion of habitualized common sense. As such, the defamiliarizing capacity of art, "which must take a variety of forms,"[18] performs a significant part in resisting the technological rationality that undergirds advanced capitalism through "the active, constitutive role of the senses in shaping reason, that is to say, in shaping the categories under which the world is ordered, experienced, changed."[19] Defamiliarization operates as a "technique of liberation"[20] (to borrow an expression from Drucilla Cornell) by reawakening a latent radical sensibility that is indirectly political through its ability to reimagine the limits imposed by habitualized common sense. In this way, defamiliarization counters repressive facticity[21] by initiating "an awakening (*anamnesis)* of memory, remembrance of things lost, consciousness of what was and what could have been [which] may provide the (artificial) basis for the remembrance of freedom in the totality of oppression."[22] Anamnesis (meaning "to recollect or remember") does not newly create radical sensibility through defamiliarization, but instead is renewed by it.

As a result, aesthetics plays a pivotal role in what Marcuse called "the Great Refusal" by recognizing and subverting the rationalized, one-dimensional common sense that makes radically alternative perspectives seem mistaken or even irrational. Through art's *dynamic autonomy* in relation to the everyday, aesthetics contributes to the Great Refusal by participating in "the desperate struggle to rejuvenate the ailing spirit."[23] Admittedly, autonomy is as fraught a concept as it is reviled by the artistic Left as a historic remnant of bourgeois liberalism.[24] I argue, however, that dynamic autonomy should not be equated with *pure autonomy* understood in terms of a detached and monadic containment, but as alterity in relation to ever-changing sociohistorical conditions. Where pure autonomy refers to a world of objects isolated from society, dynamic autonomy refers to actions, offerings, and relations that are attentively uncommon relative to the social determinations of their emergence. Fundamentally, following Marcuse, "by virtue of its aesthetic form, art is largely autonomous vis-à-vis the given social relations. In its autonomy art both protests these relations, and at the same time transcends them. Thereby art subverts the dominant consciousness, the ordinary experience."[25]

Historically, the source of the term Great Refusal has been attributed to Breton's *The Second Surrealist Manifesto* (1929);[26] however, in *Eros and Civilization* (1955) Marcuse refers to its origin in Alfred North Whitehead's series of lectures *Science and the Modern World* (1926).[27] It is noteworthy that Marcuse references both Breton and Whitehead in successive paragraphs (and Adorno in the paragraph succeeding those) to defend an "uncompromising adherence to the strict truth-value of the imagination [which] comprehends reality more fully."[28] Marcuse's notion of the Great Refusal connects Surrealism's adherence to the ultimate freedom of the imagination to Whitehead's belief in the arbitrariness of rationality. Moreover, his fusion of Breton and Whitehead foregrounds *dialectics*, which offers, in Whitehead's words, "the realm of alternative suggestions, whose foothold in actuality transcends each actual occasion. The real relevance of untrue propositions for each actual occasion is disclosed by art, romance, and by criticism in reference to ideals."[29] These elements—imagination, rationality, and dialectics—buttress Marcuse's aesthetic theory.

It is useful to briefly draw out the connection between Breton and Whitehead. The attribution of the term Great Refusal to Breton is an amalgam of inexact translations of two parallel phrases in *The Second Surrealist Manifesto*. The first is "total revolt" (*la révolte absolue*) as a "tenet of complete insubordination";[30] the second is "utter refusal" (*un refus total*) to accept "the cancer of the mind which consists of thinking all too sadly that certain things 'are,' while others . . . 'are not.'"[31] The characteristics of the "Surrealist attitude" (*l'esprit surréaliste*) model Marcuse's position on the sociopolitical value of artistic refusal, which is reflected in what Breton called the "first article" of Surrealism's charter: "a deliberate will to deal the coup de grace to that which one calls *common sense*."[32] In Whitehead, in comparison, there are two uses of the term (uncapitalized) in separate lectures, although they impart the same intention. One use speaks of the power of poetic abstraction; the other follows the Romantic view of nature as offering a poetic alternative to scientific rationality, depicting rationality's arbitrariness in general and establishing familiarity in opposition to fact. In both cases, Whitehead's "great refusal" is presented as an innate characteristic of rationality itself, which is to argue on the contrary that there are alternative forms of rationality (poetic, scientific, technological, etc.) contradicting a singular and definitive system of truth. Moreover, Whitehead's understanding of aesthetic experience is comparable to Marcuse's in two ways: first, in Whitehead's emphasis of art's reason based on "determinate negation"[33] and, second, in Whitehead's concept of the "actual occasion"[34] of experience with its emphasis on *care*—meaning both concern (to care about) and solicitude (to care for).[35] As Whitehead states, "The occasion as subject has a 'concern' for the object. And the 'concern' at once places the object as a component in the experience of the subject, with an affective tone drawn from this object and directed toward it. With this interpretation, the subject–object relation is the fundamental structure of experience."[36] It is worthy of mention that even though the Marcuse/Whitehead connection is less often cited than Marcuse/Breton, it is no less intriguing, especially due to Whitehead's revived importance through contemporary "speculative realism," which has had significant influence on recent art discourse.[37]

COMMON SENSE, COMMON NEEDS

In *One-Dimensional Man*, Marcuse examines the effects of technological rationality as playing out "on a very material and very real basis, namely on the basis of controlled and satisfied needs that in turn reproduce monopoly capitalism."[38] It is on this point that Marcuse argues that resistance can no longer be defined "simply as economic and political upheaval, as the establishment of a different mode of production and new institutions, but also and above all as a revolution in the prevailing structure of needs and the possibilities for their fulfillment."[39]

Philosopher and educator Charles Reitz shrewdly writes that *One-Dimensional Man* perpetrated something like Bertolt Brecht's alienation effect (*Verfremdungseffekt*) on its readership of the time: "Marcuse's Brechtian discourse . . . models the new sensibility he is seeking to convey. *One-Dimensional Man*, as artwork, puts American audiences off, and opens us up, by exposing this nation's concealed and catastrophic contradictions."[40] Reitz is referring to Brecht's dramatic technique that claimed opposition to Aristotelian theater's *cathartic* "pathos of distance."[41] Challenging the importance of Aristotle's dramatic elements of plot (or action), character, thought (or argument), diction, melody and spectacle,[42] Brecht's *counter*-cathartic, *anti*-Aristotelian theater inverts these elements first by twisting spectacle into banality, then instrumentalizing plot, character, and thought so that the play "no longer in any way allowed [the spectator] to submit to an experience uncritically (and with practical consequences) by means of simple empathy with the characters in a play."[43] Brecht's politically motivated inversion of Aristotelian theater was influenced by the analogous move by Karl Marx to establish historical materialism in turning Hegel's idealist dialectic upside down, "or rather it was placed upon its feet instead of on its head, where it was standing before."[44] In Brecht—as in *One-Dimensional Man*—a constellation is created that connects *estrangement*, *alienation*, and *defamiliarization* in order to challenge dominant common sense.

In Marcusean terms, common sense is established and reinforced through technological rationality's hegemonic self-presentation as objective reality regulated and replicated by our institutions, technologies, and judicial and economic structures such that refutation is made to seem *irrational*.[45] The outcome is that habitualized common sense also manipulates human needs. As such, at the root of Marcuse's analysis, technological rationality's "repressive transformation of the instincts becomes the biological constitution of the organism."[46] To counteract such external imprinting on the individual, Marcuse reiterates that the aesthetic dimension "assumes vital political importance in view of the unprecedented extent of social control perfected by advanced capitalism."[47] This argument is based on two main principles: humans are essentially caring beings and the aesthetic dimension is situated at the intersection of the imagination and critical reason.

Regarding the second of these principles, as Reitz observes, Marcuse is influenced by Brecht's strategy of putting the theatrical audience through a process of counter-cathartic alienation: "the alienation that is necessary to all understanding."[48] Counter-cathartic alienation resists the integrative and rationalized effects of catharsis that maintains repressive common sense. In *One-Dimensional Man*, Marcuse refers to this special form of alienation as "that which denotes man's relation to himself and to his work in capitalist society, the artistic alienation is the conscious transcendence of the alienated existence—a 'higher level' or mediated alienation."[49] First mentioned by Brecht in his "Alienation Effects in Chinese Acting" (1936), the concept of *Verfremdungseffekt* followed through on his earlier writings already referring to the importance of aesthetic strangeness (*befremden*).[50] As John Willett remarked, "This formula itself is a translation of [Viktor] Shklovsky's phrase *priem ostrannenija*, or 'device for making strange' and it can hardly be coincidence that it should have entered Brecht's vocabulary after his Moscow visit [1935]."[51] Brecht reframes Shklovsky's poetic estrangement device (see chapter 3) presented in the latter's essay "Art as Technique" (1917)[52] to become a didactic theatrical one, although Brecht had already been feeling his way toward a notion of strategic self-consciousness through his Hegelian/Marxist use of "alienation" (*Entfremdung*) in the essay "Theatre for Pleasure of Theatre for Instruction" (1935). The second factor regarding fundamental human care is connected to the aesthetic dimension through a practice of attentiveness via the defamiliarization of habit.

HABIT AND RATIONALITY

As a useful counterpoint to Marcuse's argument for the sociopolitical function of alienation in terms of defamiliarization (or aesthetic strangeness), American Pragmatist[53] Charles Sanders Peirce once remarked that there is no "direct profit in going behind common sense—meaning by common sense those ideas and beliefs that man's situation absolutely forces upon him."[54] While not at all dismissing the role of scrutiny (since Peirce advocates the role of doubt and criticizes the closeminded consequences of fixation), the use of common sense, in Pragmatist terms, is meant to serve the purpose of efficaciousness.[55] Peirce argues that common sense has a connection to "concrete reasonableness," which combines "logical integrity with everyday reasoning [such that] reasonableness, made concrete, could be made common, as it would be instantiated in real and in regular patterns of reasoning."[56] Like Marcuse, instincts play a central role for Peirce in connection to common-sense familiarity—not instincts so much in terms of animal urges (where Charles Darwin was careful to add that even there "judgement or reason often comes into play"[57]), but as human *habits* that can be both inherited and developed. As Peirce axiomatically writes: "The whole function of thought is to produce habits of action . . . and for what a thing means is simply what habits it involves."[58] Darwin, whose influence on Pragmatism was fundamental, explicitly links habits and instincts such that "for any habitual action to become inherited . . . then the resemblance between what originally was a habit and an instinct becomes so close as not to be distinguished."[59] This blurring of instincts and habit is what Peirce also emphasizes, when he asserts that "instincts are conscious, determined in some way toward a 'quasi-purpose' [i.e., intention] and capable of being refined by training. . . . This set of features helps us to see how it is that reason can refine common-sense *qua* instinctual response, and how common sense—insofar as it is rooted in instinct—can be capable of refinement at all."[60] As such, since instincts and habits are apt to be indistinguishable, they are equally susceptible to being rationalized, normalized, and naturalized as common sense.[61]

In agreement with Peirce's understanding of the instincts in connection to habit, but in defiance of the primary Pragmatist goal of efficaciousness, Marcuse goes *behind* common sense to locate its life-world causes.[62] In particular, Marcuse investigates how technological rationality "adjusts the rules of thought to the rules of control and domination."[63] In exercising a central tenet of Critical Theory, as first outlined by Max Horkheimer in "Traditional and Critical Theory" (1937), Marcuse examines common sense as yet another form of "the mediation of the factual through the activity of society as a whole."[64] The social research that grounds Critical Theory can be said to continue Marx's inducement of "the reform of consciousness

[that] consists entirely in making the world aware of its own consciousness, in arousing it from its dream of itself, in explaining its own actions to it. . . . In a *single word*: [it is] the self-clarification (critical philosophy) of the struggles and wishes of the age."[65] In this vein, Marcuse seeks the causes of habit and the sources of social behavior (or *ethos*) by analyzing things as they are; to expose what props things up from behind; to attend to prejudices and causes; and to see *beyond* things in the here and now, "for how can we possibly imagine that new relationships between men and things can ever arise if men continue to use the images and to speak the language of repression, exploitation and mystification."[66] For Marcuse, this critical capacity of seeing behind and beyond common sense—which his critics have erroneously reduced to utopianism[67]—connects radical sensibility to the aesthetic transformation of habitualized instincts. Marcuse's analysis of the effects of technological rationality, its hidden causes, and its immanent counterforces foreshadows important works like Edward Said's *Orientalism*, for instance, premised on human identity being "not only not natural and stable, but constructed, and occasionally even invented outright."[68] With an equal emphasis on *action*, the fundamental difference between Peirce's Pragmatism and Marcuse's practical technique of defamiliarization is the former's focus on utilizing common sense and the latter's causal analysis of common sense itself.[69]

RHETORIC AND RATIONALITY

In chapters 5 and 6 of *One-Dimensional Man*, Marcuse names *apophantic logos* as maintaining the habitualizing circularity of technological rationality.[70] This is a logic of judgments "not directly concerned with Being but rather with propositions on Being," which creates "a restriction and a prejudice with respect to the task and scope of logic."[71] The implication of this reorientation, away from dialectical practice toward *rhetorical* persuasion, is that it presents an ideological reality based on arbitrary facticity and convention with "its own logic and its own truth."[72]

In an unpublished text by Marcuse titled "Apophantic Logos. Poetic Language: Language of Negation, Absence, Silence,"[73] he argues that Western society's "universe of discourse," which encompasses and establishes common sense, is caught in a feedback loop of "its own economic and political mechanisms."[74] In this essay, Marcuse examines how technological rationality is upheld by apophantic logos that defines, constructs, and maintains its form (through the language used to describe it) in order to reveal the relative, contextual, and discursive habitualizations that are presented as objective truths. Within a philosophical context, the amorphous concept of *logos* has meant "an organizational principle of the universe" (Heraclitus), "the ability to give an account" (Plato), and, simply, "rationality" (Aristotle). In all these uses, logos interweaves our description of the reality of the world with the language we use to define it, including "words, images, gestures, tones."[75] In its apophantic manifestation, logos has the capability of being a "totalitarian terror that cancels the distinction between subject and object, man and thing, between the universal and the particular."[76] As analyzed in *One-Dimensional Man*, the apophantic logos that props up technological rationality reinforces "social habits of thought" from within "the language of total administration"[77] establishing that *what is familiar is true*. In terms of art, Marcuse argues that apophantic logos has proven to even infiltrate the imagination by diminishing it and bringing it "down from the sublimated realm of the soul or the spirit or the inner man, and translated into operational terms and problems."[78] Where Marcuse defines art in terms of its oppositional relationship with established common sense, anti-art is in harmony with it. (In chapter 2, I show how Marcuse uses the term *anti-art* in ways that are not only harmonic, but dissonant and microphonic.)

Thirty years prior to *One-Dimensional Man*, Marcuse created the template for this critique of the flattening of culture and society in his essay "The Affirmative Character of Culture" (1937). According to this argument, affirmative culture is presented as being operational (much like Peircean efficaciousness) instead of oppositional. It is ironic, on that account, that a critique of technological rationality's apophantic logos finds inadvertent support in an obscure text on scientific and common-sense operationalism.[79] An ambiguous aside by the author Anatol Rapoport links technological rationality with the pseudo-science of Social Darwinism that naturalizes brute competition: "When the predominant view of society still stems from Herbert Spencer's biological metaphor, 'the struggle for existence and the survival of the fittest,' competition appears as a benefit selection process which assures that the best men win. Accordingly, interference with competition appears as interference with the 'natural state of affairs.'"[80] Inherited by both neoliberalism and neoconservatism,[81] we may blame the Social Darwinism of Spencer for the creed of "the survival of the fittest" (which was Spencer's expression, not Charles Darwin's) in his *Principles of Biology* (1864) versus Darwin's proposition in *On the Origin of the Species* (1859) that "the mutual relations of organic beings are the most important."[82] In contrast with Spencer's corrupted version, Marcuse's critique of technological rationality aligns with the overshadowed Darwinian principle that "civilization was characterized by the prevalence of *social instincts* capable of neutralizing the eliminatory aspects of natural selection, and thought that the feeling of *sympathy* was set to be extended indefinitely."[83]

Pierre Dardot and Christian Laval call Spencer's industrialist reading of Darwin's evolutionary theory to corroborate laissez-faire capitalism "a turning point in the history of liberalism."[84] Especially influential in America and significant even in shaping the Pragmatist principle of efficaciousness, Spencer's Social Darwinism "placed a premium upon skill, intelligence, self-control, and the power to adapt through technological innovation, [which] stimulated human advancement and selected the best of each generation for survival."[85] His "scientific" worldview of right and wrong, "uniting under one generalization everything in nature from protozoa to politics,"[86] is founded on the liberal idea of the absence of interference with natural evolution and social progress. Spencer claims: "There cannot be more good done than that of letting social progress go on unhindered; yet an immensity of mischief may be done in the way of disturbing, and distorting and repressing, by policies carried out in pursuit of erroneous conceptions."[87] The function of the state, as a result, is solely "to insure that such freedom is not curbed."[88] As a by-product, Spencerian liberalism set a foundation for a range of right-wing individualist ideologies and white supremacy protectionists where he calls for "a return to natural rights, setting up as an ethical standard the right of every man to do as he pleases, subject only to the condition that he does not infringe upon the equal rights of others."[89] In effect, Spencer misconstrues Darwinism in his "System of Synthetic Philosophy" on a belief in natural self-interestedness, freedom for the powerful, and dogmatic survival of the fittest, which deplores any laws of socialist leaning (which includes caring mutual relations) that support welfare, public education, healthcare, housing regulations, state banking, and the like.[90] At its most basic, Spencer's theory champions a social *and racial* elitism, particularly suited to a business ethic that decries, while failing to take systemic responsibility for, "the artificial [*sic*] preservation of those least able to take care of themselves."[91] To see how deeply engrained this Social Darwinist influence on neoliberal ideology has become, we need look no further than recent U.S. politics where neo-fascist corporate elites sell "civic nationalism"[92] to disenfranchised populists as unveiled racism with the strong whiff of eugenics close behind.

DIALECTICAL AESTHETICS

Despite the significant barriers presented by the apophantic logos that maintains advanced capitalism, Marcuse insists that resistance is still possible: (1) through dialectical or "two-dimensional" *thought*, based on analysis and synthesis; and (2) through *practice* unfamiliar to "the established universe of discourse and action, needs and aspirations."[93] Optimally, the two should not be disentangled in practice, since the first approach cultivates radical consciousness; the second, radical sensibility. Dialectical thought—or more accurately, dialectical *materialist* thought—"retains the two-dimensionality of philosophic thought as critical, negative thinking."[94] Dialectical thought challenges the one-dimensionality of the apophantic logos that "militates against the logic of contradictions" in favor of "modes of thought which sustain the established forms of life and the modes of behavior which reproduce and improve them [by providing] a different logic, a contradicting truth."[95] The second approach refers to the aesthetic dimension that unites critical reason, imagination, and compassion.[96] Where dialectics provides a critical alternative to rhetoric (and apophantic logos), at the center of the aesthetic dimension is the technique of defamiliarization offering resistance to "one-dimensional thought and behavior"[97] through "non-conformistic artistic imagination."[98] In particular, the aesthetic dimension helps "with all its affirmation, work as part of the liberating power of the negative and would help to free the mutilated unconscious and the mutilated consciousness which solidify the repressive Establishment."[99]

Marcuse identifies defamiliarization as the catalyst for aesthetic experience, which offers the direct means of fostering radical sensibility.[100] Defamiliarization is a transformative political technique that in Seyla Benhabib's words "anticipates the radically new and the radically other."[101] Defamiliarization, therefore, demonstrates a freedom that intersects with "the universalization of the political [which] views emancipation as resolving the immanent contradictions of the existing order."[102] As a result, Marcuse's aesthetic theory unifies a socially *normative* vision (i.e., expressing what should be) on the one hand—after Immanuel Kant's pure judgment of taste wherein "the link between the object and human satisfaction is not contingent on who does the judging"[103]—and an individually *transgressive* one on the other—after Friedrich Schiller's adaptation of Kant to propose an aesthetic attitude that contradicts the rationality of dominant norms. Alongside political and economic refusals, Marcuse's emphasis on the aesthetic dimension, with defamiliarization at its center, demonstrates a *marxisant* approach, meaning it is "conversant with Marxism but not adhering to all aspects of the philosophy."[104] This *post*-Marxist shift points to individual transformation (through aesthetics) as an alternative (but also complement) to an awakened working class as the historical agent of social change.[105] At the time of his writing, based on the socioeconomic integration of the working class in the West and its Sovietization in the East, "the moral to be extracted from Marcuse is that Marxism is no longer to be regarded as a body of dogma . . . but instead as a flexible method, open to revision and reorientation over the course of time and with exposure to new socio-cultural conditions."[106]

Gathering these threads, I have emphasized that the technique of defamiliarization is at the core of Marcuse's aesthetics, which is embedded in his "philosophy of praxis," which the philosopher Andrew Feenberg defines as "the form in which the actual contradictions of social life are raised to consciousness under the horizon of the given society."[107] Furthermore, I have claimed that the technique of defamiliarization initiates practical dehabitualization in its development of a receptive capacity to ways of being outside the restrictive rationality of dominant common sense. Defamiliarization, therefore, makes a qualitative change to "primary experience" achieved through "an intensive counter-education" that repels "the instrumentalist rationality of capitalism."[108] In *The Sovereignty of Art*, Christoph Menke echoes this position also through the example of Surrealism's subversive aesthetic practices. In Menke's words: "At the margins of the (surrealist) avant-garde, it becomes clearer that art is not a utopian transcendence of reason, but rather represents a crisis for and a threat to reason . . . a crisis for our functioning discourses."[109] For Marcuse, absent of a (Surrealist) subversion of rationalized thought and behavior, art fails to deliver a defamiliarizing aesthetic experience and becomes a form of anti-art. The implications of this conclusion, as well as complications with the term itself, are addressed in chapter 2.

ANAMNESIS, SILENCE, SOCIAL-BEING

More abstrusely, regarding the premise that defamiliarization brings about a radical sensibility with transformative sociopolitical effects, Marcuse applies the concept of anamnesis, associated mainly with Plato's *Phaedo* (where we have "knowledge of the *eide* [Ideas or Forms] that we could not have acquired through the senses"[110]), in order to claim that the aesthetic dimension is a reawakening of repressed human instincts that embody *Eros*[111]—the life instinct that encompasses love, compassion, and pleasure. Eros is located in the heart (*kardia*)[112] of instinctual care: "For the life instincts are opposed to the aggressive instincts: they contain, in fact, the possibilities and conditions necessary for an improvement of life, for a greater enjoyment of life, and indeed, not against others, but with them."[113] While the Platonic concept of anamnesis entails its more esoteric pre-Socratic meaning of "rebirth,"[114] for Marcuse it would also be associated with the German *Sich erinnern*, meaning to remember or to recollect, which "literally means 'to go into oneself.' That is, in remembering one is *re-membered* or *re-collected* by returning to oneself from a state of externality, dispersion, or alienation."[115] Anamnesis, in other words, is a socially transformative response to capitalistic alienation (as self-estrangement), since "what [the aesthetic dimension] recalls and preserves in memory pertains to the future: images of a gratification that would dissolve the society which suppresses it."[116]

Marcuse further connects anamnesis to *silence* in several senses of the word: as a state rich with latent potential; as a contemplative removal from the noisy effects of the everyday; and as a "medium of communication, the break with the familiar."[117] In his essay "Freedom and Freud's Theory of Instincts," silence is presented as the moment of acknowledging our repressed instincts: "It is as though the free space which the individual has at his disposal for his psychic processes has been greatly narrowed down; it is no longer possible for something like an individual psyche with its own demands and decisions to develop; the space is occupied by public, social forces."[118] In simple terms, silence presents an opportunity to listen, reflect and then act in opposition to dominant ethos. In its multiple meanings, silence provides an opening to indeterminate alternatives through "a return to an 'immediate' art, which responds to, and activates, not only to the intellect and a refined, 'distilled,' restricted sensibility, but also, and primarily, a 'natural' sense experience freed from the requirements of an obsolescent exploitative society. The search is for art forms that express the experience of the body (and the 'soul'), not as vehicles of labor power and resignation, but as vehicles of liberation."[119]

In contrast, noise (also in its literal and metaphoric senses) is susceptible to producing repression through its association with *Thanatos*, "the companion of organized aggression."[120] Paradoxically, within the framework of technological rationality, noise that is normally the unwanted information in a system operates like a rhetorical and apophantic instrument of consent to common sense: an intentional signal of external persuasion.[121] A group of Caribbean and European Surrealists referred to this effect in "Murderous Humanitarianism" (1932) when they castigated the hypocritical, liberal colonialist character who "preaches, doses, vaccinates, assassinates and (from himself) received absolution. With his psalms, his speeches, his guarantees of liberty, equality and fraternity, he seeks to drown out the noise of his machine-guns."[122] Marcuse referred to this specious process as *repressive desublimation*, where Thanatos is held up harmoniously through an administrative form of catharsis, "the reinstatement of harmony by administrative decree, the banning of [critical] dissonance, discord, and atonality, [where] the cognitive function of art is 'brought in line.'"[123] What is cathartically produced and reproduced through technological rationality is "the ability to forget [as] the mental faculty which sustains submissiveness and renunciation."[124] Effectively, technological rationality's paradoxically harmonious noise displaces the instincts' true imaginative, erotic, and compassionate source in care as the "starting point [*arche*] of life, movement, and sensation."[125]

Returning to anamnesis, and anticipating its dismissal as a remnant of philosophical esotericism, Marcuse legitimizes it as the leitmotif of the dialectical method, which always contains within each synthesis the recollection (anamnesis) of past positions.[126] Adorno offers a similar association, in the context of his "negative dialectics," that every dialectical synthesis or "act of identification does violence to every single concept in the process. And the negation of the negation is in fact nothing other than the anamnesis, the recollection, of that violence."[127] On the actuality of anamnesis, Marcuse summarizes his reasoning in *One-Dimensional Man*:

> The Marxian vision recaptures the ancient theory of knowledge as *recollection*. . . . Recollection [*anamnesis*] thus is not remembrance of a Golden Past (which never existed), of childhood innocence, primitive man, et cetera. Recollection as epistemological faculty rather is synthesis, reassembling the bits and fragments which can be found in the distorted humanity and distorted nature. This recollected material has become the domain of the imagination, it has been sanctioned by the repressive societies in art, and as "poetic truth"—poetic truth only, and therefore not much good in the actual transformation of society. . . . They are given rather as the *horizon* of experience under which the immediately given forms of things appear as "negative," as denial of their inherent possibilities, their truth. But in this sense, they are "innate" in man as *historical* being; they are themselves historical because the possibilities of liberation are always and everywhere historical possibilities. Imagination, *as knowledge*, retains the insoluble tension between idea and reality, the potential and the actual.[128]

The placement of anamnesis within this framework of historical and dialectical materialism allows Marcuse to adapt it to the specific Marxian context of social-being (*gesellschaftlichen*

Menschen) which says we are collectively re-membered through liberated instincts realized intersubjectively as nonalienated social-being where "in his *consciousness of species* man confirms his real *social life*."[129] For Marx, the concept of social-being, actualized in ideal form through communism "as the positive transcendence of private property as *human self-estrangement*, and therefore as the real appropriation of the *human* essence by and for man"[130] is a transformation of Ludwig Feuerbach's species-being (*Gattungswesen*) where "the reflecting individual carries the consciousness of the species within himself."[131] Marcuse argues that this "socio-ontological"[132] application of anamnesis is ultimately a *bio-ontological* one—where the preconditions for liberation manifesting in individual needs are repressed and manipulated through external influence, then reinforced through habit. Hence, Marcuse believes that an aesthetic experience, defined as an encounter with defamiliarization, can recollect our essence of social-being. For Marcuse, social critique must also include a (Freudian) instinctual level, not just a (Marxian) sociohistorical one, since "the economic and political incorporation of the individuals into the hierarchical system of labor is accompanied by an instinctual process in which the human objects of domination reproduce their own oppression."[133] Marcuse points to technological rationality's influence even over the unconscious—foreshadowing his critique of Surrealism's tendency to fetishize psychic automatism (*automatisme psychique*)—which left unacknowledged results in an internal "psychic Thermidorian"[134] tendency toward self-defeat, "a dynamic at work that internally negates possible liberation and gratification and that supports external forces of denial."[135]

Drawing upon Peirce's fellow (though famously adversarial) Pragmatist William James to compare Marcuse's practical sense of habitualized instincts, he declared that "habit diminishes the conscious attention with which our acts are performed."[136] This Jamesian principle connects the degree of attentiveness to the strength of habit alongside a second principle that recognizes that habit decreases behavioral and cognitive friction, since "habit simplifies the movements required to achieve a given result, mak[ing] them more accurate and diminishes fatigue."[137] Humans, according to James, possess a *plasticity* that is constituted by "a structure weak enough to yield to an influence, but strong enough not to yield all at once." That being so, plasticity is related to habit formation and conservation where "each relatively stable phase of equilibrium in such a structure is marked by what we may call a new set of habits."[138] James' idea of plasticity becomes a historical and sociopolitical factor in his argument for the "ethical implications of the law of habit." In its formation and conservation of behavior, the so-called law of habit is "the enormous fly-wheel of society, its most precious conservative agent."[139] As an instrument to maintain the status quo:

> It alone is what keeps us all within the bounds of ordinance, and saves the children of fortune from the envious uprisings of the poor. It alone prevents the hardest and most repulsive walks of life from being deserted by those brought up to tread therein. It keeps the fisherman and the deck-hand at sea through the winter; it holds the miner in his darkness, and nails the countryman to his log-cabin and his lonely farm through all the months of snow; it protects us from invasion by the natives of

> the desert and the frozen zone. It dooms us all to fight out the battle of life upon the lines of our nurture or our early choice, and to make the best of a pursuit that disagrees, because there is no other for which we are fitted, and it is too late to begin again. It keeps different social strata from mixing.[140]

Where James underscores the historically *conservative* significance of the law of habit, in contrast, Marcuse identifies the habitualized instincts as the site of *revolutionary* potential (just as he sees redirected operationalism as producing new forms of social cohesion).[141] For that reason, it is important to linger on some relevant concepts of history, since the distinctions between historicism, historicity, and historical materialism are significant in the way Marcuse sees how plasticity of the instincts practically affects social transformation. Where history, in general, is an account of the events and characters of the past, *historicism* holds that a retrospective interpretation of the past allows more objective insight than the past's direct experience. Among the many versions of historicism—from Aristotle's *On Interpretation* to Hans Georg Gadamer's *Truth and Method*—Wilhelm Dilthey's hermeneutic critique of scientific reason (which was an influence on and later target of criticism by Martin Heidegger) proposed that a poetics of historical interpretation was able to represent human experience more fully allowing for a better determination of the future. Heideggerian *historicity*, in comparison, is particular to its existential treatment in *Being and Time*, where he presents the proper interpretation of history in connection to "authentic" Being (*Dasein*).[142] Heidegger uses the hermeneutics of historicism to revise the past to fit an "unconcealment"[143] of an authentic present and to unfold this interpretation into the future.

Heideggerian historicity, therefore, is a metaphysics of Being that applies ontology to destiny: a "process of happening as a form of motility."[144]

In comparison, influenced by the historicist tradition that claims a scientific (not poetic) application, Marxist *historical materialism* is an analysis of the relations of production in the context of their implicit and explicit socioeconomic causes. Historical materialism "recognizes that the ostensible and also the really operating motives of men . . . are by no means the causes of historical events, that behind these motives are other motives, which have to be discovered from outside, from out of philosophical ideology, into history."[145] In Engels's words, as the inverse of Hegelian idealism, historical materialism contends that "matter is not a product of mind, but mind itself is merely the highest product of matter."[146] This position is a development from the "old materialism" (says Engels of Feuerbach) that remains essentially idealist in its moralistically pragmatic judgment of "everything according to the motives of the action."[147] Regarding human activity this view only provides a superficial picture, which "takes the ideal driving forces which operate there as ultimate causes."[148] In contrast, the "new materialism" (of Marx and Engels) investigates the external forces behind human will to find "what are the driving forces of these driving forces."[149] Historical materialism, moreover, is a rejection of the (Hegelian) idealist means to the obtainment of truth—which impossibly requires "an absolute break with sensuous consciousness"[150]—in favor of identifying, in Engels's words, "the driving forces which—consciously or unconsciously, and indeed very often unconsciously—lie behind the motives of men in their historical actions and which constitute the real ultimate driving forces of history."[151] From the historical materialist standpoint, Hegel's blind spot was his failure to acknowledge his own self-consciousness (*Selbstbewußtsein*) as also including sensuous consciousness (as a *body* in specific circumstances).[152]

Ultimately, a conflation of these poetic and philosophical views of history—comprised of Heideggerian historicism and Marxist historical materialism—form Marcuse's position that "a qualitative change must occur . . . in the infrastructure of man (itself a dimension of the infrastructure of society)."[153] The consequence is that Marcuse's idea of history is a fusion of approaches that share a "method of continuous and radical concretion . . . able to grasp appropriately the historicity of human existence."[154] As Richard Wolin and John Abromeit write in their introduction to *Heideggerian Marxism*: "In Marcuse's view it seemed clear that 'historicity' represented the essential link between existentialism and historical materialism."[155] Nevertheless, Marcuse's conflated concept of history retains the problem of Heideggerian historicist grasping of Being over the lived history of beings.[156] The result is that if not well grounded in a historical materialist consciousness and lived bodily experience, historicity's overreaching conclusions, as evidenced by Heidegger's heinous and unapologetic embrace of Nazism, based on ontological pretentions, are just a "specious metaphysical obfuscation."[157]

PRACTICAL AESTHETICS

In part, I believe Marcuse's conflated notion of history was a factor in his inability to communicate his aesthetic theory persuasively. Where Marcuse advocated that "we have to direct our attention to the historical character of art . . . art as such, not only its various styles and forms, [but as] a historical phenomenon,"[158] in his 1967 lecture at the School of Visual Arts, he confusingly shifts away from art emerging from within concrete historical circumstances to abstract notions of aesthetic form.[159] Despite what members of his SVA audience would have accepted as *One-Dimensional Man*'s effective means of articulating "what young radicals felt was wrong with society,"[160] his lecture tends toward the use of abstract historicist terms, compromising the practical aesthetic technique of defamiliarization. As a result, Marcuse's SVA lecture was seen to have failed on the levels of applicability and relevance. Not only did Marcuse seem to ambiguously endorse *and* condemn anti-art, but also he defaults to speaking of art "mutatis mutandis"[161] instead of with specific reference to any of the contemporary practices that were characteristic of artistic radicality. As a result, Marcuse turns his SVA audience off. From the perspective of the artistic avant-garde, his reliance on historicity was dismissed for what was received as an anachronistic Eurocentrism and an abstract perspective on art production, instead of the real struggle of artists within their existing environments.[162] For instance, as recalled by Fluxus artist Henry Flynt, Ben Morea (the founder of the anarchist art "street gang with analysis" Black Mask) aggressively challenged Marcuse during the question period after the SVA lecture with criticisms of the philosopher's ineffectual aesthetic theory removed from actual pressing sociopolitical concerns.[163]

In order to defend the practical elements of Marcuse's aesthetics via defamiliarization it is necessary to address not only the unfair assessments of anachronism and irrationalism by his art world critics (see "Coda: Misreading Marcuse's Aesthetics"), but also the inaccurate conclusions by his political adherents who downplayed or dismissed his position regarding the practical effects of aesthetic transformation. As first principle—it must be stressed—Marcuse's application of the aesthetic dimension to political action is one that he insisted is *limited.* Unequivocally, Marcuse asserts that beyond art's ability to reconnect with repressed Eros—the "libidinal energy, in struggle with aggressive energy, striving for the intensification, gratification, and unification of life and the life environment"[164]—the political responsibility of the artist *as artist* ends.

> Art can do nothing to prevent the ascent of barbarism—it cannot by itself keep open its own domain in and against society. For its own preservation and development, art depends on the struggle for the abolition of the social system which generates barbarism as its own potential stage: potential form of its progress. The fate of art remains linked to that of the revolution. In this sense, it is indeed an internal exigency of art which drives the artist to the streets—to fight for the Commune, for the Bolshevist revolution, for the German revolution of 1918, for the Chinese and Cuban revolutions, for all revolutions which have the historical chance of liberation. But in doing so he leaves the universe of art and enters the larger universe of which art remains an antagonist part: that of radical practice.[165]

This position is central to Marcuse's aesthetics, which is central to his politics, so it must be repeated: The radical, antagonistic, *internal exigency* of art prepares the artist for direct action beyond art. While similar to Adorno's position that "all that [the artist] is able to do, and perhaps on the verge of despair, is contradict the enchained society through unchained art,"[166] Marcuse argues in practical terms that "the rest is not up to the artist. The realization, the real change which would free men and things, remains the task of political action; the artist participates not as artist."[167] On the surface, this may seem paradoxical, especially considering Marcuse's reputation for endorsing the New Left's credo: "From moral outrage to radical vision."[168] The foundation of Marcuse's position on the relationship between aesthetics and political praxis, however, is consistent and clear: the aesthetic dimension is *potentially* political through its ability to open up and radicalize our sensibility and attentiveness. Summarized in "Art in the One-Dimensional Society," he writes: "Art discovers that there are *things*; things and not mere fragments and parts of matter to be handled and used up arbitrarily, but 'things in themselves'; things which 'want' something, which suffer, and which lend themselves to the domain of Form, that is to say, things that are inherently 'aesthetic.' Thus art discovers and liberates the domain of sensuous Form, the pleasure of sensibility, as against the false, the formless and the ugly in perception which is repressive of the truth and power of sensibility."[169]

AESTHETICS AS ANALOGOUS POLITICS?

Even though Marcuse's SVA lecture tends toward historicity with detrimental results, it is equally indicative of his fundamental belief in the general socio- and bio-ontological effects that the aesthetic dimension has on instinctual transformation.

Despite this fact, Marcuse's SVA audience was left with the impression that his aesthetic theory was a reiteration of Romantic irrationalities and platitudes (such as "freedom of appearance is one with beauty")[170] that resulted in only impractically *analogous* associations between art and politics. I argue this is incorrect based on his advocacy for the *technique* of defamiliarization (which is also overlooked in Schiller).[171] Marcuse's association with Romanticism—beyond Marcuse's admiration of Schiller or through his own droll self-confession as "an absolutely incurable and sentimental romantic"[172]—is true however in the specific sense of his adherence to artistic alienation as something intentionally incompatible with the established social order. Similar criticisms of Whitehead for philosophical "irrationalism" (in particular, by the philosopher and neoliberal proponent Karl Popper)[173] and Breton for aesthetico-political "irrationalism" (by the French Communist Party)[174] are also directed at Marcuse for his "irrational" aesthetics that are seen as relying on a merely analogous connection between art and politics, instead of a practical and realistic one.

At root, these criticisms stem from a deeply embedded belief that art is categorically separate from politics and any claims to the contrary can only be excusable through analogy. This antagonism is established in the history of European aesthetics—established in Alexander Gottlieb Baumgarten's *Aesthetica* (1750–1758)—that separates art and the everyday according to formal, technical, and experiential limits. For Baumgarten, aesthetics is "the science of knowing the beautiful" (which was to be established separately alongside *logic*), yet with his novel contribution that "beauty no longer resided in the object contemplated but in the mind of the observer."[175]

Baumgarten further separates aesthetics from ethics because the former relies on uncertainty arrived at through emotions and sensations instead of the precise concepts of reason. Pithily, for Baumgarten, a poem's separation from everyday uncertainty is captured in his phrase *oratio perfecta sensitive*: "sensuously complete speech." Kant's *Critique of Judgment* and Schiller's *On the Aesthetic Education of Man* thereafter take up Baumgarten's categorical separations to reestablish a relationship between reason (in which logic is only one part) and sensibility (aesthetics) mediated by a new ethics of the beautiful (which encompasses "plenitude, magnitude, truth, clarity, certitude and a lively movement or living power of cognition and 'unity within diversity' in the work of art"[176]) only able to *analogously* relate to everyday experience. Founded on Baumgarten's original arguments, Schiller amplifies the relationship between aesthetics and analogous politics in his second equation of beauty with freedom, where "the idea of moral beauty is essentially metaphoric, based upon but not reducible to physical beauty."[177] Due to this metaphorical oversight, it is evident why Marcuse favors the mediating role that Schiller gives to aesthetics to unite reason (concerning the limits of thought) and the senses (concerning the limits of perception).[178] As applied by Marcuse, the capacity of Schiller's mediating aesthetics to both form and transform habit seems surprisingly pragmatic and material.[179] A crucial passage in Schiller's "Twentieth Letter" in *On the Aesthetic Education of Man* reinforces this assessment: "The mind passes from sensation to thought through a middle disposition in which sensuousness and reason cancel each other out [*gegenseitig aufheben*]. This middle disposition, in which our nature is constrained neither physically nor morally and yet is active in both ways, preeminently deserves to be called a free disposition; and if we call the condition of sensuous determination the physical, and that of rational determination the logical and moral, we must call this condition of real and active determinacy the *aesthetic*."[180] From the outset, however, the argument of analogy—which claims that "the moral and aesthetic realms *seem to be like* one another, or that sensible movements *appear* to be manifestations of freedom"[181] only because one believes oneself to be free via a tenuous "aesthetic attitude to the existing world"[182]—has restricted discussions on the actual and practical effects of artistic defamiliarization.[183] Indeed, Marcuse extracts from Schiller his remorse over the loss of a human communal spirit,[184] and emphasizes that the production of radical sensibility via the technique of defamiliarization leads back toward "a vital, biological drive for liberation, and with a consciousness capable of breaking through the material as well as ideological veil of the affluent society."[185]

Based on perceived metaphoric overreach,[186] critics have remained skeptical about Marcuse's claim for the sociopolitical effects of the aesthetic dimension viewing it as a category mistake. Where Marcuse argues that radical sensibility can "show the way back to a unified and total humanity,"[187] his critics insist this way back from aesthetics to the everyday is politically ineffective reserved as it is to mere analogy. Andrew Feenberg, for instance, argues: "This attempt to employ a non-formalistic intuitive understanding modeled on aesthetic principles is unsuccessful. Outside the sphere of actual artistic production, it ceases to be a true subject of practice."[188] Further, Feenberg argues that the aesthetic dimension limits the "'action' of the subject . . . to yet another form of contemplation, not calculating reason, but aesthetic appreciation."[189] For Feenberg, this insolubility is due to the fact that "artistic practice . . . fails because it has so little impact on the social world that is founding for it."[190] Charles Reitz offers a similarly skeptical critique of the actual social effectiveness of aesthetics by stressing Marcuse's "catastrophic pseudodialectic of art and life" that "admits only of a polar reciprocity or circularity; hence, the sweeping oscillation between the art-against-alienation thesis and the art-as-alienation position."[191] Feenberg and Reitz's views of the dubious practical effects of the aesthetic dimension echo the earlier dismissals of the Marxist critic Paul Mattick whose critique of Marcuse continued to rely heavily on a revolutionary "labor metaphysic" (as C. Wright Mills phrased it in "Letter to the New Left")[192] initiated by the disaffected working class.[193] Although sharing Marcuse's fight for the attainment of a "human society"[194]—that is, wanting the end of repressive capitalist values[195]—Mattick, Feenberg, and Reitz doubt any actual intersection of aesthetics and politics. Martin Jay, though critical of Marcuse's "totalizing notion of the 'Great Refusal' as a kind of aesthetic metapolitics,"[196] comes closer to capturing Marcuse's vision "between the aesthetic and practical spheres . . . as a noncolonizing interpenetration that may be re-established on the level of everyday experience."[197]

The partial though significant influence of Schiller on Marcuse has marked him as a Schillerean on the whole. The criticism of Marcuse for committing the same category mistake as Schiller is unwarranted, since Marcuse's aesthetic theory fundamentally does *not* connect "the moral and aesthetic realms, the noumenal and phenomenal domains, simply in virtue of an analogy, or purely on the basis of metaphor."[198]

On the contrary, Marcuse argues that art has a *practical* relationship to politics through defamiliarization's offering an antagonistic "counterimage of what occurs in social reality"[199] to produce indirect and indeterminate—which is not the same as analogous—effects on praxis. This practical link through defamiliarization confronts "dehumanization at the place of entrance, there where the false consciousness takes form (or rather: is systematically formed) [by] stopping the words and images which feed this consciousness."[200]

2 PARADIGMS OF ANTI-ART

In "Art in the One-Dimensional Society," Marcuse uses the term *anti-art* in various ways that have caused a range of critical misinterpretations. His application of the term is not singular, but *dialectical* and refers to: (1) *non-art* and (2) *art from art*. A focus on the prefix "anti-" in anti-art has caused his critics to emphasize negativity as falsity, pessimism, and censure (in the first sense) over negation in terms of avant-gardist succession (in the second sense). In order to present anti-art in Marcuse's full use, I perform a stereophonic reading inspired by Albrecht Wellmer's "stereoscopic" analysis of Adorno and Horkheimer's *Dialectic of Enlightenment*, "which would restore a latent three-dimensional image out of a manifest two-dimensional one."[1] To this end, I examine Marcuse's use of two contrasting anti-art paradigms—the harmonic (non-art) and the dissonant (art from art)—plus his indication of a third unified paradigm—the microphonic—which emerges from within his dialectical framework.

THE HARMONIC PARADIGM

> Not disintegration but reproduction and integration of that which is, is the catastrophe.
> —Herbert Marcuse, *The Aesthetic Dimension* (1978)

The *harmonic paradigm* of anti-art uses familiar language to present an ideological position. In this way, it is reactionary.[2] Despite its intentions of political dissent, its mode of representation "has fallen prey to the process of integration."[3] Consequently, harmonic anti-art undermines art's dynamic autonomy and forfeits its aesthetic transformation of the instincts. In Marcuse's words: "The more immediately political the work of art, the more it reduces the power of estrangement and the radical, transcendent goals of change."[4] In defense of this principle, he adds: "The artist's desperate efforts to make art a direct expression of life cannot overcome the separation of art from life. . . . Nor can these differences be bridged by simply letting things happen (noises, movements, chitchat, etc.) and incorporating them, unaltered, into a definite 'frame' (e.g., a concert hall, a book). The *immediacy* thus expressed is false inasmuch as it results from a mere abstraction from the real-life context which establishes this immediacy."[5]

As such, does Marcuse's disapproval of harmonic anti-art not contradict his endorsement of direct political action? Does this contradiction not seem as philosophically irreconcilable now as it was vexing to his 1967 SVA audience of artists and activists? On what grounds does Marcuse base his criticism of directly political anti-art that *mimics* political action as being "consciously and methodically destructive, disorderly, negative, and nonsensical"?[6] Moreover, is it not ironic that harmonic anti-art was practiced by some of the most vocal adherents in the arts to his sociopolitical analyses? While applicable to the theatrical activism of collectives from the 1960s like Black Mask, Guerrilla Art Action Group, and Up Against the Wall Motherfucker (with the slogan "Armed Love"),[7] Marcuse's archetype for harmonic anti-art was The Living Theatre, a long-running, overtly political nomadic anarchist theater group, influenced by Vsevolod Meyerhold, Erwin Piscator, Antonin Artaud, Bertolt Brecht, Jerzy Grotowski, and Joseph Chaikin[8] (figure 2.1). While Marcuse rejects harmonic anti-art on *formal* grounds because it does not assert "the degree of autonomy

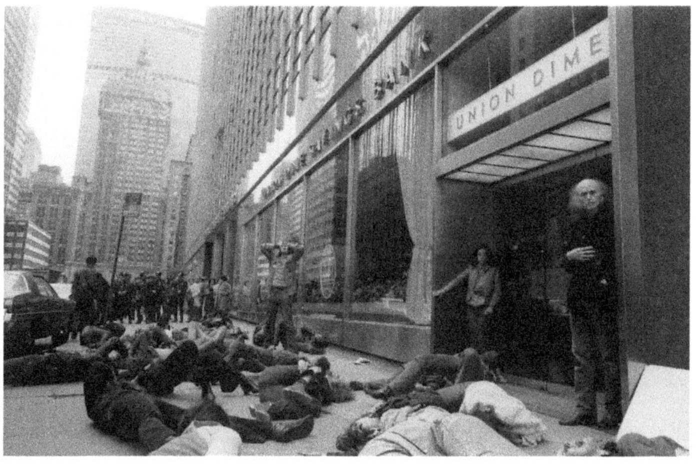

Figure 2.1
Anti-war demonstration, The Living Theatre performs the Plague scene from "Mysteries" on Park Avenue in New York City, May 10, 1972. Gianfranco Mantegna Papers, D-191, Special Collections, UC Davis Library. *Photo credit:* Gianfranco Mantegna

which withdraws art from the mystifying power of the given and frees it for the power of its own truth . . . represented only in an *estranging* form,"[9] he was explicit about his sympathy for its anti-establishment *political* objectives, confessing (in response here to The Living Theatre) that his "criticism is fraternal, since we share the same struggle."[10]

Julian Beck, a founding member of The Living Theatre with Judith Malina, describes the group's approach in the following way: "I hold up the mirror till my arms ache. It falls on the heads of the spectators, leaving them bleeding and marred. Or it does nothing. I hold up a mirror which is only a crumbling ikon of shit, and I am buried under it. A mound of dung upon the stage where no man ought to look. A unique life of nothing."[11] The Living Theatre views guerrilla theater as the means to change culture by changing perception "so that the usefulness of the revolution can be comprehended."[12] This is captured in their central tenet that "the essential trip is the voyage from the many to the one."[13]

In contrast, Marcuse's vision is the inverse: the voyage is from the one to the many. He argues that "the guerrilla theatre of today, The Living Theatre, may serve as an example of self-defeating purpose,"[14] since harmonic anti-art relinquishes art's defamiliarizing effects "to a degree to which it makes itself part of real life, it loses the transcendence which opposes art to the established order—it remains immanent in this order, one-dimensional, and thus succumbs to this order. Precisely its immediate 'life quality' is the undoing of this anti-art and of its appeal. It moves (literally and figuratively) here and now, within the existing universe, and it terminates in the frustrated outcry for its abrogation."[15] By mimicking the everyday, The

Living Theatre sacrifices defamiliarization through its immediacy of purpose and its integration into the established view of reality. Marcuse's criticism of harmonic anti-art, therefore, recalls how a dynamically autonomous aesthetic dimension *indirectly* overflows into the everyday through a recalibration of instinctual energy (figure 2.2).

Through this process, the aesthetic dimension is "transcendent in a sense which distinguishes and divorces it from any 'daily' reality we can possibly envisage."[16] Instinctual transformation is achieved through art's dynamic autonomy wherein "the artistic alienation makes the work of art, the universe of

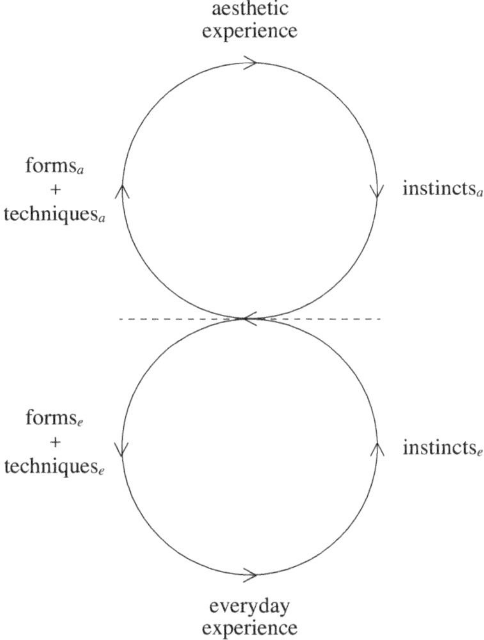

Figure 2.2
The energetic overflow of the instincts

art, essentially unreal—it creates a world which does not exist, a world of *Schein*, semblance, appearance, illusion. But in this transformation of reality into illusion, and only in it, appears the subversive truth of art. In this universe, every word, every color, every sound is 'new,' different—breaking the familiar context of perception and understanding, of sense certainty and reason in which men and nature are enclosed."[17]

A comparison between Beck's manifesto "The Seven Imperatives of Contemporary Theatre"[18] and Marcuse's aesthetic dimension and the characteristics of radical sensibility reflects their points of overlap (or solidarity) and divergence (figure 2.3). Points (*iii–vi*), which are connected to aspects of Eros, mainly find equivalents in both The Living Theatre and Marcuse: participation, play, and bodily freedom. Point (*v*), however, separates The Living Theatre's emphasis on sexuality, which is "a partial drive, libidinal energy confined and concentrated in the erotogenic zones of the body,"[19] from Marcuse's emphasis on Eros as total "libidinal energy, in the struggle with

	The Living Theatre's "Seven Imperatives of Contemporary Theatre"	**Marcuse's aesthetic dimension and radical sensibility**
i	In the streets	Defamiliarization not integration
ii	Free; Accessible	Non-conformist
iii	Open participation	Methexis; Counter-catharsis
iv	Spontaneous creation	Play instinct (*Spieltrieb*)
v	Physical life; Bodily (sexual) liberation	Eros; Care; Life instinct (*Liebestrieb*)
vi	Increase of conscious awareness	Non-repressive sublimation
vii	Theater as action; Art as direct politics	Dynamic autonomy; Art as indirect politics

Figure 2.3

A comparison of the aesthetic principles of The Living Theatre to those of Herbert Marcuse

aggressive energy, striving for the intensification, gratification, and unification of life and the life environment."[20] In relation to aesthetic *form*, points (*i*), (*ii*), and (*vii*) reveal Marcuse's main disagreements with harmonic anti-art. Specifically (*i–ii*): The Living Theatre desires to bring theater to the streets while Marcuse requires that revolutionary praxis "in the streets" take place not as artist but *after* the aesthetic transformation of the instincts. While (*vii*), regarding political practice, the immediacy of The Living Theatre's "acting as action" or "politics as art" tends toward imitative politics. For Marcuse, art is indirectly political by its conscious and mediated subversion of common sense, through its dynamic autonomy, such that "art by itself in its own inner process and procedure tends toward the political dimension, without giving up the form of art itself."[21] The harmonic anti-art of The Living Theatre, in contrast, *reproduces* common sense.

Where the (anti-) artistic strategy of The Living Theatre is the performance of direct politics, Marcuse's aesthetic dimension envisions art as a form of politics that is preparatory. The aesthetic dimension affects political activity as afterimage, as an energetic overflow into practices that embody Eros and social-being.[22] In Marcuse's words: "The liberated consciousness would promote the development of a science and technology free to discover and realize the possibilities of things and men in the protection and gratification of life, playing with the potentialities of form and matter for the attainment of this goal."[23] Along with such a qualitatively transformed reality, in which the everyday intersects with the aesthetic dimension, there would coincide the end of technological rationality. It would be the age of the "new type of man" formed with a new "biological need in a new system of life . . . [and] a construction of a qualitatively new environment, technical and natural, by an essentially new type of human being."[24] Art would have fulfilled its political function, "not as 'political art', not politics as art," but as a *catalyst* of radical sensibility that translates to building (not just modeling[25]) the "architecture of a free society."[26] Similarly, the ideal society for Marx could exist only after the overcoming of false consciousness and only then could one realize the essential freedom encapsulated in the maxim: "From each according to his ability, to each according to his needs."[27] Prior to this, humanity must struggle, in Marxian terms, through its prehistory, which is "the history of man prior to his liberation in a free society."[28] For Marcuse, the preponderance of harmonic anti-art is indicative at best of the ongoing need for societal change.

In "Art in the One-Dimensional Society," Marcuse asks, how can harmonic anti-art subvert the rationality of the everyday if it is using the same language as the everyday? Harmonic anti-art demonstrates an anti-aesthetic self-defeat where its apophantic form has blurred the boundaries of art and the everyday without a defamiliarizing effect.[29] Harmonic anti-art, therefore, operates undialectically, in the same way Adorno famously critiques "committed" art that "even when politically radical, already contains an accommodation to the world."[30] Adorno's critique of committed art is a response to Jean-Paul Sartre's "For Whom Does One Write?" In this essay, Sartre defines the committed artist as one who "tries to achieve the most lucid and the most complete consciousness of being embarked, that is, when he causes the commitment of immediate spontaneity to advance, for himself and others, to the reflective. The writer is, par excellence, a mediator and his commitment is mediation."[31] Sartre presents committed literature as delivering a *direct* judgment on current social issues through a literary form that aims to explicitly stimulate the reader to action while not sacrificing the novel's artistic merit. In *Aesthetic Theory*, Adorno challenges Sartre's confident proclamation of effectively performing both goals by arguing that "artworks are, as synthesis, analogous to judgement; in artworks, however, synthesis does not result in judgement; of no artwork is it possible to determine its judgement or what its so-called message is. It is therefore questionable whether artworks can possibly be *engagé* [committed], even when they emphasize their engagement. What works amount to, that in which they are unified, cannot be formulated as a judgment, not even as on that they state in words and sentences."[32] Committed art, according to Adorno, is victim to its didactic form: "All commitment to the world has to be canceled if the idea of the committed work of art is to be fulfilled . . . proclaimed commitment only subjugates art from the outside, hence only illusorily."[33]

Influenced by both Sartrean commitment and Adorno's critique of it, Marcuse views the dynamically autonomous artwork as a revolt of the instincts.[34] Marcuse expands on Adorno's critique of committed art to reflect the bio-ontological associations in habit and instinct where "the political 'engagement' [commitment] becomes a problem of artistic 'technique,' and instead of translating art (poetry) into reality, reality is translated into a new aesthetic form. The radical refusal, the protest, appears in the way in which words are grouped and regrouped, freed from their familiar use and abuse. *Alchemy of the word*; the image, the sound, creation of another reality out of the existing one—permanent imaginary revolution, emergence of a 'second history' within the historical continuum."[35] According to Marcuse, therefore, harmonic anti-art's use of familiar forms and techniques reifies dominant rationality instead of subverting it. As explicit commitment, it reproduces the everyday, instead of offering "a new language of different components and an unfamiliar grammar."[36] In sum, harmonic anti-art mimics praxis, which both sabotages the potential of dynamically autonomous art and the politics that harmonic anti-art wishes to realize.[37]

THE DISSONANT PARADIGM

> A successful work . . . is not one which resolves objective contradictions in a spurious harmony, but one which expresses the idea of harmony negatively by embodying the contradictions, pure and uncompromised in its innermost structure.
>
> —Theodor Adorno, *Prisms* (1967)

The *dissonant paradigm* of anti-art is the antithesis of the harmonic paradigm. Philosophically underscored by Hegel's "negation of negation" as the "acting (and, indeed, the knowing-acting) ego that really can sublate, can remove that which is 'posited,'"[38] dissonant anti-art progresses *immanently* ("by virtue of inner-aesthetic development") through the formal negation of previous artistic negations. Like Adorno's negative dialectics that "rests on the texts it criticizes,"[39] the dissonant paradigm is based on art from art, the well-established modernist adherence to the avant-garde's successive subversions of subversive precedents.[40] Wellmer identifies three basic criteria of Adorno's dissonant aesthetic theory framed by negative dialectics: semblance (or mimesis), autonomy, and immanence.[41] Adorno's negative dialectical aesthetics is not only driven by the negation of negation, which rejects the possibility of a final *affirmative* synthesis, but also rejects dialectical affirmation in general as a form of "positivity" (such as positive thinking, philosophical positivism, and so on) that claims to establish a stable and final truth. From Adorno's perspective, affirmation *fetishizes* the positive and puts a halt to critical negation. As Wellmer remarks: "Adorno has tried to characterize this self-conquest of the concept as the incorporation of a 'mimetic' moment into conceptual thought. Rationality and mimesis must come together to deliver rationality from its irrationality."[42]

For Adorno, the experimental musical activities of Arnold Schönberg's "Society for Private Musical Performances" (*Verein für musikalische Privataufführungen*) epitomize dissonant anti-art's immanent quest for the "self-conquest of the concept." The Schönberg Circle also exemplifies the immanent framework that is contrary to The Living Theatre's resistance to pure artistic autonomy. Using the example of Schönberg, Adorno upholds a modernist continuation of the Romantic ideal that "all art constantly aspires towards the condition of music."[43] On the one hand, Romantic art is expected to reach *beyond* its formal limits (as in the Wagnerian *Gesamtkunstwerk*) while leaning toward an immaterial (or invisible)[44] concept quintessentially captured in music; on the other hand, modernist art is expected to remain *within* its formal limits to realize a categorical purity. Modernist music extends the Romantic artistic ideal, by operating radically within Western musical limits (as in Schönberg's twelve-tone technique), just as other modernist art forms are expected to aspire to the condition of music *and* operate within their particular formal limits (as in, for example, Ad Reinhardt's refrain about painting that "the one subject of a hundred years of modern art is that awareness of art itself, of art preoccupied with its own process and means, with its own identity and distinction"[45]). Adorno fuses "the beyond" and "the within"—the transcendent and the immanent—as criteria for pure dissonant artistic autonomy. The abandonment of one or the other of these essential criteria defeats art's truth-value, according to Adorno, which is the principle that art must refuse integration into the everyday.

As such, dissonant anti-art relies on its *difficulty* as a form of negation, reiterating the basic definition of poetic language presented by Russian Formalists that "in poetry, communication is not really important"[46] (see chapter 3). Similarly, for Adorno, where "direct communicability to everyone is not a criterion of truth,"[47] dissonant anti-art opposes harmonic anti-art's communicative immediacy. In Marcuse's words, dissonant anti-art "excludes all accommodation [to the everyday] and leaves literature as literature [that is, art as art]. And as literature, the work carries one single message: to make an end with things as they are. . . . This is the passing of anti-art, the reemergence of form."[48] Dissonant anti-art combines the notions of immanence and pure autonomy as it takes on the purpose to which "it acts; and this law or rule is the art or technique of a thing."[49] Regarding immanence, which frames the process of dialectical negation, dissonant anti-art is like "exact fantasy; fantasy which abides strictly within the material which [is presented] to it, and reaches beyond them only in the smallest aspects of their arrangement: aspects, granted, which fantasy itself must originally generate."[50] The historical reliance of exact fantasy differs from immaterial fantasy (or imagination) alone. As Adorno describes, the connection between imagination (as transcendence) and materiality (as immanence) is that "fantasy cannot be the mere capacity to escape the existing by positing the nonexisting as if it existed. On the contrary, fantasy shifts whatever artworks absorb of the existing into constellations through which they become the other of the existing, if only through its determinate negation. . . . Art transcends the nonexisting only by way of the existing; otherwise, it becomes the helpless projection of what in any case already exists. Accordingly, fantasy in artworks cannot be restricted to the sudden vision."[51]

In dissonant anti-art's transcendence of the nonexisting by way of the existing, down to "the smallest aspects" of a form's constitution, it embodies qualities of the philosophical *monad*. In Adorno's words, "the position of the absolute monad in art is both resistance to spurious socialization and a willingness to endure even worse."[52] In particular, dissonant anti-art develops autonomously and operates hermetically like a monad, which has "no windows through which anything could come in or go out."[53] Monadically, dissonant anti-art "is both the result of the process and the process itself at a standstill. . . . At once a force field and a thing. Artworks are closed to one another, blind, and yet in their hermeticism they represent what is external."[54] In a sense, through its hermeticism, dissonant anti-art subscribes to something essentially *magic*[55] about art "which converts the negative into being."[56] Dissonant anti-art expresses awareness of its "power not as the positive that looks away from the negative [but] the power only by looking the negative in the face and abiding with it."[57] Its monadic character, therefore, re-echoes early modernist standpoints on the *symbol* as supporting art's hermeticism: "Everything that is sacred and that wishes to remain so must envelop itself in mystery."[58] Adorno reiterates this hermetic power as a form of secular transmogrification of the object: "Every work of art still bears the imprint of its magical origin. We may even concede that, if the magic element should be extirpated from art altogether, the decline of art itself will have been reached."[59] Unlike the "symbolic politics"[60] of harmonic anti-art like The Living Theatre, dissonant anti-art's pure autonomy and its social agonism develop out of this relationship with exact fantasy's negation of the everyday.

Adorno and Marcuse share the view that "ever since Art left the magical stage, ever since it ceased to be practical, to be one 'technique' among others . . . it assumed a Form of its own, common to all arts. . . . This Form corresponded to the new function of Art in society."[61] Fundamentally, Marcuse is allied with Adorno's criticism of harmonic anti-art due in part to its disavowal of the remnants of art's "magical character." In opposition to Adorno, however, Marcuse acknowledges the role of negation as artistic refusal when it is in service to the aesthetic experience of defamiliarization, which need not embrace a singular avant-gardist development. Following the Adornian view, adherence to dissonant anti-art ultimately is a formal and experiential dead-end. Like the discomfort of atonality that can be overcome through familiarization, even Adorno's "estimate of the negative, critical element in Schönberg's type of music [declined], especially after the twelve-tone row became a more rigid imperative of composition to his followers."[62]

Paradoxically, Adorno's aesthetic theory grounded in negative dialectics reaches an impasse via its progressive negations, in the inexorable circularity of immanent critique, when enchained to the monadic art form. The immanent negation of previous negations eventually empties out any further development, at which point the axiom "the greatest strictness is also the greatest freedom"[63] ironically necessitates an absolute depletion of form. In the 1960s, escape acts by dissonant anti-artists like Charlotte Posenenske, Christopher D'Arcangelo, Lee Lozano, Robert Huot, Raivo Puusemp, and others demonstrate the exhaustion of formal progress when the immanently negative aspect of pure autonomy is fetishized.[64]

THE MICROPHONIC PARADIGM

> The avant-gardistic negation was not negative enough.
> —Herbert Marcuse, "Some Remarks on Aragon: Art and Politics in the Totalitarian Era" (1945)

The *microphonic paradigm* is (1) the unification of dissonant anti-art and (2) the affirmation of aesthetic experience through the subversion of dominant technē (that is, technology and techniques).[65] This marks the threshold between artistic and extra-artistic defamiliarization, which claims a rejection of common sense through nonconformist artistic imagination. The microphonic paradigm addresses the diremption (or sharp division) of the aesthetic and everyday dimensions without relinquishing art's dynamic autonomy. In this way, a Marcusean microphonic paradigm bridges instinctual and social forces that are attentive to technological rationality's repressive causes and asserts the dynamic autonomy of art within a noncolonizing interpenetrative framework.

As such, the microphonic paradigm offers a paradigmatic distinction between Marcuse and Adorno through Marcuse's focus on technē beyond Adorno's focus on the dissonant monadic form. While Marcuse agrees with Adorno that "the relationship between art and society has its place in its approach and its development, not in the immediate partisanship, in today's so-called commitment,"[66] he rejects Adorno's aversion to new art forms undermining art's pure autonomy.[67] Where Adorno's position against the use of technology in art exemplifies the *modern* dualistic epistemological paradigm that extends elements of Romanticism, Marcuse's alternative position tends toward the *postmodern* by interconnecting social habit and technē.[68] Adorno flatly rejects the recuperation of technology for productive social ends and censures its incorporation into art, since "only in the medium of technology, man and nature become fungible objects of organization. . . . In other words, technology has become the great vehicle of reification; reification in its most mature and effective form."[69] Marcuse, in contrast, suggests that the subversion of technē addresses the dead-end of dissonant anti-art, while effectively resisting technological rationality through its nonconformism with habitualized instincts.

Ironically, Marcuse's affirmative refusal initially requires the production of negating forms. This contradiction exposes the actual differences (nascent in Brecht) between alienation—as a *rift* between subject and object—and defamiliarization—which *bonds* subject and object through a strengthened tolerance for the unfamiliar. On this distinction, Marcuse's contribution to the problems of technology, foreseen in *Capital*, is reframed through the effect defamiliarization has on instinctually transformed technique. Where Adorno values dissonant anti-art based on its negation of the mundane and its progressive and purely autonomous formal negation of prior artistic negations, Marcuse shifts away from the monadic art *object* toward defamiliarization as the *technique* of producing aesthetic experience. In this sense, Marcuse's aesthetics move from the spatial to the spatio-temporal, or more clearly, which shifts from the historically transcendent to the transgressively historical.

The tension between the specific structure of the artwork and its reflection of technē is what Fluxus artist Dick Higgins describes as "intermedia"[70] (a key term of Fluxus, with pedigree not only in Duchamp's readymade, in John Cage's incorporation of indeterminacy, but also in John Dewey's "multiform"[71]). Higgins emphasizes opposition to an artistic "compartmentalized approach."[72] Alan Kaprow similarly characterizes intermedia as nonhierarchical in its emphasis on "context rather than category; flow rather than work of art"[73]—where "contemporary artists are not out to supplant recent modern art with a better kind; they wonder what art might be. Art and life are not simply commingled; the identity of each is uncertain."[74] Marcuse is close to both Higgins and Kaprow in his embrace of a plasticity of habits, categories, and disciplines. Where the hybrid approach of intermedia suggests a similarity to the dialectical sublation of thesis and antithesis, in his essay "Intermedia" (1965) Higgins emphasizes that an intermedial technique is not limited to a determinate dialectical framework, but is indeterminate and pluralistic.[75] Regarding this shift, Marcuse's aesthetic theory unknowingly overlaps with Fluxus, which rejects the primacy of categorical art objects (*pure autonomy*) in favor of a wide range and varying degree of defamiliarizing aesthetic experiences (*dynamic autonomy*).[76]

As a distinct quality inherent to aesthetic experience, Marcuse's understanding of the effects of defamiliarization as applied to technē are akin to the effects of *de-reification*, which is "art as making and remaking of 'things,' playing with the possibilities of matter. . . . It is supposed to redefine that which is, to free perception from the range and shape of objects making up our repressive universe."[77] Where for Adorno "the rational and mimetic combined break through the crust of reification,"[78] Marcuse's deeper critique of reification—what Jay calls "the key to a Marxist or neo-Marxist analysis of culture"[79]—is in connection to the integrated instincts, which have become "debilitatingly comfortable" through technological rationality's repressiveness.[80] As Marcuse had already pursued almost a quarter century before *One-Dimensional Man* in "Some Social Implications of Modern Technology" (1941): "Technics hampers individual development only insofar as they are *tied* to a social apparatus which perpetuates scarcity, and this same apparatus has released forces which may shatter the special historical form in which technics is utilized."[81] Technē, consequently, must be dynamically untied from technological rationality to achieve the compassionate and attentive development of the individual toward social transformation.

STOCKHAUSEN

In his SVA lecture, Marcuse refers to Karlheinz Stockhausen's subversive use of technology in his electronic and electro-acoustic works as exemplary of a artistic microphonic paradigm. Stockhausen's work is presented as breaking with the modernism of Schönberg by choosing, from Adorno's derogatory perspective, to "willful[ly] ced[e] to crude material . . . which extends from the hybridization of the arts to the happenings."[82] Specifically, Adorno rejects the aleatoric, electronic, and ready-made elements of the post-Schönbergian "new music" of Stockhausen (and Cage, including the Happenings influenced by him).[83] In contrast, the Marcusean microphonic paradigm acknowledges Stockhausen's electro-acoustic approach as being representative through technique of a historical consciousness: "The present situation of art is, in my view, perhaps most clearly expressed in Thomas Mann's demand that one must revoke the Ninth Symphony. . . . As far as one can go in revocation of the Ninth Symphony, I think Stockhausen has achieved it. And if the revocation of the great art of the past can only be another work of art, then we have the process of art from one Form to another, from one style to another, from one illusion to another."[84] Adorno's inability to accept the music of Stockhausen (and Cage) reveals his aesthetic boundaries, described by Wellmer as the susceptible relationship between the modern *subject*'s "flexible organizational form of a 'communicatively fluid' ego-identity,"[85] in parallel with the potential for the modern *form*'s "expansion of subjective limits . . . as well as a potential for reification."[86]

Stockhausen's electronic studies such as the *Mikrophonie* series and *Spirale* negate musical conventions while they also experiment with extra-musical technology and techniques, literally "synthesizing" technē and the dissonant anti-art form. Upon close analysis, these electronic studies are organized "down to the micro-acoustical level of the basic sounds" in order to separate "the simplest of electro-acoustical raw material."[87] Using electronic filters, "'white noise' is separated further into 'coloured noise' to split up the 'white noise' into bands of noise of any given breadth and density."[88] The first suite of electro-acoustic works in the 1960s included *Mikrophonie I* (1964), which is composed for six players using tam-tam, two microphones, two filters and potentiometers; *Mikrophonie II* (1965) for chorus, Hammond organ and four ring modulators; and *Mixture* (1964–1967) for orchestra (later chamber ensemble), sine-wave generators, ring modulators, and loudspeakers. By 1967, the year of Marcuse's SVA lecture, Stockhausen had formulated *groups* and *moment forms*. Groups are "a new development in the 'spatial deployment of instrumental music," theorized to replace "points" of sounds, and constituted "groups of sounds, of noises and of combined sound and noise [as] wholly autonomous units."[89] Moment forms are "individual and self-regulated, and able to sustain an independent existence. The musical events do not take a fixed course between a determined beginning and an inevitable ending, and the moments are not merely consequents of what precedes them and antecedents of what follows; rather the concentration of the Now—on every Now—as if it were a vertical slice dominating over any horizontal conception of time and reaching into timelessness, which I call eternity: an eternity which does not begin at the end of time, but is attainable at every *moment*."[90]

While Adorno rejects Stockhausen's electronic works on formal grounds, claiming his reliance on indeterminacy relinquishes compositional control and the use of unorthodox technological instrumentation willfully cedes to "crude materialism," Marcuse allows tactics like moment forms to release the the radical potential that is latent in technē. Stockhausen's *Mikrophonie* series "searched for closer conjunctions between electronic and instrumental music"[91] through "the separation of the musical process into three independent areas (production, presentation and transformation of sounds) making possible a continuous combination of all the experience of instrumental practice with that of the techniques of electronic sound."[92] Stockhausen even implies his electro-acoustic works manifest care (*Sorge*) by "composing the act of composing."[93] Consequently, the *Mikrophonie* series emphasizes musical defamiliarization across energetic levels through "vibrations that are normally inaudible . . . made audible by means of an active process of auscultation [listening to sounds of the inner organs] with microphones (in much the same way as a doctor uses a stethoscope); in contrast to its previous passive function as an extremely faithful recorder of sounds, the microphone is used actively, as musical instrument."[94]

Despite Stockhausen's intermedial experimentation, and his challenge to the formal purity of modernist precedents through technical means, mysticism (not magic) informs his conceptual approach. The composer Cornelius Cardew refers to this tendency in Marcusean terms as an expression of "*repressive tolerance* . . . where its abstruse, pseudo-scientific tendencies were encouraged in ivory tower conditions."[95] In his essay "Stockhausen Serves Imperialism" (1972), Cardew strongly criticizes Stockhausen for "slipping off into cosmic consciousness that removes [him] from the reach of the painful contradictions that surround [him] in the real world."[96] In two ways, through his compositional mysticism, Stockhausen ultimately deviates from a historical materialist critique. First, Stockhausen perpetuates the bourgeois myth of genius. In Cardew's words: "Concurrent with the development of capitalistic private enterprise we see the corresponding development in bourgeois culture of the individual artistic genius. . . . We see Stockhausen adopting all the hallmarks of the genius of popular legend: arrogance, intractability, irrationality, unconventional appearance, egomania."[97] Second, since the myth of genius is a primary characteristic of bourgeois culture, Stockhausen remains influenced by neoliberal values. In his criticism of Stockhausen's composition *Refrain* (1959)—which allows the performers to freely play with the circular musical score (using a transparent strip with tempo instructions attached to the center of the page)—Cardew refers to "the true character of the piece as part of the superstructure of imperialism . . . in that it promotes a mystical world outlook which is an ally of imperialism and an enemy of the working and oppressed people of the world."[98]

More dramatically, the artist Henry Flynt chastises Stockhausen for his cultural imperialism through what he views as the composer's Adornian rejection of folk music and jazz.[99] In reference to a 1958 lecture given by Stockhausen at Harvard, Flynt printed Stockhausen's remarks on flyers that dismissed jazz as "primitive . . . barbaric . . . beat and a few single chords" on flyers for two separate protests, organized by Flynt and fellow Fluxus artist George Maciunas, against Stockhausen performances in New York City.[100] The first protest (which included Maciunas, Flynt, Ben Vautier, Takako Saito, and Ikuko Iijima) on April 29, 1964, was at The Town Hall performance space in New York City; the second protest (which included

Maciunas, Flynt, Saito, Tony Conrad, Alan Marlow, and Marc Schleifer) on September 8, 1964, was at the Judson Hall. Both demonstrations were organized under the title of Action Against Cultural Imperialism (AACI) and targeted Stockhausen's "white aristocratic European supremacy" for his "repeated decrees about the lowness of plebian music and the racial inferiority of non-European music."[101] These criticisms of cultural imperialism in Stockhausen's music are crucial in exposing the cultural biases of European dissonant avant-gardism and, due to his endorsement of Stockhausen (in "Art in the One-Dimensional Society"), for identifying Marcuse's referential limits.

PROTESTING THE PROTEST

On Flynt's invitation, LeRoi Jones (aka Amiri Baraka) attended the Judson Hall protest against Stockhausen, but "chose to observe the event from across the street."[102] His dissent from the performative protest led by Flynt and Maciunas strongly resisted both Stockhausen's Adornian pronouncements about jazz and also the Fluxus fetishization of "non-European" music. Jones's *protest of the protest* demonstrates the limits of a singular (or dissonant) European artistic avant-garde even when that avant-garde is protesting its own white Eurocentric prejudices.[103] Significantly, Jones's protest of the protest represented a refusal of the historical and structural exclusion of Black artists from the white-washed art world establishment.[104]

Jones's protest of the protest was a radical act of refusal that recalls Cedric J. Robinson's groundbreaking study of the Black radical tradition. Robinson's book *Black Marxism: The*

Making of the Black Radical Tradition "challenges our *common sense* about the history of modernity, nationalism, capitalism, radical ideology, the origins of Western racism, and the worldwide Left from the 1848 revolutions to the present."[105] Robinson presents the Black radical tradition as "a negation of Western civilization, but not in the direct sense of a simple dialectical negation. It is certain that the evolving tradition of Black radicalism owes its peculiar moment to the historical interdiction of African life by European agents."[106] Robinson locates one of the ideological seeds of the Eurocentric devaluation of non-European cultures, and specifically the erasure of African cultures, in the following passage from Hegel after the philosopher's brief mention of slavery in the Americas: "At this point we leave Africa, not to mention it again. For it is no historical part of the World; it has no movement or development to exhibit. Historical movements in it—that is in its northern part—belong to the Asiatic or European World."[107] In Robinson's words, "the Eurocentrism that Hegel displays in these passages has proven to be neither anachronistic nor idiosyncratic. He would be echoed by legions of European scholars (and their non-European epigoni) in a myriad of ways into the present century. The tradition persisted and permutated."[108]

To evaluate the *actual* universality of Marcuse's aesthetic dimension, his own predilection for the white European avant-garde must be examined. It is important to acknowledge that Marcuse emerged from the same Hegelian patrilineage that Robinson criticizes (and Jones resists citing the influences of Aimé Césaire and Frantz Fanon against cultural integration)[109] and mostly defaults to a European bias in his cultural references (as seen in his comparison of Stockhausen's formal and technical usurpation of Bach's "Ninth Symphony"). Even though Marcuse consistently shows solidarity with radical universes of discourse (recalling his criticism of apophantic logos) such as the "Hippie subculture" (including the folk music of Bob Dylan) but also aspects of African American culture that enact "a systematic linguistic rebellion, which smashes the ideological context in which the words are employed and defined, and places them into the opposite context—negation of the established one."[110] Affirming Robinson's critique of a Eurocentric supremacism, from within its tradition, Marcuse refers to African American linguistic subversions as a significant demonstration of defamiliarizing "some of the most sublime and sublimated concepts of Western civilization, desublimat[ing] them, and redefin[ing] them."[111]

Where Marcuse regularly cites Surrealism as the quintessence of artistic radical sensibility, the limits of the most loyal representatives of the movement (like Breton and Benjamin Péret) are exposed by the challenges brought to their cultural assumptions and habitualized expectations by Black artists informed by Surrealism (and Marxism) like Césaire, Jones/Baraka, Richard Wright, and Ted Jones.[112] A historical comparison here is illuminating: Where the Communist Party *expelled* Breton for his aesthetic radicalism, Césaire *resigned* from the Communist Party because of its unwillingness "to support effectively the black peoples in their present and future struggle—their struggle for justice, for culture, for dignity, for liberty."[113] Césaire's resignation, and Jones's protest of the protest, are revealing refusals of not only the dominant sociocultural structures of exclusion, but the unacknowledged racial prejudices of the Eurocentric artistic avant-garde.

In principle, the microphonic paradigm I associate with Marcuse expands the validity claims on art (and dissonant anti-art) without relinquishing the dynamic autonomy of aesthetic experience. In demonstrating art's political and practical potential through technē's potential for radical nonconformism, Marcuse's aesthetic position unifies the theoretically dissonant paradigm of Adorno and, in solidarity, the political objectives, although not the form, of the harmonic paradigm. Nevertheless, Marcuse's limits are exposed by his bias toward Breton and Stockhausen—representatives of white Eurocentric avant-garde traditions—which is not a question of his sympathies, but the extent of his attention and concern. To reecho Jones: "The entire technology of the West, is just that, the technology of the West. Nothing *has* to look or function the way it does."[114]

3 DEFAMILIARIZATION

> Surrealism pays tribute to the essential estrangement of art.
> —Herbert Marcuse, ""Letter to the Chicago Surrealists" (1973)

Defamiliarization refuses "to accept as final the limitations imposed upon freedom and happiness by the reality principle, in its refusal to forget what *can be*."[1] As a technique, it operates at the intersection of poetics and dialectics. Owing to Surrealism's adherence to defamiliarization, Marcuse views the movement as exemplifying a revolutionary "meta-language"[2] through the efforts of negating social norms and established habits. Breton's lecture titled "Surrealist Situation of the Object" cites the revolutionary necessity of defamiliarization when he writes that art must strive "to make the pleasure principle hold clearer and clearer sway over the reality principle. This search tends more and more to liberate instinctive impulses."[3] Contrary to the conventional academic emphasis on Surrealism and Dada "overcome[ing] the distances between art and everyday life, artists and audience,"[4] defamiliarization permits their *separation* in a dynamically dialectical sense to reveal their mutual influence.

For Marcuse, defamiliarization is the characteristic of art that brings about aesthetic experience embodying the development "of consciousness and of unconsciousness lead[ing] to making us see the things which we do not see or are not allowed to see, speak and hear a language which we do not hear and do not speak and are not allowed to hear and speak."[5] He argues that defamiliarization challenges existence as it is and frees sensibility from dependence on common sense. Summarized in *The Aesthetic Dimension*, Marcuse states: "Art breaks open a dimension inaccessible to other experience, a dimension in which human beings, nature, and things no longer stand under the law of the established reality principle. Subjects and objects encounter the appearance of that autonomy which is denied them in their society. The encounter with the truth of art happens in the *estranging language and images* which make perceptible, visible, and audible that which is no longer, or not yet, perceived, said, and heard in everyday life."[6]

As an artistic technique and essential element of aesthetic experience, defamiliarization challenges habitualized common sense, which for Marcuse substantiates the aesthetic dimension's *promesse du bonheur*.[7] This phrase, first cited by Marcuse in his essay "The Affirmative Character of Culture," is a shortened version of Stendhal's original footnote to *De L'Amour* (1822) ("la beauté n'est que la promesse du bonheur"), which subtly states that beauty is *only the promise* of happiness, *not its guarantee*. More specifically, Stendhal's syntax inverts the relationship so that the *hope* of happiness may promise beauty, rather than beauty promising happiness. In Marcuse's words, the aesthetic dimension promises the hope of the "construction of the beautiful not as beautiful objects or places but as the Form of the totality of life—society and nature."[8] In practice, like hope's mere promise of beauty through happiness, the aesthetic dimension beyond art is not guaranteed through defamiliarization alone.[9]

FORMALIST POETICS

In his 1967 SVA lecture, Marcuse invokes Viktor Shklovsky, "one of the great Russian 'Formalists' who wrote at the time of the Bolshevik Revolution,"[10] in his allusion to defamiliarization (*ostrananie*). In "Art as Technique" (which Marcuse had read in French in 1965 as "L'art comme procédé"),[11] Shklovsky first theorizes defamiliarization as a means of distinguishing poetic language from the language of the everyday. He draws a strong line between these two types of language and how they are assessed. As a method of formal analysis, Shklovsky applies the phenomenological technique of bracketing (*epoché*),[12] borrowed from Edmund Husserl's *Logical Investigations*,[13] to isolate instances of poetic language to analyze its defamiliarized form in relation to the prosaic. In his SVA lecture, without naming him directly, Marcuse quotes Shklovsky at length: "Art exists in order to give the sensation of life, to feel the object, to experience that a stone is a stone. The aim of art is the sensation of the object as vision and *not as familiar object*. Art "singularizes the objects"; *it obscures the familiar Forms*, and it increases the difficulty and duration of perception. In art the act of perception is an end in itself and must be prolonged. Art is a means of experiencing the becoming of the object; that which is already there is of no importance to art."[14]

In "Art as Technique," Shklovsky connects formalism and phenomenology by arguing that poetic language produces "an aesthetic feeling" in the reader or perceiver, which we may call aesthetic experience as it appears in the German philosophical tradition. For Marcuse, Shklovsky's central premise is that there is a determinate relationship between aesthetic experience and the alteration of familiar forms. Shklovsky's assertions about defamiliarization reinforce a central tenet of modernist poetics—namely "poetry is *formed* speech"—while affirming the phenomenological principle that "the object not only performs, it also signifies its function."[15] Thus, defamiliarization acts in two meta-linguistic ways: (1) by performing or "playing the role" of its discursive function, which is always historically situated, and (2) by signifying through the negation of dominant language, which is systemically and socially determined.

Allowing these aspects of formalism and phenomenology to merge inside a historical materialist framework, the political condition of art manifests for Marcuse from "within the medium of experience while subverting the familiarity of the medium: estrangement from within. The possible modes of such subversion are circumscribed by the given historical situation (in the development of art as well as society)."[16] From the standpoint of *orthodox* Marxism, Marcuse's application of Shklovsky's concept of defamiliarization constitutes an anti-revolutionary aesthetics because of its formal experimentalism—which is the same argument applied to Surrealism when Breton tried vainly to propose a Surrealist Marxist aesthetics at the First All-Union Congress of Soviet Writers in 1934.[17] Marcuse's aesthetic theory criticizes the paradoxical and fetishized absolutism of Soviet Marxist aesthetics that upheld revolutionary politics and denounced revolutionary (which is to say, dissonant avant-gardist) formalism. We see this counter-position as the subject of Marcuse's book *Soviet Marxism*[18] as well as in the subtitle of *The Aesthetic Dimension: A Critique of Marxist Aesthetics.* The latter especially can be seen as Marcuse's retaliation to the Soviet rejection of Russian Formalist and Surrealist defamiliarization as well as a sophisticated criticism of propagandistic art in its authorized form as Socialist Realism.

Marcuse upholds Breton as the paragon of an *indirect* political imaginary in Surrealism's "unlimited capacity to say no."[19] Under the influence of Breton, Marcuse envisions a Surrealist aesthetic dimension where "such a world could (in a literal sense!) embody, incorporate, the human faculties and desires to such an extent that they appear as part of the objective determinism of nature and causality through freedom. . . . Breton has made this idea the center of Surrealist thought."[20] Even though Breton was convinced of Surrealism's suitability for the socialist cause—as "the conception of individual revolt: force and unlimited negation transformed into a positive revolutionary consciousness"[21]—for orthodox Marxism, Surrealism was too strange and too difficult (or difficult because it was strange) to effectively communicate Communist Party ideology. Nevertheless, Breton was convinced that Surrealism took Marx's statement literally that "the world has long since possessed something in the form of a dream which it need only take possession of consciously, in order to possess it in reality."[22] Thus, the Surrealists considered their research into psychic automatism as tapping into a "revolutionary consciousness"[23] beyond the conventions even of the Marxist revolutionary establishment. As Péret declared, "The poet can no longer be recognized as such unless he opposes to the world in which he lives a total non-conformity."[24] Here, Péret alludes to the "affairs" of past Surrealists—like the Bolshevization of Louis Aragon, Paul Eluard, and Tristan Tzara—who had "proclaimed their submission of culture to the accomplishment of the social revolution."[25] In the opinion of Péret and Breton, the Surrealist deserters of aesthetic defamiliarization relinquished art's greater revolutionary potential to the historically, ideologically, and aesthetically reductionist polemics of Soviet propaganda.

DIALECTICAL CONSCIOUSNESS

Even though for Marcuse Surrealism is a model of artistic nonconformism, he challenges its absolute adherence to psychic automatism as the counter-technique that claims to access an unconscious level of unadulterated freedom. As Marcuse writes: "The surrealistic emphasis on automatism, on the creativity of the unconscious, is fallacious."[26] In this respect, he finds the Surrealist attitude to be naively "undialectical" with its disregard of the effects that external forces have on automatic behavior.[27] In Adornian terms, this is the Surrealists committing "bad negation" with its overreliance on chance—the variation of automatism that knowingly relinquishes control over the determinable results of a known process—where "individual associations, in their necessity, are not conveyed starting from the articulated image."[28] Surrealism's undialectical psychic automatism does not demonstrate, in Adorno's words, "behavior that takes possession of 'consistency' [*Stimmigkeit* =

coherence] by wholly belonging to it."[29] That is to say, psychic automatism succumbs to the same revolutionary presumptions as harmonic anti-art (like The Living Theatre) and the "anti-disciplinary politics" of the New Left's "ridiculing of political commitment, sacrifice, seriousness and coherence."[30]

The dialectical artist, in comparison, possesses consistency and coherence within the "larger question as to the historical element in all art."[31] The dialectical consciousness of artistic production must intersect with history, such that the artist awakens to "a consciousness that changes itself along with reality, on which it knows itself to be dependent, and in which it still intervenes."[32] Materially, to question art's historical purpose is to question its place logically, not only in a diachronically dissonant response to the cultural expressions that preceded it, but also as synchronically emerging from contemporaneous art and politics. Teleologically, dialectical art through technē is also a demonstration of the subversive ends it hopes to achieve: "These propositions may indicate to what extent the aesthetic dimension is a potential dimension of reality itself and not only of art as contrasted with reality. The *telos* of art is actually to achieve the end of its usefulness as an instrument of opposition, depend[ing] on the alienating force of the aesthetic creation: on its power to remain strange, antagonistic, transcendent to normalcy and, at the same time, being the reservoir of man's suppressed needs, faculties and desires, to remain more real than the reality of normalcy."[33]

For Marcuse, Surrealist automatism performs an undialectical and incoherent second nature where "the conscious processes of confrontation [between the Id, Ego, and Superego] are replaced to an increasing degree by immediate, almost physical reactions in which comprehending consciousness, thought, and even one's own feelings play a very small role."[34] That is, there is no guarantee that psychic automatism's "degree of instinctual freedom to be allowed and the modifications, sublimations, and repressions to be carried out"[35] will bypass the effects of "rational unfreedom, rational domination."[36] A *non-repressive* instinctual unconsciousness (see chapter 4) does not necessarily exist without first developing a dialectical consciousness that challenges habitualized common sense. Instead of psychic automatism being a means of instinctual liberation, the Surrealists ignored that the unconscious instincts are also affected by external habitualization. This repeats Shklovsky's view where "we see that as perception becomes habitual, it becomes automatic. Thus, all of our habits retreat in the area of the unconsciously automatic."[37] Overall, through the Surrealists' research into techniques of psychic automatism, what they failed to consistently consider is the extra-psychic sociogenic "reciprocal production of subject and object."[38] Even though Marcuse acknowledges that Surrealism's intentions most closely approach his vision of artistic refusal, his ultimate assessment of Surrealism is based on psychic automatism's possible "reification and automatization of the ego."[39] As an artistic version of *repressive desublimation*, automatism does not necessarily liberate repressed freedoms, but instead may repeat socially constructed unfreedom in a more insidious form.

CRITIQUE OF CATHARSIS

Breton and Péret summarized the Surrealist desertions of Aragon, Eluard, and Tzara in terms of *guilt*—"the 'moral authority' of internalized values and norms"[40]—in which "the former Surrealists who have become functionaries of the Communist Party or aspire to become such, people who, doubtless in order to get themselves forgiven for their past trouble-making, have abandoned all critical sense and are anxious to be examples of the most fanatic obedience by being ever ready to contradict on order what they have affirmed on order."[41] In like manner, guilt is tied to the psychoanalytic process of *catharsis*, originally a formal component of Aristotelian tragedy, where the spectator is meant to identify through pity and fear with the protagonist's downfall due to error (*hamartia*). The process of catharsis affectively and effectively is meant to cause identification with the fate of the tragic hero to avoid carrying out similar shame (*aidōs*) themselves. This process of identification is established through guilt. In "Ancient Tragedy's Reflection in the Modern," Søren Kierkegaard translates hamartia not as error but more akin to a proto-existential guilt: "The sorrow of Greek tragedy is deeper because the guilt has the ambiguity of the aesthetic. In modern times the pain is greater. It is a fearful thing to fall into the hands of the living God, that is what one might say about Greek tragedy. The wrath of the gods is terrible, yet the pain is not so great as in the modern tragedy, where the hero suffers all his guilt, is transparent to himself in his own suffering of his guilt."[42] As a stimulant of guilt, Aristotelian tragedy works upon "pity and fear accomplishing the catharsis of such emotions."[43] As a result, the *administrative* use of guilt through pity and fear works to reaffirm dominant rationality through the repression of nonconformity. Seen as potentially detrimental to smooth social functioning, the citizenry's misdirected "excess"[44] (or energetic overflow) of reason and the emotions is managed through theatrical catharsis by prompting guilt-identification with societally shameful action as a precaution against likemindedness (*philia*) in the everyday.

Marcuse viewed the theatrical purge of subjective excess as a parallel to the smooth functioning of the democratic unfreedom of the "totally administered world."[45] In *One-Dimensional Man*, as Charles Reitz observes, Marcuse envisions late capitalistic society as an all-encompassing stage where the mimetic/cathartic effects of production and consumption both represent and reinforce the dominant ideology that is present in the process of production itself—not just the processes of production, but "the products themselves indoctrinate ensuring the ideological social relations of which they manifest."[46] As Marcuse summarizes the use of catharsis to maintain advanced capitalism: "This technical-administrative collectivization appears as the expression of objective reason, that is, as the form in which the whole reproduces and extends itself. All freedoms are predetermined and preformed by it and subordinated not so much to political force as to the rational demands of the apparatus."[47] Thus, Reitz's identification of the Brechtian anti-Aristotelian effects of *One-Dimensional Man* were likely intentional, even though Marcuse expressed skepticism about the extent that Brecht's alienation effect produces the same degree of radical sensibility as defamiliarization.

Brecht's tactic of amplifying banality—instead of aesthetic defamiliarization that "communicates truth not communicable in any other language; *it contradicts*"[48]—is liable to reify, not edify. Of similar mind to Marcuse, Adorno asks of Brecht: "How is it that art, whose a priori gesture protests against vulgarity, is yet capable of being integrated with the vulgar?"[49]

Here, the vulgar is not the obscene, but *vulgaris*: the commonsensical and familiar "workaday bustle and the practical individual."[50] Both Adorno and Marcuse question the actual effects of Brecht's *Verfremdungseffekt* due to its "theoretical slippage into a kind of left-utilitarianism,"[51] which relies on a de-aestheticized, banalized, gestic strategy through its covertly critical reproduction of the everyday. Although Brecht brought forward the notion of *Gestus* as "a moment demanding special attention [where] representation (mimesis) reveals itself to be imbedded in history and is simultaneously opened up to new interpretations,"[52] its presumptive effect is susceptible to reenforcing, instead of undermining, social norms through a "deliberately formless expression [that] 'banalizes' inasmuch as it obliterates the opposition to the established universe of discourse."[53]

BODILY RESISTANCE

While Marcuse's use of the body is political through practices of rebellion (including but not limited to sexual freedom), in the context of art, he is allied with Adorno's resistance to the sensuous manipulation of emotion and affect through the cathartic use of pathos.[54] As Wellmer summarizes, reason and representation (or mimesis) are "the moving principles of Adorno's aesthetics"; where reason is "the dialectic of subjectification and reification," and mimesis is "the dialectic of aesthetic semblance."[55] Due to the body's vulnerability to affective persuasion, Adorno argues that aesthetic experience must be protected from emotion and affect, since catharsis provides "fictional feelings in which no one is actually participating and thus . . . neutraliz[es] these feelings."[56] Specifically, Adorno rejects pathos, emotion, or embodied knowledge as effects of a cathartic guilt that can wrongly lead to irrational thought and action.[57] In this context, Adorno even derides laughter, an outburst of pleasure, as acquiescing to the status quo: "The only comical thing remaining is that along with the sense of the punchline, comedy itself has evaporated. . . . The most extreme crudity completes the verdict of laughter, which has long since participated in its own guilt."[58] Recognition of our susceptible bodies provides Adorno with a general argument in terms of guilt against cathartic experience, for its supplying both guilty pleasure and guilt by association. As he summarizes, "The purging of the affects in Aristotle's *Poetics* no longer makes equally frank admission of its devotion to ruling interests, yet it supports them all the same in that this ideal of sublimation entrusts art with the task of providing aesthetic semblance as a substitute satisfaction for the bodily satisfaction of the targeted public's instincts and needs: Catharsis is a purging action directed against the affects and an ally of repression."[59] Where guilty pleasure is seen to bypass reason through an appeal to the emotions, guilt by association (which is the intention of catharsis) tends to reify common sense. The former is forced to recognize a sensuous body, while the latter produces an undialectical social body.

The excessive fear of catharsis, therefore, revolves around mimesis, which in relation to catharsis is the theatrical element of enactment (although much more than this since it has been called the "most baffling of all words in [Plato's] philosophical vocabulary"[60]). The well-known argument in Book X of Plato's *Republic* is that the expulsion of artists from the utopian city-state is due to art's mimetic deception and counterfactual threat to authoritative truth. Plato's rejection of art is based on two criticisms of mimesis: (1) the artist produces representations that are "twice removed from truth";[61] and (2) because they appeal to the emotions, which "destroys reason."[62] Plato's fear is in the potential effects of mimesis on the reproduction of error (hamartia). In its original sense, mimesis refers to "the enactment of deeds and experiences, whether human or divine."[63] In this way, the artist "can let his imagination run wild and 'make anything,' just like a 'sophist.'"[64] In "The Problem of Dialectics" Marcuse's interpretation of mimesis in Plato's *Phaedo* is similar to Adorno's in its recognition that the body's susceptibility to pathos (that is, emotion and affect) is considered a site of vulnerability: a "source of endless trouble" introducing "a turmoil and confusion and fear into the course of speculation, hindering us from seeing the truth," in which we will "make the nearest approach to knowledge when we have the least possible concern or interest in the body, and are not saturated with the bodily nature."[65]

Plato's classical argument is based on the idealist principle that truth must be separated from the body such that its realization is in thought or most purely at the moment of one's death—or even in dreaming "upon the separation of soul from the body."[66] "True philosophers," argued Plato, "and they only, study and are eager to release the soul [and] live as nearly as they can in a state of death."[67] In other words, truth is not bodily. The merging of idea and soul requires the body's essential sublimation (i.e., the literal vaporization from solid to gas, from body to spirit)—ultimately making the purified "no place" of utopia qualitatively and quantitatively an accurate nondestination.[68] The Platonic valorization of immateriality finds its origin in this fear of embodied knowledge, affective immediacy, and pathos—which explains the unbreachable distance between the abstract Platonic Form and its concrete real-world particulars (like the separation between the Kantian noumena and phenomena). In terms of the expulsion of the artist from the body politic, it is the banishment of artistic mimesis that attempts to remove the threat of emotive and affective tendencies from *all bodies*.[69]

In response to Platonic idealism, by the readmission of the artist to the citizenry, Aristotle materially transforms mimesis as an instrument of civil maintenance through his logical "allopathic-homeopathic" social application of catharsis.[70] Aristotelian tragedy effectively instrumentalizes the characteristics of mimesis and catharsis by acknowledging their affective means of persuasion: affectation (mimesis) and affect (pathos) are used as instruments for rationalizing truth through a "disturbance and confusion" of bodily immediacy.[71] As W. Hamilton Fyfe writes in his preface to *Poetics*: "Aristotle meets Plato's hesitation with hard *common sense*. Of course, emotions are dangerous in the body politic. But what good is done by ignoring them or by heaping legislation on the safety-valve? We must face them as facts and use art as their medicine. The soul, like the body, needs an occasional purge."[72]

On this account, Aristotle performs a rational readjustment of the notion of "purgation" in his proto-reception theory by making theater's cathartic representations embody both creation and reception—or analogously, production and consumption—while becoming a structural element that defines tragedy itself: "What it is to be a pitiable and fearful event is to be an event capable of inducing pity and fear in the audience. But pity and fear are clearly not the proper effects of tragedy: it is merely a necessary step along the route toward the proper effect."[73] According to Aristotle, the proper effect of catharsis is "mastery" (*enkrateia*) of oneself in service to civic harmony via guilt, which is an administrative instrument of repression.

COUNTER-CATHARTIC ÆFFECT

To summarize with Adorno, "The doctrine of catharsis imputes to art the principle that ultimately the culture industry appropriates and administers. The index of its untruth is the well-founded doubt whether the salutary Aristotelian effect ever occurred; substitute satisfaction may well have spawned repressed instincts."[74] Against this classical backdrop viewed through Adorno's critique of catharsis, Marcuse's aesthetic theory can be understood through a notion of counter-catharsis, which *guiltlessly* opposes the "technical-administrative collectivization that appears as the expression of objective reason"[75] where "individuation is almost synonymous with apathy and even guilt."[76] Counter-catharsis intertwines the aesthetic tactics of Shklovsky, Breton, and Brecht that bring about resilience to the cathartic "annihilation of the I in the face of art."[77] As in its classical use, technological rationality relies on catharsis to instinctually regulate "the coordination of the individual within the whole."[78] For Marcuse, due to this administratively limited notion of freedom, catharsis must be resisted through a counter-cathartic refusal that revives social-being against its harmonizing "palmed-off cultural surrogate."[79]

As a form of self-defense, counter-catharsis is a resilient act of æffect[80]—an affective and effective mode of resistance that redefines aesthetic experience in terms of "counter-administration."[81] Where Aristotelian catharsis has the administrative function as a tool of persuasion, Marcusean counter-catharsis refuses the preservation of the established order by æffectively resisting it. Where Shklovsky discusses the parallel relationship between art and the everyday in which "the purpose of the parallelism . . . is to transfer the usual perception of an object into the sphere of a new perception,"[82] Marcuse conveys the æffective transformation of the instincts capable of opening radical alternatives to habitualized common sense.

Through æffective defamiliarization, Marcuse argues that counter-catharsis brings about "a qualitatively different sensibility"[83] that begins with a *shudder*. Like the Surrealist concept of *frisson*, where experience is seen for "what it presently is,"[84] the shudder that precedes counter-catharsis "reveals truths, energies, and mechanisms that are hidden and repressed."[85] Against the hegemony of the everyday, counter-cathartic aesthetic experience offers a "transactional, interpenetrative framework and its capacity to create a sense of continuity with the world."[86] Through art's "defiance, indictment, and protest,"[87] this is an instinctual return-crossing of a threshold[88] that leads from aesthetic experience to practical action.[89]

In Freudian terms, the shudder is a moment of "counter-transference" (the *objectification* of the life instincts: Eros) in resistance to repressive rationality (the *reification* of the death instinct: Thanatos).[90] Where "the resistance is the limitation that is usually experienced as voluntary and conscious, although it has an involuntary and unconscious side as well . . . the transference is the limitation that is usually experienced in an involuntary and unconscious fashion, though it too can be made conscious and experienced as voluntary."[91] The Surrealist frisson embodies the Freudian psychoanalytic function of dialectical negation (which is also psychoanalytically nascent in Hegel's negation as the realization of critical self-consciousness; the hypostatized force that reveals *Geist*). Psychoanalytic negation "proceeds from the understanding to dismemberment (*Zerrissenheit*) because the analytic understanding *tears its objects apart*; and thence to the negative, because the understanding negates and does away with the *familiar* form of that which it analyzes."[92] In Freud, "the performance of the function of judgement is not made possible until the creation of the symbol of negation [*verneinen*] has endowed thinking with a first measure of freedom from the consequences of repression."[93] In this way, the counter-cathartic shudder is a bodily and "an existential and sociological category"[94] where the transformation of the instincts manifests in a conscious and unconscious revolt against everyday practices, such that it opposes the ego-weakness manipulated by capitalism and exploited through catharsis. As described by Marcuse, the shudder is a radical moment of resistance to the "technical-administrative collectivization"[95] of catharsis, which is the "psychic correlate of the social overpowering of the opposition, the impotence of criticism, technical coordination, and the permanent mobilization of the collective."[96]

Cathartic *shock*, in contrast, sustains common sense that opposes the shudder, because it "does not break the oppressive familiarity with destruction; it reproduces it."[97] Shock is an instrument of integration that administers the emotions toward a massification of consciousness like "group therapy which, temporarily, removes inhibitions."[98] Marcuse illustrates shock's desired effects as a "constant sonarization: sounds and noises and cries, first for their quality of vibration and then for that which they represent," then asks: "Has not the audience, even the 'natural' audience on the streets, long since become familiar with the violent noises, cries, which are the daily equipment of the mass media, sports, highways, places of recreation?"[99] As in The Living Theatre's principle of the voyage from the many to the one, the cathartic effect of harmonic anti-art reinforces a reification of the subject, such that "'the group' becomes fixed (*verdinglicht*)[100] by absorbing the individuals; it is 'totalitarian' in the way in which it overwhelms individual consciousness and mobilizes a collective unconscious which remains without social foundation."[101] In its most extreme, catharsis is used to stupefy like the shock therapy of disaster capitalism, which thrives in authoritarian contexts.[102]

4 INSTINCTUAL CRITIQUE

Marcuse shifts the stakes of a critical art practice from institutional critique to *instinctual* critique. Alexander Alberro defines institutional critique as the range of artistic strategies of the late 1960s and 1970s that unite "the tension between the theoretical self-understanding of the institution of art and its actual practice of operation [and] the need for a resolution of that tension."[1] Alberro's definition leans on Benjamin Buchloh's retrospectively authoritative essay "Conceptual Art 1962–1969: From the Aesthetic of Administration to the Critique of Institutions," which presents his particular version of shared forms, methods, aims, and actors of conceptual art and institutional critique. Second- and third-wave institutional critiques—represented by Andrea Fraser's "From the Critique of Institutions to the Institution of Critique" (2005) and Pascal Gielen's "Institutional Imagination" (2013)—retain the basic premise of the operational tensions present within Buchloh's narrative with the addition, in Fraser's case, of acknowledging the artist's complicity in defining the institution; and for Gielen, the more affirmative view that "accepts the institution as its ally."[2]

Less than a year after Marcuse's lecture "Art in the One-Dimensional Society," Lawrence Weiner executed an early work of institutional critique that enacted critical negation through a form of removal. Weiner's work *A 36" X 36" REMOVAL TO THE LATHING OR SUPPORT WALL OF PLASTER OR WALL BOARD FROM A WALL* (1968) was installed in the exhibition *January 5–31, 1969*, organized by Seth Siegelaub at a rented office space in New York (McLendon Building, 44 East 52 Street) (figure 4.1). In *Writings 1973–1983 on Works 1969–1979*, artist Michael Asher relates Weiner's statement of removal to his own strategy of subtraction, first attempted by Asher at Lisson Gallery in 1973 (figure 4.2). In this installation, Asher "cut an architectural reveal, ¼ inch wide and 1½ inches deep, into the wall at floor level, around the perimeter of the room."[3] Through these early works of removal and subtraction by Weiner and Asher, they establish themselves as exemplars of institutional critique. In relation to Weiner's earlier work, Asher states:

> The creation of a pictorial or sculptural sign traditionally involves the *addition* of materials to an initial support until some sort of resolution is brought about. The work at the Lisson Gallery ("August 24-September 16, 1973") reversed this process by creating a mark or sign through a process of material subtraction, in which existing materials were withdrawn from the architectural support. This procedure of material withdrawal was similar to that used by Lawrence Weiner in several works he did in 1968 in which he removed materials from gallery floors and walls. . . . At that point in the historical development of art, any process that involved the adding, structuring, or assembling of materials on a support

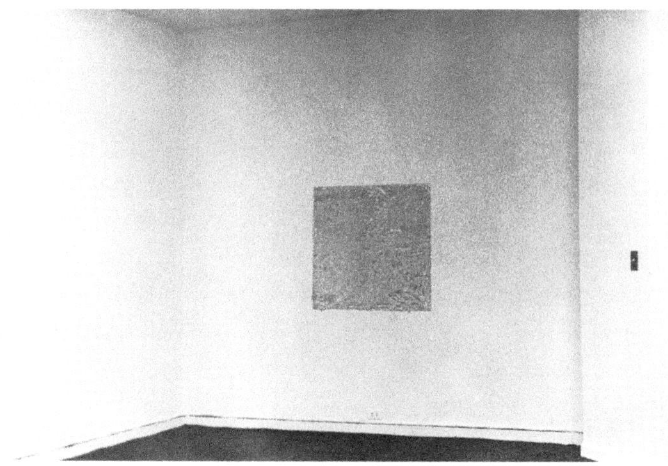

Figure 4.1

Lawrence Weiner, *A 36" × 36" REMOVAL TO THE LATHING OR SUPPORT WALL OF PLASTER OR WALL BOARD FROM A WALL* (1968). © Lawrence Weiner. Photograph by: Seth Sieglaub. Digital Image © The Museum of Modern Art/Licensed by SCALA /Art Resource, NY

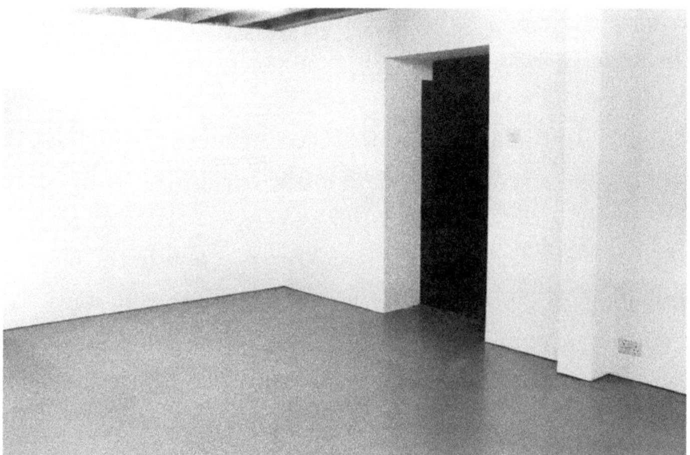

Figure 4.2

Michael Asher, Lisson Gallery, London, August 24–September 16, 1973. Installation view, northeast, with entry/exit passage. For this work, Asher cut an architectural reveal, 1⁄4 inch wide and 1 1⁄2 inches deep, into the wall at floor level around the perimeter of the room. Photograph by: Nicholas Logsdail. © Michael Asher Foundation

> was acceptable within aesthetic practice. The procedure of withdrawing material interrupted and questioned the continuation of that practice. The additive process was partially the result of the traditional avant-garde concern for innovation, whereby materials were synthesized and contextualized in a manner that was alien to their own materiality and method of production. In this work, the subtraction of materials from the site of both, production and reception, disclosed and defined the structure of the production, as well as its contextual determination.[4]

Buchloh strongly supports both Weiner and Asher's strategies of negation, which create experiences of "*perceptual* withdrawal" tied to "its institutional location, since the physical inscription into each particular surface inevitably generates contextual readings dependent upon the institutional conventions and the particular use of those surfaces in place."[5] Buchloh equates effective institutional critique with a dialectical sense of anaesthesia, as an antithesis of aesthetic experience. Similarly, Weiner's removals and Asher's subtractions "negate the specularity of the traditional artistic object by literally withdrawing rather than adding visual data in the construct."[6] This act of perceptual withdrawal, as Buchloh writes, "operates at the same time as a physical (and symbolic) intervention in the institutional power and property relations underlying the supposed neutrality of 'mere' devices of presentation. The installation and/or acquisition of either of these works requires that the future owner accept an instance of physical removal/withdrawal/interruption on both the level of institutional order and on that of private ownership."[7]

ADMINISTRATIVE SMOOTHNESS

The opening lines to *One-Dimensional Man* refer to societal smoothness in pejorative terms: "A comfortable, smooth, reasonable, democratic unfreedom prevail[ing] in advanced industrial civilization, a token of technical progress."[8] Through artistic negation, Buchloh endorses interventionist practices that *anti*-administratively (which is not to be confused with *non*-administratively) manifest something like social friction, as expressed by Adorno in a letter to Marcuse, against "the smooth transition to the totally administered world."[9] Buchloh assigns a label of frictional anti-administration to a particular set of artists, including Weiner and Asher, who arose partly from "the different readings of Minimal sculpture (and of its pictorial equivalents in the painting of Mangold, Ryman, and Stella) and in the consequences the generation of artists emerging in 1965 drew from those readings—just as the divergences also resulted from the impact of various artists within the Minimalist movement as one or another was chosen by the new generation as its central figures of reference."[10] More than a decade earlier, Robert Pincus-Witten identifies this Post-Minimalist immaterial ("conceptual") tendency in works of the period that continued the Minimalist "attachment to the 'pre-executive,' the intellectual."[11] Buchloh repeats Pincus-Witten's observation that a "rationalistic strain maintained and generated an ever more sharply honed, up-front intensification of the theoretical and analytical bases of art."[12] A Post-Minimalist institutional critique, therefore, "destabilized the boundaries of the traditional artistic categories of studio production, by eroding them with modes of industrial production in the manner of

Minimalism . . . that went further in their critical revision of the discourse of the studio versus the discourse of production/consumption."[13] These immaterial and anti-administrative gestures of "minimalization," insists Buchloh, dismantle "the conventions of visuality" to establish "an aesthetic of administration."[14] Buchloh adheres to the Adornian dialectical logic of dissonance where the antithesis of dominant administration produces a progressive sublation (or synthesis) of an anti-administrative aesthetic. Buchloh argues that the resultant institutional critique redefines not only artistic forms through reductive minimalization, but also *aesthetic experience* beyond conceptual art's general challenge to "the traditional concepts of visuality,"[15] to "operate at the level of the aesthetic 'institution.'" In his words, this means "a recognition that materials and procedures, surfaces and textures, locations and placement are not only sculptural or painterly matters to be dealt with in terms of a phenomenology of visual and cognitive experience or in terms of structural analysis of the sign (as most of the Minimalist and post-Minimalist artists had still believed), but that they are always already inscribed within the conventions of language and thereby within institutional power and ideological and economic investment."[16]

This conception of institutional critique consciously *illustrates* its inescapable domination of the total administrative apparatus by taking on its own administrative character, even if in terms of its negation through either administration's folding into aesthetics or the inverse. In comparison, Buchloh's version of institutional critique is distinct from Joseph Kosuth's logocentric "analytic" conceptual art,[17] which is akin to self-consciousness for its own sake. Ironically, Buchloh offers an

Adornian critique of Kosuth's (Wittgensteinian) approach by claiming that the latter does more to entrench institutional rationality than he does to critique it, while overlooking the same result in his own position. Buchloh's argument rests on similar grounds of surface versus depth: "This is to say that in 1968 artistic production is still the result, for Kosuth, of artistic intention as it constitutes itself above all in self-reflexiveness."[18] Thus, Buchloh asserts that deeper than the mere self-reflexiveness of conceptual art, institutional critique is conscious of its cultural "performance of daily bureaucratic tasks."[19]

Buchloh's claims for institutional critique are twofold: (1) it "demands the receiver to take a critical position within the material world";[20] and (2) it transforms aesthetic experience into one that is equivalent to a *cognitive* registration of administrative dominance. Institutional critique turns "the violence of that mimetic relationship back onto the ideological apparatus itself, using it to analyze and expose the social institutions from which the laws of positivist instrumentality and the logic of administration emanate in the first place. These institutions, which determine the conditions of cultural consumption, are the very ones in which artistic production is transformed into a tool of ideological control and cultural legitimation."[21] The end result is that institutional critique rests on a razor's edge of integration into the system that it opposes through its adherence to the antithesis of administration as the primary means of critiquing awareness of its own integrated position. Through institutional critique's conscious anti-aesthetic (or anaesthetic) use of its systemic integration, it is illustrative of integration and therefore performative of actual critique by reorienting aesthetic experience mainly toward cognition, "purging itself entirely of imaginary and bodily experience" while "liquidating even the last remnants of traditional aesthetic experience."[22]

AESTHETIC ANTI-UTOPIANISM

Buchloh's version of institutional critique further aims to resist any of the "utopian" qualities he saw contained in adjacent art practices.[23] While critical of Kosuth's logocentric approach, Buchloh also identified a disagreeable utopianism in other conceptual practices for demonstrating an "acute sense of discursive and institutional limitations, its self-imposed restrictions, its lack of totalizing vision, its critical devotion to the factual conditions of artistic production and reception without aspiring to overcome the mere facticity of these conditions."[24] Buchloh finds these practices have an affinity with what he ascribes to "Marcuse's Freudo-Marxist philosophy of liberation."[25]

To support this claim, he uses contemporaneous artistic and curatorial examples. As illustrating what Buchloh believes to be an intersection of pseudo-critical conceptual art and naive utopianism, he identifies artist Robert Barry's *Some Places to Which We Can Come, and for a While, "Be Free to Think About What We Are Going to Do" (MARCUSE)* (1971–continuing)—also known as the *MARCUSE PIECE* (figure 4.3) with its reference to the "Solidarity" section of Marcuse's *An Essay on Liberation.*[26] Barry's piece, first shown at Gallery Sperone in Italy in 1971 as text on the gallery wall,[27] and then continued to other venues listed on the announcement card, I argue on the contrary performs concrete negation *and* affirmation in a way that promotes both a transgression of consciousness and the potential for conscious transgression.

ROBERT BARRY
30. MÄRZ - 8. APRIL 1971

SOME PLACES TO WHICH WE CAN COME, AND FOR A WHILE,
"BE FREE TO THINK ABOUT WHAT WE ARE GOING TO DO." (MARCUSE)

EINIGE ORTE, WOHIN WIR KOMMEN KÖNNEN UND EINE WEILE
„FREI SEIN DARÜBER NACHZUDENKEN, WAS WIR TUN WERDEN." (MARCUSE)

1. GALLERIA SPERONE, TURIN
2. GALLERIA SAN FEDELE, MAILAND
3. ART & PROJECT, AMSTERDAM
4. YVON LAMBERT, PARIS
5. PAUL MAENZ, KÖLN
6.

Figure 4.3

Robert Barry, *MARCUSE PIECE* (1971–continuing). © Robert Barry. Image courtesy of the artist

From the curatorial standpoint, Buchloh criticizes the agendas of Seth Siegelaub and Lucy Lippard. Siegelaub's utopianism is presented as resulting from simplistic Productivist leanings (even though Siegelaub had in mind a very different reading of Marxism emphasizing equivalency between *all forms* of labor/technē),[28] which not only are unable to evade "the rigorous control of forces governing and structuring the art market by displacing the supposedly unique art object,"[29] but also succumb to an *unacknowledged* integration into the administered world. Lippard, in comparison, is said to uphold the "dematerialized post-aesthetic phase" of conceptual art, which for Buchloh is utopian (since it is not dissonant) in that it "supersedes self-conscious, self-critical art that answers other art according to a deterministic schedule."[30]

In the cases of Barry, Siegelaub, and Lippard, Buchloh's critique of "utopianism" must be judged in relation to his own overreach for the ultimate importance of negation, which like Adorno, he does not recognize as a dead-end strategy. Buchloh bristles when conceptual negation is not dissonant enough and laments "that the specular regime, which conceptual art claimed to have upset, would soon be reinstated with renewed vigor"[31] and its work subsumed rapidly into the system under attack. Andrea Fraser describes this in lucid terms: "Institutional critique has always been institutionalized. It could only have emerged within and, like all art, can only function within the institution of art."[32] Contrary to Buchloh's perspective, Lippard is "involved with opening up rather than narrowing down . . . which offers a "curious kind of Utopianism . . . which indirectly advocates a *tabula rasa*; like most Utopias, it has no concrete expression."[33] This opening up is conceptual art's promotion of a *nonhierarchical* aesthetic experience based on the claim that "intellectual and aesthetic pleasure can merge in this experience when the work is both visually strong and theoretically complex."[34] Similarly, Siegelaub's decentralized organizational efforts in the 1960s and 1970s—such as the "Untitled (Xerox Book)" (1968) and "The Artist's Reserved Rights Transfer and Sale Agreement" (1971)[35]—must be recognized for redefining not just art *forms*, but also the experience of art through platforms using new *techniques* of distribution, reception, and interpretation.

The shift to technique brings Siegelaub and Lippard into a Marcusean framework,[36] but not the fabulated "Freudo-Marxist" caricature Buchloh presents. Siegelaub's response to Buchloh's insistence on framing critical art dissonantly as "litanies of negation"[37] is by means of a communication model of sharing information across a wide field "in relation to its historical moment."[38] This includes artists, critics, curators, dealers, art journals, filmmakers, pop bands, movements, political uprisings, student protests, revolutionary newspapers, and military missions to name but a few.[39] In this way, both Siegelaub and Lippard present an alternative to Buchloh's upholding of orthodox Marxist tenets and Adornian elitisms, while also foregrounding the aim of transformative social cohesion. As Siegelaub summarizes: "The generalization of this search for new forms of popular creativity, and new possibilities of individual and collective expression, enrichment and liberation, in many respects, is often at odds with certain prevailing Left political practices and ideas which arose during the formative period of industrial capitalism. . . . In short, a historically-defined project of liberation, which despite its often heroic character, in practice tended to be constructed from the 'top' to 'bottom,' from center to periphery, from the one to the many."[40]

FREUDO-MARXIST ENERGIES

Buchloh's critique of Barry, Siegelaub, and Lippard for their Marcusean "Freudo-Marxist philosophy of liberation" requires a clarification of Freudo-Marxism itself. Freud's own rare glossing of Marxism is a useful starting point mainly for its suggestiveness rather than any real shared ambitions with Marx (or Marx with Freud).[41] In "The Question of *Weltanschauung*," Freud modestly discusses Marx, stating that he, Freud, feels "the liveliest regret" for his "inadequacy" of knowledge on Marx; yet he then demonstrates his understanding of Marxist concepts in his brief analysis of Marxism on the following points. First, Freud disagrees with a dialectical understanding of natural evolution, especially regarding its "prophetic" tendencies. As he states, "I am far from sure that I understand these assertions aright; nor do they sound to me 'materialistic' but, rather, like a precipitate of the obscure Hegelian philosophy in whose school Marx graduated."[42] Second, Freud expresses disbelief that "psychological factors can be overlooked where what is in question are the reactions of living human beings."[43] Third, he agrees with "the sagacious indication of the decisive influence which the economic circumstances of men have upon their intellectual, ethical and artistic attitudes,"[44] but a communist utopia does not spell out how the "total satisfaction of needs" will be laid out; Freud understands that human needs are not always compatible and "therefore always a difficulty to every kind of social community."[45] Fourth, Marxism is ideological and requires force when confronted with resistance: "It is impossible to do without compulsion in education, without the prohibition of thought and without the employment of force to the point of bloodshed."[46]

Marcuse's actual Freudo-Marxism distorted by Buchloh presents not an abstract utopianism, but a practical critique of habitualized instincts where art confronts the historical materialist essence that constitutes the interrelationships between humans and things. As Marcuse states, "Art stands against history, withstands history which has been the history of oppression, for art subjects reality to laws other than the established ones: to the laws of the Form which creates a different reality—negation of the established one even where art depicts the established reality."[47] In terms of the instincts, Marcuse expands on *energy* as it appears in both Marx and Freud in the "very often unconscious motives which set in motion great masses, whole peoples, and again whole classes of the people in each people."[48] On the one hand, he applies a Marxist view of energy as (material and immaterial) labor—not only regarding production, relations of exchange, public and private laws, and means of communication, but also the instinctual relations that are susceptible to administrative (and cathartic) manipulation.[49] On the other, he draws upon Freud's theory of the instincts, in which the idea of energy is native to the category of the aesthetic. Freud describes an instinct as "arising from sources of stimulation within the body, that it operates as a constant force and that the subject cannot avoid it by flight, as is possible with an external stimulus. We can distinguish an instinct's source, object and aim. Its source is a state of excitation in the body, its aim is the removal of that excitation; on its path from its source to its aim the instinct becomes operative psychically. We picture it as a certain quota of energy which presses in a particular direction."[50]

The psychodynamism of the Freudian instincts (or drives)[51] includes the life instinct (*Liebestriebe*; *Eros*) and the death instinct (*Todestriebe*; *Thanatos*).[52] As Freud describes: "The aim of the first of these basic instincts is to establish ever greater unities and to preserve them thus—in short, to bind together; the aim of the second, on the contrary, is to undo connections and so to destroy things."[53] In terms of energy, Marcuse associates Eros with the instincts that "liberate the life protecting and life enhancing potentialities of matter" and Thanatos with those that are "governed by a reality principle which subjugates, on the social scale, aggressive energy."[54]

In "Art in the One-Dimensional Society," Marcuse presents the energy of Eros as that which lends itself to "construction of the beautiful, not as beautiful objects of places but as the Form of a totality of life—society and nature. The beautiful as Form of such a totality can never be natural, immediate; it must be created and mediated by reason and imagination in the most exacting sense."[55] Eros confronts the "aggressive energy" of Thanatos through aesthetic mediation (recalling Schiller), which provides a transformation of the instincts through the re-emergence of anamnestic energy connecting the subjective and the social worlds. Here, potential (*dynamis*) meets actuality (*energia*) as a "symbolic event which announces the transition from everyday life to an essentially different medium, the 'leap' from the established social universe to the estranged universe of art; this is the occurrence of *silence*."[56]

Marcuse's Freudo-Marxist instinctual critique opposes the repression of energy that has rendered the administered life-world a total "economic-technical coordination which operates through the manipulation of needs by vested interests [through] . . . a specific system of production and distribution."[57] His characterization of repression in this way allows for its application to all forms of authoritarianism, whether as the technological rationality analyzed in *One-Dimensional Man* or the Stalinism he analyzes in *Soviet Marxism*. Instinctual critique probes more deeply than institutional critique (of Buchloh and, by implication, Adorno) into the causes of oppression, and repression, by analyzing institutional critique *below* "the structure of production" and "its contextual determination."[58] It recognizes that individual needs have been integrated into a repressive system that falsely determines and habitually reinforces the limits of reason and the senses.

Furthermore, it determines *progress* through the administered repression of the instincts. As Marcuse states: "The more civilization progresses, the more powerful its apparatus for the development and gratification of social needs becomes, the more oppressive are the sacrifices that it has to impose on individuals in order to maintain the necessary instinctual structure."[59] Such is the framework of instinctual critique and the backdrop of its procedures, where "the repressive transformation of the instincts becomes the biological constitution of the organism: history rules even in the instinctual structure; culture becomes nature as soon as the individual learns to affirm and to reproduce the reality principle from within himself, through the instincts."[60]

SUBLIMATION AND DESUBLIMATION

At the center of instinctual critique, Marcuse argues that radical sensibility is capable of being recaptured, and common sense challenged, through acts of *non-repressive sublimation*. This term relies on an understanding of its development through stages of sublimation and desublimation. "Sublimation of instinct," writes Freud, "is an especially conspicuous feature of cultural development; it is what makes it possible for higher psychical activities, scientific, artistic or ideological, to play such an important part in civilized life."[61] Freud's belief that sublimation oscillates via the Ego between subjectivity (Id) and society (Superego) influenced Marcuse's Freudo-Marxist synthesis in which instincts and sociocultural forms are mutually reinforcing. In *Eros and Civilization*, Marcuse defines *culture* as the result of the sublimation of repressed instincts. Specifically, in terms of aesthetics: "Artistic alienation is sublimation. It creates the images of conditions which are irreconcilable with the established Reality Principle but which, as cultural images, become tolerable, even edifying and useful."[62] Pyschosocially, sublimation is the "culturally promoted processing of frustrated instinctual desires."[63] As Marcuse writes:

> (1) the aesthetic transformation reveals the human condition as it pertains to the entire history (Marx: pre-history) of mankind over and above any specific condition; and (2) the aesthetic form responds to certain constant qualities of the human intellect, sensibility and imagination—qualities which the tradition of philosophical aesthetics has interpreted as the idea of beauty. By virtue of this transformation of the specific historical universe in the work of art—a transformation which arises in the presentation of the specific content itself—art opens the established reality to another dimension: that of possible liberation. To be sure, this is illusion [*Schein*] but an illusion in which another reality shows forth. And it does so only if art *wills* itself as illusion: as an unreal world other than the established one. And precisely in this transfiguration, art preserves and *transcends* its class character. And transcends it, not toward a realm of mere fiction and fantasy, but toward a universe of concrete possibilities.[64]

Desublimation, in contrast, is a *deconstructive* response—that is, both constructive and destructive—to sublimated cultural expression. In an ideal form, desublimation would allow for "the recovery of a large part of the instinctual energy diverted to alienated labor, and its release for the fulfillment of the autonomously developing needs of individuals."[65] Yet, desublimation is subject to deeper internal tensions, since it is sublimation's antithesis, carrying with it sublimation's repressive traces. Constructively, it may connect aesthetic experience with a bio-ontological notion of anamnestic instincts of care; destructively, it can double-down on the repressed instincts that are already promoted. In this way, desublimation is both repressive and non-repressive. *Repressive desublimation* reproduces dominant rationality by keeping the expression of critique within a familiar framework. Marcuse refers to repressive desublimation as integrated and reactionary.[66] As introduced in chapter 2, Marcuse associates the harmonic paradigm of anti-art with repressive desublimation through its "premature harmonies, ignoring the persistence of social contradictions."[67] Thus, even in the critical, yet integrated, use of everyday language, harmonic anti-art is a cathartic form (and institutional critique its dissonant opposite, by illustrating the administratively repressive aspects) of repressive desublimation that ultimately reproduces and reinforces its common-sense framework. Critically, these harmonic forms signal the ongoing need for alternative ways of being and doing dominated by the "exchange ethic of capitalism."[68] Repressive desublimation, in Marcuse's words, "preserves the consciousness of the renunciations which the repressive society inflicts upon the individual, and thereby preserves the need for liberation."[69] That is to say, due to its dialectical character, repressive desublimation still plays a useful role through its *anticipatory* need for resistance in the present.[70] As Marcuse writes in *An Essay on Liberation*: "In its negativity, the desublimating art and anti-art of today "anticipate" a stage where society's capacity to produce may be akin to the creative capacity of art, and the construction of the world of art akin to the reconstruction of the real world—union of liberating art and liberating technology. By virtue of this anticipation, the disorderly, uncivil, farcical, artistic desublimation of culture constitutes an essential element of radical politics: of subverting forces in transition."[71] Nevertheless, repressive desublimation only remains a criticism of the existing sublimated culture on familiar terms, so it tends to manifest repression again in an unacknowledged form. This is not just the Freudian civilizing expression of the repressed libido, but an agglomeration of false freedoms offered from the limited options within established rationality. Where sublimation is an expression of repressed Eros, repressive desublimation is the actual expression of Thanatos masquerading as Eros—which in terms of sublimation is the return of the repressed.

Non-repressive sublimation, alternatively, is the dialectical synthesis of sublimation and repressive desublimation, which "would not destroy the 'spiritualized' manifestations of human energy but rather take them as projects for and possibilities of happy satisfaction [Eros]."[72] Not as cultural reaction via cathartic release, but rather a counter-cathartic "fundamental change in the content and goal of civilization . . . that presupposes fundamentally changed social and cultural institutions."[73] In his preparatory notes to "Beyond One-Dimensional Man" (1968), Marcuse presents non-repressive sublimation as a "reintegration into civilization of human faculties, needs and satisfactions which have been reduced, mutilated and distorted in the tradition of exploitative civilization. . . . This [stage of] desublimation is a revolt only against the repressive aspects of a culture which fostered the false consciousness, the hypocritical morality, the administered forms of fun and elevation, the self-righteous submission to the management of human relations in our society."[74] Non-repressive sublimation is the process associated with radical sensibility that is a "search for a *sensuous culture*, 'sensuous' inasmuch as it involves the radical transformation of man's sense experience and receptivity: their emancipation from a self-propelling, profitable, and mutilating productivity. But the cultural revolution goes far beyond a revaluation in the arts: it strikes at the roots of capitalism in the individuals themselves."[75]

In non-repressive sublimation, therefore, there is a qualitative change to the instincts that allows energy to overflow from defamiliarized aesthetic experience to everyday uncommon sense. From within a Freudo-Marxist framework, Marcuse further entwines the psychobiological life instinct (*Lebenstrieb*; Eros) with Schiller's idealist-materialist play instinct (*Spieltrieb*) to situate non-repressive sublimation in terms of a bio-ontological human essence.[76] What Marcuse calls "the apparatus of need-gratification . . . that reproduces the individuals themselves in the form of labor power"[77] is further extended through sensuous *play*. The manifestation of dehabitualized instincts through non-repressive sublimation is subject to the "free play of faculties" in the inherent "pacification of nature"[78]—that is, human nature's bio-ontological potential for compassion. In practice, *Spieltrieb* and *Lebenstrieb* together constitute the defamiliarized work in its release of habitually repressed instinctual energy by demonstrating care for "the present with the hope for the future."[79] This instinctual transformation through defamiliarization operates at energetic levels that attentively interconnect the individual to others, to which

Marcuse attributes three affirmative, non-repressive psychosocial effects:

(1) the consciousness of the individual is extended beyond the limits imposed by the requirements of domination;
(2) the individual's imagination recaptures its creative power to project possibilities of human freedom—not only in terms of fiction, poetic truth, but also of "real," political truth;
(3) the sensibility and sensitivity of the individual have their share in the aesthetic reconciliation of the environment.[80]

5 THE HUMAN DIMENSION

> Law and order are always and everywhere the law and order which protect the established hierarchy; it is nonsensical to invoke the absolute authority of this law and this order against those who suffer from it and struggle against it—not for personal advantages and revenge, but for their share of humanity.
>
> —Herbert Marcuse, "Repressive Tolerance" (1965)

In 1930s Paris, coteries of diasporic Caribbean and African students informed by Marxism and Surrealism confronted their European political and artistic influences. One group consisting of Aimé Césaire, Léopold Senghor, and Léon Damas gave birth to the Négritude movement in their journal *L'Étudiant noir*. Césaire coined the term in his essay "Racial Consciousness and Social Revolution" (1935)[1] and explored it in more depth in his long poem *Cahier d'un retour au pays natal* ("Notebook of a Return to My Native Land") (1939). A few years prior to *L'Étudiant noir* a different intellectual circle of Martinican students based in Paris—consisting of Étienne Léro, Thélus Léro, René Ménil, J. M. Monnerot, Michel Pilotin, Maurice-Sabas

Quitman, Auguste Thésée, and Pierre Yoyotte—published *Légitime défense* (1932) which offered a scathing anti-colonial critique, also from within the frameworks of Marxism and Surrealism, of "the constraints and restrictions, the extermination of love and confinement of dream, generally known under the name of Western civilization."[2] The poets and intellectuals associated directly or adjacently with the Négritude movement agreed: on the one hand, that anti-colonialism must be a central concern of Marxism for radical societal change to occur;[3] and, on the other, that the range of Surrealism's "domain of the Marvelous" must be extended beyond the European imagination.[4] In recounting the artistic aims of Négritude, for instance, René Ménil wrote that its poetic texts "distort French Surrealist form in order to establish another form in a new literary structure imposed by Caribbean socio-historical circumstances at a particular date."[5] Published after *Légitime défense* during the occupation of Martinique during the authoritarian, Nazi-collaborating Vichy regime's governance, Ménil joined with Aimé and Suzanne Césaire to co-produce the Martinican journal *Tropiques* (1941–1945), which courageously actualized Adorno and Marcuse's submissions that, despite the horrors of Auschwitz, liberation still has a home in art.[6]

Through the anti-colonial and counter-poetic perspectives of the Césaires, Ménil, and others associated with Négritude, a radical form of historical materialism was reapplied both to Marxism and Surrealism in dynamic and concrete ways by acknowledging the *actual* experiences of African-Caribbean diasporic subjects under colonialism instead of the ideological tendencies of Marxist essentialism and Surrealist exoticism.[7] To add internal complexity to this account, it must be emphasized that Négritude, despite its significant steps toward a decolonial consciousness, underwent scrutiny by its participants and affiliates who pointed to the movement's own instances of essentialism, cultural abstractness, and political instrumentalization.[8] Frantz Fanon, a student of Aimé Césaire's, provides one of the most trenchant and complex critiques of Négritude's presentation of an abstract "essence"[9] to stress instead "the historical, contingent character of how racialized subjectivities are created."[10] In *Black Skin, White Masks*, Fanon proposes three approaches to human study: the ontogenic (the individual organism), the phylogenic (the species) and the sociogenic.[11] The last relates to "what emerges from the social world, the intersubjective world of culture, history, language, and economics. In that world, Fanon reminds us, it is the human being who brings such forces into existence."[12]

In sociogenic terms, one of the most toxic habitualizations is that race is an inborn category with hierarchical human consequences,[13] instead of an externally imposed structure with oppressive motivations. Equally pernicious is the commonsense belief that humans are separate from nature, instead of being of it, allowing for technological rationality to exploit such arbitrary and hierarchical separations.[14] Racial inequality and technological superiority, therefore, are intersecting myths that have been used to serve colonial and capitalist exploitation. In Sylvia Wynter's words, this is based on the narrative of the "Western bourgeois liberal humanist *homo oeconomicus*," which provides a "monohumanist conception of our being human, its overrepresentation as the being of being human itself."[15] The invention of race creates artificial hierarchies based on differences in phenotype (physical appearance and cultural traits) and genotype (genetic code) with an arbitrary blurring of the two to justify the oppression of some based on the hypervaluation of others. Through this "auto-instituted, not-genetically restricted fictive mode of eurosociality"[16]—where "racial constructions are leeches on all manifestations of human ways of living: language, sex, labor (material and aesthetic), socializing (reciprocal recognition), consciousness, and the 'soul'"[17]—*racism* has been administered through policies, practices, and technologies established on myths of white Anglo-Saxon supremacism and enforced through hegemonic discrimination and brutality.[18] Safiya Umoja Noble's analysis of the algorithmic racial profiling of search engines, Simone Browne's historical examination of racism through visible and invisible surveillance, and Ruha Benjamin's examination of anti-Black racism built into digital programming provide critical contemporary examples that urgently expand the fundamental Marcusean analysis of technological rationality discussed throughout this book.[19]

Race, though a pseudo-scientific categorical invention, historically has become entrenched as a sociogenic reality through the many racist technologies of oppression. The extraction of natural resources—such as gold in the sixteenth century by European interlopers into West Africa—arose hand in glove with *dehumanization*, establishing the infrastructure for the Atlantic slave trade that supplied the brutal physical labor in the British and French colonies, at the same time as the colonial robbery of Indigenous lands in the Americas. From the early 1500s, "the growth of European mercantile activities generally influenced the fortunes of the privileged in society while, at the same time, stimulating the expansion and diversification of slavery in various coastal societies in West Africa."[20] Before race was pseudo-scientifically instituted to consolidate power in the hands of the colonial establishment, in seventeenth-century Virginia for example, to suppress organized resistance by enslaved African *and* European bond-laborers, the ruling class created the first of a series of constitutional principles that elevated whiteness over blackness establishing race as "the primary badge of status."[21] This invented common sense through racial oppression for exploitative human and industrial profits—what Cedric J. Robinson explores in *Black Marxism* as *racial capitalism*[22]—began as myth, then turned into policy to be enforced by law, perfected by technology, practiced through habit, and sedimented in instinct.

Racism, to be clear, is a historical and ideological product in which it is "the theory and the practice of applying a social, civic, or legal double standard based on ancestry, and to the ideology surrounding such a double standard."[23] In its subtler forms, (overlapping with and reinforced by its explicit systemic manifestations) implicit biases and aversive racist tendencies are *ambivalent* to structural change at best.[24] Truly undoing the sociogenic reality of racial oppression, which is "epistemologically and humanly structured,"[25] requires social acknowledgment and individual attention to the mutually supportive explicit and implicit common-sense structures that add up to establish the dominant "tape of the world."[26] Thinking of racism in terms of sociogenic habitualization is by no means to downplay the overabundance of agents and practices that have upheld historical and systemic prejudice. On the contrary, an emphasis on habit exposes the potential for systemic transformation from within the sociogenic arbitrariness of established common sense.

As William David Hart asserts, "The world chooses the self before the self makes choices. Racial identification and racist practices are among the social realities that habituate, condition, position, and educate the emerging self before it makes any choices at all."[27] Echoing Marcuse's fundamental analysis, Hart attests that habits shape the instincts.

> Race and racism are about habit formation. . . . Habits are affected by concepts. But their effects are typically slow, highly mediated, and ambiguous. While affected by concepts, habits resist them as well—especially when rooted in the noncognitive, unconscious, or irrational mind, or when created by rituals, routines, and disciplines that orient bodies in social space. Here one might recall the elaborate racial etiquette, including a racist *pathos of distance* enforced by violence, which defined relations between black and white in Jim Crow America. Addressing these kinds of problems and the habits and affects they create require much more than conceptual work. This requires *habit deformation and reformation* and creating the kind of structures that make this rehabituation possible.[28]

I read Hart's reference to "a racist pathos of distance enforced by violence" as a grotesque, though historically reinforced, comparison of racist sociogenic practices to the real-world application of catharsis. Recall that Brecht's anti-Aristotelian theater is based on a rejection of catharsis, which embodies the "pathos of distance,"[29] due to its administrative manipulation of the emotions and the bodily effects of purgation for the maintenance of the established common-sense rationality. In the case of Hart's suggestion of *racial* catharsis, numerous questions mount: Who administers the catharsis and upon whom is it administered?

Whose guilt is being purged and for what purposes? Which mimetic order is being presented for reproduction and maintenance? Whose mastery (*enkrateia*) is being served and why?

NON-REPRESSIVE INTOLERANCE

Marcuse's concept of repressive tolerance applies directly to racial catharsis. In his essay "Repressive Tolerance" (1965), Marcuse argues that "the realization of the objective of tolerance would call for intolerance toward prevailing policies, attitudes, opinions, and the extension of tolerance to policies, attitudes, and opinions which are outlawed or suppressed."[30] He reframes the choice of tolerance (as inattentiveness and avoidance) to known injustices as an act of submission to dominant common sense that endorses the perpetration of a systemic inequlity. Infamously, however, "Repressive Tolerance" is remembered more as an endorsement of violence, or more accurately *counterviolence*, than it is for its fundamental intolerance to systemic inhumanity.[31]

Marcuse's argument for counterviolence, however, must be recontextualized as *self-defense*. "On the question of violence," writes Marcuse, "I can only repeat what I have already said; that in existing society violence is institutionalized to an absolutely monstrous extent and the primary question is first of all, 'From whom does the violence come?' In any event, in a period of incipient counterrevolution—violence comes first of all from the existing society and that from this point of view the opposition is confronted with the question of counterviolence, the violence of defense but definitely not the violence of aggression."[32] A reflection on Marcuse's position on counterviolence as self-defense is enhanced by drawing upon Judith Butler's inquiry into nonviolence, which she frames in this way: "What starts, then, as an apparently moral argument about whether to be for or against violence quickly turns into a debate about how violence is defined and who is called 'violent'—and for what purposes."[33] The question of what constitutes the status of the "self" is of central importance to both Marcuse's defense of counterviolence and Butler's inquiry into the terms of self-defense. Butler breaks down the inquiry into two separate but related issues: "Given that self-defense is very often regarded as the justifiable exception to the norms guiding a nonviolent practice, we have to consider both (a) who counts as such a self and (b) how encompassing is the 'self' of self-defense."[34] Self-defense is not just the physical defense of the self, but of the status of *selfhood*. As Butler writes, "For lives not considered grievable (those treated as if they can be neither lost nor mourned), dwelling already in what Frantz Fanon called 'the zone of non-being,' the assertion of a life that matters . . . can break through the schema [of dehumanization],"[35] which fails to regard self-defense as the defense of selfhood.[36]

In a 1970 letter to Angela Davis,[37] Marcuse acknowledges her impact on his formulation of repressive tolerance in regard to the necessity of the "violence of defense" in the face of the systemically habitualized "violence of aggression."[38] Davis, who studied under Marcuse at Brandeis University at the time of his writing "Repressive Violence," impressed upon him the necessity of self-defense in the face of systemic violence (as a continuation of colonial violence)[39] as she enacted through her own activism with the Communist Party and the student resistance groups Sozialistische Deutsche Studentenbund (SDS) in Germany and the Student Nonviolent Coordinating Committee and later the Black Panther Party in America. Marcuse's defense of counterviolence as self-defense, therefore, is more akin to counterforce that intimates only reluctant (or qualified) support for *physical* conflict.

In this way, Marcusean counterviolence points back to his fundamental belief in Eros expressed in its historical materialist form as anamnestic social-being. Marcuse writes, "The strange myth according to which the unhealing wound can only be healed by the weapon that afflicted the wound has not yet been validated in history: the violence which breaks the chain of violence may start a new chain. And yet, in and against this continuum, the fight will continue."[40] As such, Marcuse's sense of counterviolence resists the framework of violence itself. Again, this perspectival shift affirms a forceful self-defense as a defense of selfhood—which relates directly to the work of Fanon. First introduced in existential and psychoanalytic terms in *Black Skin, White Masks* as "the zone of nonbeing,"[41] Fanon's *The Wretched of the Earth* (1961) lays out the imperative for counterforce toward the liberation of all oppressed peoples.[42] An excerpt from Fanon's critical tour de force encapsulates a notion of counterforce in the name of salvaging essential human dignity: "From the moment that you and your like are liquidated like so many dogs, you have no other resource but to use all and every means to regain your importance as a human being. You must therefore weigh as heavily as you can upon the body of your torturer in order that his lost soul may finally find once more its universal dimension."[43]

Wynter refers to the sweeping dehumanization depicted in *Wretched of the Earth* as the racist demarcation of "those 'outside' the *referent-we* of *homo oeconomicus*."[44] Wynter, born at the time of Fanon and a generation before Davis, develops a stylistically poetic counter-narrative and perspicacious sociogenic critique of the racist normalization of the "monohumanist conception of our being human" by presenting her "own Fanonianly adapted hindsight hypothesis."[45] Wynter does this by unpacking the "governing tape that has been made to be reflexly and subjectively experienced . . . as if it were indeed a *bio-instinctually experienced* one."[46] Building on Fanon, Wynter develops a sociogenic critique of the ontology of humanness by *defamiliarizing* habitualized common sense—enframed by racist and sexist myths—to present a praxis of being "hybridly" human that "challenges the single biocentric model of liberal monohumanist *Man*."[47] Historically, Wynter points to the social movements of the 1960s, as "really the first opening phase of the dynamic in which the series of 'isms' (initiated by the Black antiapartheid struggle for civil rights, women's rights/feminism, indigenous and other of-color rights, gay and lesbian rights, and so forth) had erupted to challenge Man's episteme, its truth, and therefore its biocentric descriptive statement."[48] Wynter's sociogenic critique shares the counterforce of Fanon and Davis through a "counterhumanist"[49] expansion on Marcuse's belief in the sociopolitical impact of aesthetic defamiliarization.

LIVED AND PROFOUND EXPERIENCES

As with Marcuse's critique of apophantic logos, Wynter directs our attention to the "sociogenically encoded and semantically activated"[50] influence on our "unquestioned, genre-specific, *normalcy of being human*."[51] In contrast, Adorno's aesthetics succumbs to what Wynter identifies (reechoing Robinson's criticism of the foundations of Western thought) as "the *referent-we*'s fictively instituted autopoiesis"[52] (what Butler calls "politically consequential forms of phantasmagoria"[53] and Karen Fields and Barbara Fields refer to as "invisible ontology"[54]) when maintaining two *distinct* types of experience: profound experience (*Erfahrung*) described as being conscious of a comprehensive social experience and lived experience (*Erlebnis*) as being subjective, immediate and vulnerable to external manipulation.[55] Adorno asserts that "full comprehending experience (Erfahrung), which terminates in judgment on the non-judging work, demands a decision and, by extension, the concept [whereas] lived experience (Erlebnis) is exclusively an element of such comprehending experience and faulty because it is subject to persuasion."[56] Moreover, he presents not only a necessary division of (aesthetic) experiences, but also a *hierarchy* with Erfahrung superior to Erlebnis: "This subjective experience (Erfahrung) directed against the I is an element of the objective truth of art. Whoever experiences (*erlebt*) artworks by referring them to himself, does not experience them; what passes for experience (Erlebnis) is a palmed-off cultural surrogate."[57]

Adorno's insistence on this distinction can be viewed as the "fictively instituted" privileging of a homogenized ideal human subject derived from the figure of "the West's liberal monohumanist *Man*."[58] Wynter, alternatively, views ethico-aesthetic experience as a mutual reciprocity between lived and profound experience, which takes on an important double meaning regarding self- and social-consciousness. In other words, Wynter emphasizes that lived experience and social experience are not distinct but *relational.*[59] Wynter's counterhumanism is based on defamiliarizing "the West's hitherto secular liberal monohumanist conception of our being human, its overrepresentation as the being of being human itself."[60] Thus, Wynter derives the profundity of lived experience from the "multiplicity of genres of being human."[61] Wynter's correction to the Adornian distinction between profound and lived experience should be seen as a fundamental critique of "our *present* order of knowledge—an order of knowledge that is indispensable to the continued reproduction of our present neoliberal/neo-imperial, secularly biocentric, global order of words and of things."[62]

PHRONESIS

In *One-Dimensional Man*, Marcuse performs a parallel critique to that of Wynter by revealing the sociogenic myth that is the basis of technological rationality, which is the "social mode of production"[63] that is "organized in such a way that the existing system in the highly industrialized capitalist countries is very largely held together by [it]."[64] He urges, first, attentiveness to sociogenic habit and, second, a refusal to conform to its repressive common sense. From the perspective of technē, this implies the evocation of *phronesis* that guides technologies of production and their relationality to humans and the environment through practical wisdom and ethical action—in other words, by giving equal care to both profound and lived experience.

As a result, phronesis connects to defamiliarization through attentiveness that is "sharp enough to see into the idiosyncrasies of the situation, the subtleties of a complicated and slightly unprecedented situation."[65] Wynter refers to this as "minding

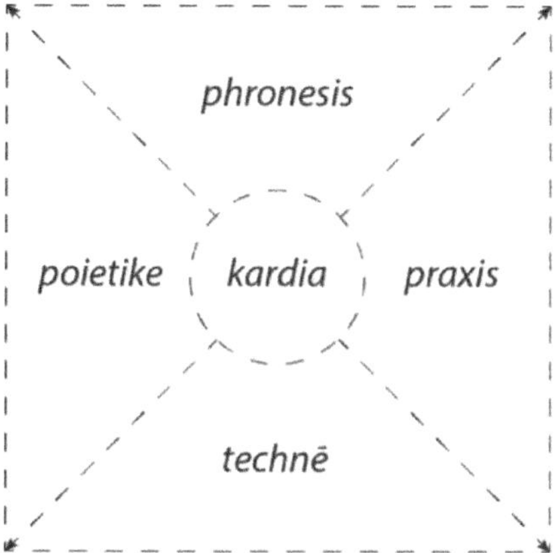

Figure 5.1
A re-membering of realms of being

about those *outside* our specific and particular *referent-we* perspectives and worldviews."[66] In a Marcusean sense, "minding about" is equivalent to the attentiveness that is concurrent with defamiliarized aesthetic experience. Structurally, therefore, defamiliarization as a technique of care, is at the heart (*kardia*) of praxis, technē, phronesis, and *poietike* (art, in general) due to its practical and ethical attentiveness (figure 5.1). Defamiliarization effectively reconnects the realms of poietike with praxis, originally separated in the Aristotelian categories of *poiein* ("to produce") and *prattein* ("to act"). John Wall explains the lasting impact on Western thought of Aristotle's separation, in book VI of *Nichomachean Ethics*, of phronesis and poietike:

> While *phronesis* and *poietike* have in common that, in contrast with theoretical wisdom, they both deal with "things which admit of being other than they are" ("the realm of coming-to-be"), *phronesis* "is itself an end," namely "good action,"

> whereas *poietike* "has an end other than itself," namely a work of art or a product (Aristotle, book VI, 1140b, 5–6). This in essence means that *phronesis* has to do with action in its own right, *poietike* with action as a means to something else. The result is that the one belongs to the realm of ethics, or the goods internal to action, the other the realm of aesthetics, or goods produced by or imitative of action. This distinction—which echoes in a milder form Plato's famous expulsion of the poets from his ideal moral republic—has had, and continues to have, a profound influence in Western moral thought.[67]

Practically and theoretically the effect of defamiliarization on and beyond aesthetics is, in Marcusean terms, an anamnestic re-membering of "things which have been prematurely separated [that] must once again be drawn together."[68]

CARE-STRUCTURE

At the heart of the human dimension is the technique of defamiliarization, which in turn is an act of care. Reciprocally, a consciousness of care is also a demonstration of it, which for Marcuse gives rise to social-being through care (*Sorge; sorgen*) as solicitude (to care for) and concern (to care about) as presented in Heidegger's care-structure (*Sorgestruktur*) central to his concept of Being (*Dasein*) in *Being and Time*[69] (figure 5.2). In Heidegger's words, "care, as a primordial structural totality, [which] lies 'before' every factical 'attitude' and 'situation' of Being [*Dasein*], and it does so existentially *a priori*; this means that it always lies *in* them."[70] Simply, *Dasein* is founded on care, which is a form of attentiveness that motivates human will.[71] Careful and attentive inquiry expresses fact or factuality (*Tatsächlichkeit*) as

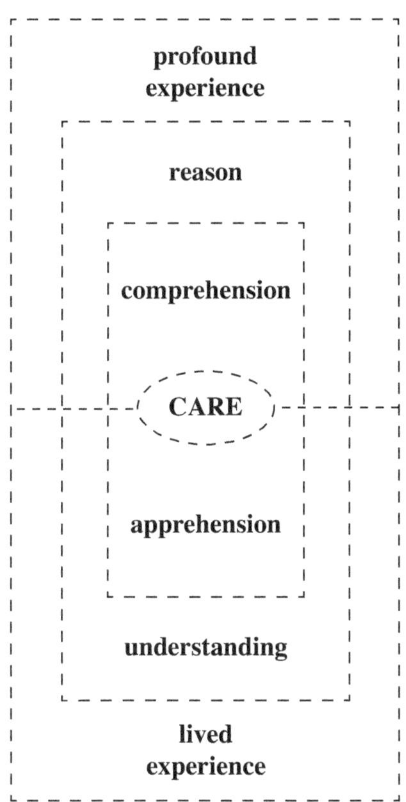

Figure 5.2
Heidegger's care-structure

opposed to facticity (*Faktizität*),[72] the "understanding already available to us."[73] Through the connection to care (*Sorge*) and *Dasein*, Heidegger seeks "to work out the question of Being adequately" by making "the inquirer—transparent in his own Being. The very asking of this question is an entity's mode of *Being*; and as such it gets its essential character from what is inquired about—namely, Being."[74]

Where care as both solicitude and concern is ontological, by steering thought and behavior toward a radically "new sensibility" (*Bewusstseinsenleitung*),[75] the pseudo-care of facticity remains within the ontic, familiar, and commonsensical "sphere of the Real": "Ontologically, care is not to be derived from Reality or to be built up with the categories of Reality."[76] In other words, care is not automatically derived from the familiar, but emerges from an attentive, defamiliarizing inquiry that leads to an understanding of what establishes common sense.

In Heideggerian terms, care opens up a "clearing" to potential worlds,[77] which connects care to *willing* and ultimately refers it to unrealized potential (*dynamis*).[78] The pseudo-care of technological rationality, in contrast, is anchored to a limited form of possibility as *wishing*, restricted to that which is merely possible based on common-sense familiarity. Wishing provides the false sense of willing, bound to familiar and common-sense ontic options, resulting in a deformation of *Dasein* through a fundamental "modification of the care-structure."[79] The break with pseudo-care is through attention to the factual relationality of lived and profound experience that allows the defamiliarized crossing of habitualized limits.

By remaining dynamically autonomous, defamiliarization attends to the unrealized potential in the details of material circumstances by seeking, respecting, and nurturing uncommon sense. As Marcuse argues, defamiliarization provides "the radical subversion of technology's prevailing direction and organization"[80] where "the revision is suggested, and even necessitated, by the actual evolution of contemporary societies."[81] In this way, defamiliarization draws together phronesis and poietike to become a technique of care that is both aesthetic and ethical.

It allows "technique . . . to become art and art would tend to form reality: the opposition between imagination and reason, higher and lower faculties, poetic and scientific thought, would be invalidated. Emergence of a new Reality Principle: under which a new sensibility and a desublimated scientific intelligence would combine in the creation of an *aesthetic ethos*."[82] Marcuse understands this as an *ethico-aesthetic* transformation of the instincts, the dynamic emergence of a multidimensional, radical sensibility open to the unfamiliar.[83] Thus, the ostensibly formal poetic technique first theorized by Shklovsky becomes for Marcuse ethico-aesthetic technē that connects to praxis, poietike, and phronesis.

With defamiliarization at its core, Marcuse's ethico-aesthetic theory goes beyond mere formal aesthetics to provide phenomenological and historical frameworks that establish care as the foundation for instinctual transformation. In applying the Heideggerian care-structure to Marxist social analysis, Marcuse reconceives the notion of "enframing" (*Ge-stell*), which links *Dasein* and "man's ordering attitude"[84] to the revolutionary potential from within given historical conditions. Enframing, a central concept in Heidegger's essay "The Question Concerning Technology," includes but truly exceeds its technological context. Enframing is both framework and platform; it has the characteristics of a framework as context, but also a platform as an infrastructure with "monopolistic tendencies."[85] Broadly speaking, Heidegger presents enframing as the given limits of rationality: "Enframing, as a challenging-forth into ordering, sends into a way of revealing. Enframing is an ordaining of destining, as is every way of revealing. . . . It is from out of this destining that the essence of all history [*Geschichte*] is determined."[86] Despite the restrictions of enframing on common sense, a consciousness of the limits of enframing offers "a challenging claim which gathers man thither to order the self-revealing as standing reserve."[87] Associated to the concept of enframing is "standing reserve" (*Bestand*), an inventory of the accessible means of being and knowing (including available language and concepts) for deployment and revision, not just as stockpile, but as an intrinsic part of the enframed possibilities always already on call for possible use. A consciousness of (which is "a challenging claim" to) the limits of enframed rationality—such as a specific acknowledgement of the repressive limits of technological rationality—allows for the possibility of crossing the threshold of its epistemological and phenomenological limits. Ultimately, therefore, crossing the threshold of enframed limits requires a distinctive break from common sense. While

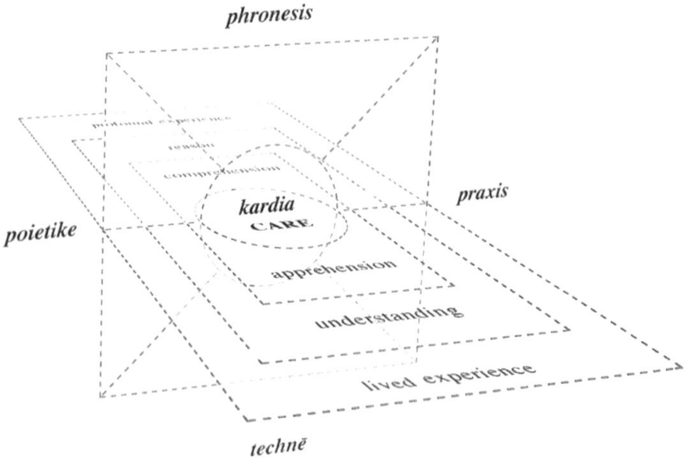

Figure 5.3
The human dimension

Marcuse returns to Heidegger to adapt his care-structure to frame radical sensibility as emerging from the aesthetic dimension, Wynter extends Marcuse's adaptation of the care-structure relationally and multidimensionally (figure 5.3).

PLASTICITY

For Marcuse, care as both concern and solicitude is central to radical sensibility. "Care for human existence and its truth makes philosophy a 'practical science' in the deepest sense, and it also leads philosophy—and this is the crucial point—into the concrete distress [*Bedrängnis*] of human existence."[88] Catherine Malabou expresses this dual transgression of consciousness and conscious transgression in terms of productive silence (as does Marcuse) such that "if form crosses the line, then serenity is possible."[89] In a modification of Malabou's observation, where Marcuse identifies defamiliarization as the central technique that develops ethico-aesthetic instincts, Malabou refers to *plasticity*, which goes beyond habitualized sociogenic frameworks *from within them*, by "crossing thresholds without changing ground."[90] With respect to dehabitualization, writes Malabou, our "suppleness and plasticity constitutes what, in a thing, can change."[91]

Through a merger with habit, Marcuse applies plasticity to the instincts "which [Freud's] theory presupposes should suffice to refute the notion that the instincts are essentially unalterable biological substrata: only the *energy* of the instincts and—to some extent—their *localization* remain fundamentally unchanged."[92] In comparison, in *Principles of Psychology*, William James writes about plasticity as "the possession of a structure weak enough to yield to an influence, but strong enough not to yield all at once. Each relatively stable phase of equilibrium in such a structure is marked by what we may call a new set of habits."[93] Applied to aesthetics, James's plasticity of a system to create new habits parallels Malabou's crossing of thresholds and Marcuse's use of aesthetic defamiliarization to recalibrate the instincts. For Marcuse, this adjustment is a *supra*-transgressive event; the intersection of past and present (and potential) futures.

From within Pragmatist aesthetics, John Dewey addresses the significance of counterfactual plasticity necessary for aesthetic experience that disrupts invariable and arrhythmic "aesthetic vulgarity . . . due to the monotony caused by regular repetition of forms, uniformly spaced"[94] and the "humdrum,"[95] meaning "any product whose quality is not of the very 'easy' sort that exhibits dislocations and dissociations of what is usually connected."[96] In distinguishing aesthetic experience as something autonomous—under the influence of James's "habituation" on the one hand, and Peirce's "prejudices and prejudgments" based on particular experiences on the other—Dewey places great emphasis on alterations to familiar perceptions in their *temporal* context of occurrence (or recurrence) as well as in their *intensity*. In the common-sense language of Pragmatism, Dewey writes: "The new idea must be generated out of the old; it has its basis in them; and in the end its justification is found in the completion and organization which it contributes to them."[97] While expressed in terms of rhythm and energy, Dewey's perceptual notion of aesthetic experience emphasized its *progressive* disruption (reflecting his praise of Darwinian evolution) of familiar experiences through "doing and undergoing"[98] whereby, at least on the level of its perception, "in a distinctively aesthetic experience, characteristics that are subdued in other experiences are dominant."[99] For Marcuse, this is synonymous with the instinctually transformative effects of defamiliarization, while for Wynter, defamiliarization means crossing familiar thresholds *by changing ground.*

METHEXIS AND AMBIVALENCE

The aspirations of ethico-aesthetic experience include its application to collective participation (*methexis*) in which "a group stands to its immanent collective soul. . . . The one can go out into the many; the many can lose themselves in reunion with the one."[100] Methexis refers to an active organization of individuals against preimposed common-sense limits, just as the multitude of particular defamiliarizing aesthetic forms and techniques are able to challenge the dominant notion of a monohumanist experience. Where common sense is maintained cathartically through repressive tolerance and the administration of what Adorno calls the "subjugation of the particular,"[101] methexis is an act of counter-cathartic collectivism that defines the praxis of being human. In the radically democratic terms of Wynter, methexis means the "transcosmogonic" participation of all "hybrid" individuals in the definition of a human dimension: "whether white or non-white, black or non-black, now cognitively empowered to, as Fanon urges us, 'tear off with all [our] strength, the shameful livery put together by centuries of incomprehension.'"[102]

In Marcuse's late essay "Ecology and the Critique of Modern Society," he concludes that a fundamental "radical character structure" in the individual is necessary for radical social change.[103] Like the development of radical sensibility through defamiliarized aesthetic experience, Marcuse defines the radical character structure in Freudo-Marxist terms as "a preponderance in the individual of life instincts or erotic energy over the death instinct or destructive drives"[104] demonstrating a "a nonconformist consciousness."[105] In practice, however, he confesses that even a radical shift in individual consciousness does not necessarily move beyond *ambivalence*, a state of concurrent conflicting beliefs toward some end goal.[106]

To overcome ambivalence, effective resistance exists methectically in "groups which cut across social classes—for example, the student movement, women's liberation, citizen initiatives, ecology collectives, and so on."[107] He emphasizes that art's dynamic autonomy relies on an acknowledgment of the conscious and unconscious repressive effects of administered catharsis prior to participation in political defamiliarization emerging from care. Thus, aesthetic experience in Marcuse's sense points to participatory, counter-cathartic action (as opposed to cathartic integration) where a multiplicity of subjects participate in a collective nonhierarchical transgression of common sense.[108] Michael Hardt and Antonio Negri describe this as "the plural ontology of politics"[109] that preserves "the continuing development of a collective consciousness informed by the historical struggles for liberation and motivated by the shared sense of obligation to preserve the collective being, the ontological totality."[110] Davis, too, phrases such pluralistic politics similarly, such that "any theory or political strategy that pretends to possess a total theory of freedom, or one that can be categorically understood, has failed to account for the multiplicity of possibilities, which can, perhaps, only be evocatively represented in the realm of culture."[111] In agreement with Davis, the counterforce that is ultimately needed is to "build a mass movement and develop actions through which any and everybody who is opposed to injustice can add their voices to the outcry."[112]

Ultimately, what follows from the analysis pursued in the preceding chapters? Why is it *important* to develop a radical sensibility? Why does habitualization make it *difficult* to develop such a character structure? How is such a character structure *developed* through defamiliarization? How does such a character structure still need to be *applied*? Significantly, this last question refers to the challenge to overcome ambivalence even after the habitualizing forces behind common sense are identified. Marcuse knows that aesthetics cannot overcome political ambivalence alone, but he acknowledges its potential and wills for a collective participation "through estrangement and the subversion of consciousness,"[113] where "the sensibility, sensitivity of the individual has their share in the aesthetic reconciliation of the environment."[114]

By tracing the philosophical and historical roots of Marcuse's aesthetics, I have tried to address the relevance and practicality of his claims for art's radical ethico-aesthetic effects. Of central importance, Marcuse insists that art (and anti-art) is *not* direct politics, since ambivalence must still be overcome through collective action. Beyond the indirect political effects that aesthetic defamiliarization has on habitualized instincts by caring for the uncommon, concrete social change still requires methectic will: "In this sense, it is indeed an internal exigency of art which drives the artist to the street . . . but in doing so he leaves the universe of art and enters the larger universe of which art remains an antagonist part: that of radical practice."[115]

Wynter, in terms of aesthetics, reframes this necessary work as deconstructing "our particular genre-specific auto-speciating, always already storytelling chartered/encoded 'descriptive statement' of being human."[116] In this way, for Marcuse and Wynter, defamiliarization provides a practical aesthetic technique that can subvert repressive common sense producing indirect political effects *without* determinate results. By revisiting Marcuse's aesthetic theory, and by extending it through Wynter's decolonial, anti-racist, and feminist perspectives, the hope is that defamiliarization will newly resonate. At the heart of Marcuse's ethico-aesthetic theory is defamiliarization that is connected to care as solicitude, concern, attentiveness, willing, and minding. Defamiliarizing aesthetic experience, therefore, profoundly increases the plasticity of our lived experience in relation to the lived experiences of others, beyond ours worlds enframed by habitualization, yet awaiting the overcoming of ambivalence. As Marcuse affirms: "Art breaks open a dimension inaccessible to other experiences, in which human beings, nature, and things no longer stand under the law of the established reality principle. Subjects and objects encounter the appearance of that autonomy which is denied them in their society. The encounter with the truth of art happens in the estranging language and images which make perceptible, visible, and audible that which is no longer, or not yet, perceived, said, and heard in everyday life."[117]

CODA: MISREADING MARCUSE'S AESTHETICS

Some of the main commentators in the 1960s and 1970s on Herbert Marcuse's aesthetics—including the art critics Ursula Meyer, Jack Burnham, Harold Rosenberg, and Gregory Battcock—often raised questions about the connection he makes between art and politics. What exactly is it about art's "internal exigency"[1] that links it with political practice? How can art's indirect political character have actual political effects? Can these political effects be measured, identified, or nurtured? Ultimately, must the artist step outside of art (that is, become a non-artist or harmonic *anti*-artist) to engage in direct political activity? A main purpose of this book has been to address such questions by closely analyzing Marcuse's aesthetic theory to show his overlooked relevance to the discourse on contemporary art and politics. This coda looks at some of the main criticisms and misreadings of Marcuse's aesthetics specifically by Meyer, Burnham, Rosenberg, and Battcock and, in the process, applies some of the terminology and issues that were addressed in depth in the preceding chapters.

Marcuse's essay "Art in the One-Dimensional Society" was published in the periodical *Arts Magazine* in May 1967. In the same year, art historian George Kubler published "Style and the Representation of Historical Time" in the multimedia magazine *Aspen* (no. 5+6, "The Minimalism Issue"), which was a synopsis of his admired, but now mostly forgotten, book titled *The Shape of Time: Remarks on the History of Things* (1962). There are strong affinities between Marcuse and Kubler in the former's notion of "radical sensibility" and latter's category of "radical human invention." Curiously, however, Marcuse's aesthetic theory has mainly been viewed as anachronistic and conservative while, at the time, Kubler's was seen as innovative and progressive. It is known, for instance, that Kubler influenced artists such as Robert Smithson, Robert Morris, Asger Jorn, Brian O'Doherty, and Ad Reinhardt (who even wrote a review of Kubler's book for *Art News*).[2]

At the core of *The Shape of Time* he presents two models of human invention: the production of tools based on changing needs and the production of artworks beyond immediate needs. Where the first signifies inventions to serve some utility, the second refers to inventions of "non-instrumental use."[3] Art's non-instrumentality, however, does not mean it is of lesser value than useful invention. On the contrary, aesthetic invention is the "channel to the universe," since it "alters the sensibility of mankind [and when] the capacity of that channel can be increased, knowledge of the universe will expand accordingly."[4] Where human inventions take on varying degrees of expansion, the most transformative is non-instrumental "radical invention,"[5] which "discards ready-made positions, [such that] the investigator constructs his own system of postulates and sets forth to discover the universe they alone can disclose."[6] While the invention of artworks and tools are "among ways of altering the set of the mind," it is exclusively radical artistic invention that alters the governing "system of postulates" that construct common sense. While tools are limited to solving matters at hand, radical artistic inventions, in their non-instrumentality, confront "elements already given to the observer."[7] As Kubler colorfully puts it, artworks challenge given limits through "a difficult tour de force [and] a lapse of propriety surrounded by the frightening aura of a violation of the sanctity of routine."[8]

Despite similar conceptual conclusions, including art's capacity to alter "given limits" and "ready-made positions," Marcuse's aesthetic theory was ignored or misunderstood by art critics due to, I argue, his conceptual density and through cumulative and repetitive misinterpretations. In addition, assessments of Marcuse's aesthetics were overshadowed by his sociopolitical writings and his association with the New Left. Harold Rosenberg, for example, fully reduced Marcuse's position to the New Left's failed political ambitions. (Such a representation was not unique to Rosenberg, however, since post-May 1968 resentments developed, for various reasons, among even his staunchest political adherents.)[9] Most damagingly, the artist, critic, and prolific anthologist Gregory Battcock's "Marcuse and Anti-Art" series in *Arts Magazine* (1969), as well as his essay in *Idea Art* titled "Art in Service to the Left" (1973), deformed Marcuse through his misunderstanding of Marcusean themes (like Eros and anti-art) resulting in the promulgation of error and caricature in numerous publications. Even the efforts of more astute art world interpreters, such as Ursula Meyer and, to a lesser degree, Jack Burnham also assisted in obfuscating Marcuse's aesthetics through overdetermined readings of anti-art (Meyer) and technology (Burnham).

A closer examination of these four critics reveals many of the prejudices that have endured and devalued Marcuse's aesthetic theory into the present. Meyer's "Eruption of Anti-Art" (1973) analyzes anti-art in the context of Marcuse's *An Essay on Liberation*. Meyer presents Marcuse as having "resuscitated the concept of anti-art, radicalizing it substantially by extending it to the purely political arena . . . and places anti-art in streets and marketplaces and not in galleries and museums." This simplification, however, stigmatized Marcuse as endorsing political anti-art on *formal* grounds. Meyer falsely presents Marcuse as wholeheartedly celebrating the aesthetic qualities of "graffiti, posters, and guerilla theatre actions that played a significant role in catalyzing the revolutionary impact [of the May Rebellion]."[10] On the contrary, Marcuse insists that direct political forms of anti-art reproducing the language of the everyday undermine the indirect political potency of defamiliarization that "rebels against the dictates of repressive reason."[11]

Burnham, a sympathetic reader of Marcuse's aesthetic theory, is especially concerned as a curator with replicating what he termed a "Marcusean analysis" of art and technology.[12] Burnham even brushed up against Marcuse in *On the Future of Art* (1970), a collection of essays that included Burnham's "The Aesthetics of Intelligent Systems" alongside Marcuse's Guggenheim lecture "Art as a Form of Reality." At times, Burnham adopts a Freudo-Marxist lexicon that imitates Marcuse in his critique of direct political anti-art, asking for instance: "Are we so far into Thanatos that the next upheaval can only be the death of illusionary revolution?"[13] In particular, Burnham's fascination with art and technology is remembered in the exhibition he curated at the Jewish Museum titled *Software* (1970), which "presented the results of scientific experiments, conducted by research teams and scientists, alongside projects born out of the conceptual art movement. . . . Detached from the heightened optimism toward media at the time, he criticizes Marshall McLuhan's theories and says that man-machine interaction encourages invention and creativity while also alienating the worker."[14] Yet, in his eventual disenchantment with the lack of art world enthusiasm for a "post-industrial" direction that should have merged art and technology, Burnham inaccurately enlists Marcuse for its cause. Within his Marcusean analysis, he inquires: "Why have others so bungled its use in producing new art forms? Is it possible that the schism between art and sophisticated technology is far deeper than we suspect, that, in fact, these differences may lie embedded in the neural programs of artists' and scientists' minds?"[15] In the end, Burnham's application of Marcuse to postindustrial art exemplifies the "technological fetishism"[16] that is an inverted wish that technology would change art and not, as Marcuse argues, that a radical sensibility must change technē—including techniques as social modes of production and behavior.

More polemically, Harold Rosenberg misinterprets Marcuse's fundamental arguments, even though he shares his perspective on harmonic anti-art at times. In the collected essays in *The De-Definition of Art*, Rosenberg criticizes the emergence of the "post-artist," which in some ways intersects with Marcuse's criticism of the anti-artist who undialectically seeks to blur the boundaries between art and the everyday. Rosenberg argues that "the artist without art, the beyond-art artist, is not an artist at all, no matter how talented he may be as an impresario of popular spectaculars."[17] In his essay "Set Out for Clayton!," he illustrates his thesis using the performance work of Vito Acconci and the "living art" of Robert Morris, which represents a wide-ranging "breakdown of the barriers between art and life as a radical assault on bourgeois culture."[18] According to Rosenberg, Acconci and Morris represent the extremes of "a situation that offers a role to everyone, regardless of talent or training," resulting in art's "de-definition" (which is also a "deskilling")[19] such that "everyone is an artist."[20] Rosenberg describes this situation as a conflation of utopianism, failed social revolution, the influence of mass culture, and a systematic art world logic, which results in a reversal of Marxist identity theory wherein *social*-consciousness must precede *self*-consciousness. This inverted logic is brought about by art forms that are "gestic" (recalling Brecht) in which "relieved of inherited forms, the individual has gained the privilege of molding his own identity out of data pertaining to his body and any mode of busyness ('gestic')."[21] Artists like Acconci and Morris are depicted as performing a living art where their self-interestedness causes "the cultural revolution [to] precede the political-economic one."[22]

Furthermore, with an emphasis on *quantity* over quality, Rosenberg argues that Morris and Acconci (as well as a list of artists including Andy Warhol, Les Levine, Allan Kaprow, John Cage, Dennis Oppenheim, and Otto Piene) have made "quality superfluous." He claims that post-art at best relies on quantity (or extremism) located in gestic banality and fungible objects. Here, Rosenberg shares Marcuse's criticism of a Brechtian version of anti-art "with [its] present tendency to dissolve forms and mingle art and life"[23] for reproducing and ineffectually confronting dominant rationality. Rosenberg epitomizes Morris as embodying this triumph of banality, calling him "the leading theoretician-practitioner of an art that could be made by anyone and appreciated through hearsay."[24] While he grants that Acconci and Morris may have challenged an *art world* status quo, through an undialectical blurring of art and life they end up reproducing the *social* status quo.

Nevertheless, despite these parallels, Rosenberg ultimately misconstrues Marcuse's position and reduces it to a perspective that only "identifies 'real' art with anti-art, and anti-art with the New Left." Rosenberg propounds the erroneous view that "the radical connections of art-as-life" endear themselves to Marcuse as an artistic form of political protest. Moreover, he claims that Marcuse's contradictoriness was *anti*-avant-garde in "conflict with the negative and utilitarian art of this century since Futurism and Constructivism." To support these false claims, Rosenberg argues that Marcuse promotes "changeless standards by which to denounce the creations of free minds . . . by locating himself firmly in the academic tradition." In Rosenberg's opinion, Marcuse "splits form from content," resulting in his "overlooking the progressive deformalization of the modern imagination under the flood of random events and mass-communication patterns . . . overlook[ing], too, the great works of modernism that are improvised in one-of-a-kind forms (*Thus Spoke Zarathustra*, 'Guernica,' even the *Communist Manifesto*) or built out of raw fact (*Moby Dick*, Impressionist painting, collage)." Most egregiously, Rosenberg encourages the wholly invalid claim that "Marcuse's position is an instance of the intrinsic conservation of the contemporary Marxist outlook on art. In the name of a future new society, it rejects the changing imaginative substance of the present."[25] The accusation that Rosenberg cannot support is how the author of *The Aesthetic Dimension*, which is subtitled *Toward a Critique of Marxist Aesthetics*, can be accused of maintaining an orthodox Marxist position.

Rosenberg's depiction of Marcuse overlooks the latter's aesthetic imperative that *defamiliarization* is "the radical effort to sustain and intensify the 'power of the negative,' the subversive potential of art . . . sustain[ing] and intensify[ing] the alienating power of art: the aesthetic form, in which alone the radical force of art becomes communicable."[26] Essentially, Rosenberg erroneously represents Marcuse as a Romantic utopianist who wants "to revolutionize society but to keep art intact *above* society, in the form it presumably always had . . . art being higher than revolution . . . higher than life itself."[27] On the contrary, Marcuse's aesthetics promotes the material subversion of common sense through "a reclamation of processes refocusing art as energy driving to change perception."[28] With unfortunate effects, the straw man Rosenberg creates has only superficial resemblance to the actual Marcuse who demands that art is "an essential aspect of liberation, namely, the radical transformation of the technical and natural universe in accordance with the emancipated sensibility (and rationality) of man."[29]

Finally, the most prolific yet inconsistent and incoherent interpreters of Marcuse was Gregory Battcock. In Battcock's planned three-part series (which ended after Part II) published in *Arts Magazine* (1969) titled "Marcuse and Anti-Art," he reconstructs Marcuse's aesthetic theory mainly through his idiosyncratic reading of anti-art. It is safe to assume that Battcock was familiar with Marcuse's essay "Art in the One-Dimensional

Society," since it was published two years earlier in the same periodical, although Part I and Part II of his series only explicitly cite *An Essay on Liberation*."[30] Though attuned to certain aspects of Marcuse's critical theory that "appear within a larger philosophical context that views artistic development as an essential and revealing aspect of the new revolution in perception, in creation of the new sensibility and the inevitable trend away from reification,"[31] Battcock's inability or unwillingness to portray Marcuse's *dialectical* analysis of anti-art leads to numerous misinterpretations.

First, Battcock claims Marcuse broadly endorses anti-art that is categorically and conventionally "outside the realm of formal art" as "best conforming to the requirements for total revolutionary change."[32] His motley representatives of anti-art include the cinema of Warhol, graffiti, "sex papers," and serial art. Taking each of these examples in turn, by inference from Marcuse's writings, he would have criticized the banality of Warhol's films as fetishizing the familiar. As for graffiti and "sex papers," he would have labeled these as reactionary forms of repression or, precisely, as forms of repressive desublimation. Further, regarding Battcock's anti-art example of "sex papers," he tenaciously argues pornography is endorsed in Marcuse's rejection of conventional morality. While true in terms of a critique of rationalized *repressive* morality, Battcock over-identifies Marcuse's advocacy of Eros (as love freed from the bondage of the particular)[33] with pornography of "the new sex oriented press . . . that has engaged in the creation of a different language that is not officially acceptable."[34] From this perspective, Battcock simply reiterates the clichéd version of Marcuse as the product of an era of "free love, flower power and personal liberation"[35] and as someone who only supports anti-art that defies "'good taste' and 'common decency.'"[36] As for serial art (depending on the object of serial repetition, but taking for example Carl Andre's "Lever" [1966]), he may have conceded it was the closest on the list to offering, through repeated elements, a form of defamiliarization—although a weak Pragmatist variety, more in line with Dewey's description of aesthetic experience produced through the satisfaction of an emotional quality possessing "internal integration and fulfillment reached through ordered and organized movement."[37] Regarding Battcock's examples of anti-art, he erroneously reduces Marcuse's use of the term to one "that must not only be difficult to accept as art, but it must be unacceptable as art."[38]

Second, Battcock overplays Marcuse's association with the Romantic equation of Form and Beauty. Even though in "Marcuse and Anti-Art, Part II," he keeps to Marcuse's argument in "Art as a Form of Reality," which aligns beauty (in a metaphorical sense) with alienation (in existential and formal senses), Battcock misses the crucial parenthetical subtext. Battcock deduces that because Marcuse criticizes repressive desublimation as "formless semi-spontaneity,"[39] it follows that art should "purify"[40] reality or otherwise fail. On the contrary, Marcuse is critical of anti-art (where it mimics the language of the everyday) for not fulfilling art's necessity of *depurifying* (which is to say, defamiliarizing) familiar forms. The demonstration of defamiliarized "form," moreover, is "beautiful" insofar as it exposes the arbitrary laws of dominant rationality. Marcuse insists that art *not* reject its autonomy from the everyday, but that it must strengthen it *dynamically* in relation to socio-historical conditions. Contrary to Battcock's version of Marcuse's theory of aesthetic form, it is art's capacity for *non*-repressive sublimation via defamiliarization as a counterforce to common sense that can practically subvert habitualized instincts and, once ambivalence is overcome, result in "society as a work of art."[41]

Lastly, as a self-promotional tactic, Battcock rebrands anti-art (first in "Marcuse and Anti-Art, Part II," then later more fully in "Art in the Service to the Left?") as "outlaw art," which cannot be "conveniently housed within the framework of existent cultural, educational and even industrial corporations."[42] Battcock presents his own version of anti-art, incorrectly derived from Marcuse's dialectical sense, to defend a "diluted and in a sense hypocritical artistic activity that is better to subvert the system from within."[43] Astutely, in "Eruption of Anti-Art," Meyer defends Marcuse and detects Battcock's "romantic terminology suggestive of virile strength and stamina"[44] that judges the valuation of his outlaw art by its *unacceptability* in terms of moralistic taste ("perversion and subversion"[45]) that is beyond markets and museums. Meyer correctly criticizes Battcock for missing the multilayered "social, political, economic and psychological"[46] content of the aesthetic dimension which, to the detriment of Marcuse's legacy, often eludes his critics.

Acknowledgments

My deepest gratitude goes to Juliane Rebentisch without whose expert guidance and continual encouragement this book would not exist. I am also sincerely grateful to the members of my dissertation committee at Hochschule für Gestaltung, Offenbach—Martin Gessmann, Heiner Blum, and Barbara Fischer—for offering challenging questions and invaluable input that helped strengthen the book's arguments. A very special thanks to Nathifa Greene for agreeing to write a foreword. My conversations with Nathifa, since meeting one another at a conference of the Radical Philosophy Association in 2018, have been exhilarating.

Thank you to the long list of friends and colleagues who intentionally or unintentionally offered support and substance during the writing of this book since 2013. This list includes but is in no way limited to Bryne McLaughlin, Matthew Beattie, Clive Robertson, Ruthanne Kim Crapo, Barbarita Polster, Nicole Prutsch, Merray Gerges, Lisa Steele, Kim Tomczak, Irmgard Emmelhainz, Nassima Rayuela, James Hoff, Emily Bingeman, Alexis Lagimodière-Grisé, Andrew Cairns,

Danny Hussey, Bridget Thompson, Mitchell Wiebe, Ryan Witt, Linda Rosa Saal, Julia Sunniva, Ella Tetrault, Michael Eddy, Carmel Farahbakhsh, Adi Fleisher, Bruce Barber, and the late Sandra Alfoldy. Also, much gratitude to the many friends who offered generous hospitality during long periods of research in Germany, including Matthew and Aine Beattie, Sebastian Mühl, Mathias Windelberg, Lisa Hopf, Marina Kampka, Isabelle Hoffman, Annika Frye, Daniel Taylor, Aaron Weldon, and Sophia Erdahl.

Significant thanks to colleagues met through conferences of the International Herbert Marcuse Society, which allowed me to learn and stumble through ideas in a very supportive scholarly community. Thanks especially to Andrew Lamas, Imaculada Kangussu, and Charles Reitz for feedback and encouragement in the late manuscript phase of the book. Also, I thank Peter-Erwin Jansen, Arnold Farr, Douglas Kellner, Andrew Feenberg, Sarah Surak, Craig R. Christiansen, J. Reese Faust, and Terry Maley for informal conversations with lasting effects.

Heartfelt gratitude to the incredible undergraduate and graduate students at NSCAD University, the participants of the Gonzago Institute through the Khyber Artist-Run Centre, and the unforgettable workshop group at Hochschule für Gestaltung, Offenbach for helping to develop these ideas in real-time.

Most recently, sincere thanks to the editorial and design teams at the MIT Press. I am deeply grateful to Victoria Hindley whose encouragement and advocacy ultimately made the publication of this book possible. Thanks also to Gabriela Bueno Gibbs for her superb assistance along the way; Kathleen Caruso for her meticulous final editing; Molly Seamans for her skillful book design, and Marc Lowenthal for passing my manuscript along at the submission stage. I am also deeply grateful for the precise criticism and suggestions of the peer reviewers of the original manuscript sent to the MIT Press. Thanks also to Danielle St-Amour for providing helpful editorial work at the midpoint of the manuscript's development and to Matthew Beattie for help polishing up figure 5.3.

With enduring respect, I thank Robert Barry and the late Lawrence Weiner for permission to reproduce images of their work and for their lifetime of artistic commitment. Thanks also to the Michael Asher Foundation (especially Karen Dunbar and Roxy Gonzalez) and the School of Visual Arts (especially Beth Kleber and Dan Strodl) for permission to reproduce images from their respective archives. In addition, I wish to acknowledge the institutional support from Hochschule für Gestaltung, Offenbach, and NSCAD University, Halifax.

Finally, abundant love to Janet Leonard, Jennifer Leonard, and Anne-Sophie Vallée for their years of encouragement and input over the entire course of the book's development.

Notes

CHAPTER 1

1. For comprehensive histories of the Frankfurt School, see Jay, *Dialectical Imagination* and Held, *Introduction to Critical Theory*. For histories of the New Left, see Isserman, *If I Had a Hammer*; Miller, *Democracy in the Streets*; Breines, *Community and Organization*; Gitlin, *The Sixties*; Katsiaficas, *The Global Imagination of 1968*; McMillan and Buhle, *The New Left Revisited*; and Davis and Wiener, *Set the Night on Fire*.
2. Marcuse and Wynter both taught at the University of California at San Diego, but their time there unfortunately did not overlap (Marcuse 1965–1970; Wynter 1974–1977).
3. "This strange alliance has found its most striking form in the fact that the two names who appeared most frequently on the walls of the University of Paris were Karl Marx, the founder of socialism and André Breton, the founder of Surrealism" (Marcuse, "Beyond One-Dimensional Man," 118).
4. The concept of Négritude was first proposed by Aimé Césaire in the journal *L'Étudiant noir* (1935), then in his long poem *Cahier d'un retour au pays natal* ("Notebook of a Return to My Native Land") (1939) and later in the subsequent pages of the Martinican journal *Tropiques* (1941–1945).
5. Marcuse, *Counterrevolution and Revolt*, 87–88.

6. Marcuse, 63. The term "radical sensibility" is also developed in chapter 2 of *Counterrevolution and Revolt*, "Nature and Revolution," which is republished separately in *The Essential Marcuse*.

7. Alberro, "Institutions, Critique, and Institutional Critique," 3.

8. As asserted by Jürgen Habermas in tribute to Marcuse (Habermas, "Questions and Counter Questions," 72).

9. I use *habitualize*, which means "to become accustomed to a situation" throughout the book instead of *habituate*, which means "to make specific behaviors through habit." While both are reliant on habit formation, habitualization works unconsciously, even furtively, to normalize behavior, whereas habituation works through intentional effort.

10. Marcuse, *One-Dimensional Man*, 134.

11. Marcuse, "Failure of the New Left?," 6.

12. Marcuse, 5.

13. Marcuse, "Art in the One-Dimensional Society." In Spring 1969, Marcuse delivered a second public lecture on art and politics at the Guggenheim Museum titled "Art as a Form of Reality" published in Fry, *On the Future of Art*.

14. "Rhetoric is the counterpart to dialectic" (Aristotle, *Rhetoric*, 1354a).

15. In context, Adorno's full statement is: "The critique of culture is confronted with the last stage in the dialectic of culture and barbarism: to write a poem after Auschwitz is barbaric, and that corrodes also the knowledge which expresses why it has become impossible to write poetry today. Absolute reification, which presupposed intellectual progress as one of its elements, is now preparing to absorb the mind entirely. Critical intelligence cannot be equal to this challenge as long as it confines itself to self-satisfied contemplation" (Adorno, "Cultural Criticism and Society," 34). Here, it is relevant to note that the "task" of the New Left (or specifically the Students for a Democratic Society) was self-described as "impossible and necessary" (Gitlin, *The Sixties*, 246).

16. Marcuse, "Letters to the Chicago Surrealists," 43. On a history of the Chicago Surrealist movement, see Rosemont, Rosemont, and Garon, *The Forecast Is Hot*.

17. Marcuse, *One-Dimensional Man*, 72.

18. Marcuse, *An Essay on Liberation*, vii.

19. Marcuse, *Counterrevolution and Revolt*, 63.

20. See Drucilla Cornell's application of technē as a mode of praxis in "Derrida's Negotiations." Also see Cornell and Seely, *Spirit of Revolution*, especially the discussion of Sylvia Wynter in chapter 4.

21. The distinction between fact and facticity is a variation of the premise at the root of German idealism where "philosophy is in constant conflict with *common-sense* understanding and also those institutions in society which support it." The notion behind this is "the real world is the intelligible world (*Geistigwelt*)—the material world is a system of images which received real content only by the working of the human mind. The intelligible world as philosophy is knowledge concepts (as against the common-sense understanding of things, mere unreflective perception). . . . The state is actually a moral institution whose function is to create the conditions (pre-conditions) under which the freedom of man can operate." (Leiss, "Herbert Marcuse: Lectures on Marxian Theory and Communism, 13).

22. Marcuse, "Some Remarks on Aragon," 214.

23. Leiss, "Critical Theory and Its Future," 336.

24. See, for example, Gablik, "Connective Aesthetics."

25. Marcuse, *The Aesthetic Dimension*, ix.

26. See Bronner's "Reconstructing the Experiment," 129; and *Modernism at the Barricades*, 18.

27. Marcuse, *Eros and Civilization*, 149.

28. Marcuse, 149.

29. Whitehead, *Science*, 197.

30. Breton, "Second Manifesto of Surrealism," 125.

31. Breton, 186.

32. Breton, "A Great Black Poet," xvii.

33. Marcuse, *One-Dimensional Man*, 228.

34. Whitehead, *Science*, 197. Also see Whitehead, *Process*, 347.

35. There is a parallel formulation of care as solicitude and concern in Martin Heidegger's care-structure (*Sorgestruktur*) as presented in *Being and Time*. I discuss this subject in chapter 5 and apply it through the thought of Sylvia Wynter.

36. Whitehead, *Adventures in Ideas*, 226.

37. See Shaviro, *Universe of Things*. For the Marcuse/Whitehead connection, see Duston Moore's work on the subject, especially "Whitehead and Marcuse." Also see Taggart, "Whitehead and Marcuse."

38. Marcuse, "The Problem of Violence and the Radical Opposition," 84. Compare to the digital equivalent of "computational capitalism" in Beller, *The Message Is Murder.*

39. Marcuse, "Failure of the New Left?," 3.

40. Reitz, *Marcuse's One-Dimensional Man*, 18.

41. Adorno, "On the Fetish Character of Music," 44.

42. Aristotle, *Poetics*, 1450/15–1450.1/15.

43. Other prominent examples of anti-Aristotelian theater, based mainly on cathartic *shock*, include Antonin Artaud's "Theatre of Cruelty" and the Italian Futurists' "Synthetic Theatre," which attacked the idea of audience as "a circle of bystanders who swallow their anguish and pity as they watch the slow agony of a horse who has collapsed on the pavement. The sigh of applause that finally breaks out frees the audience's stomach from all the indigestible time it has swallowed" (Marinetti, Settimelli, and Corra, "The Futurist Synthetic Theatre," 205).

44. Engels, *Feuerbach*, 96.

45. Compare to Antonio Gramsci's examination of *hegemony* in *The Prison Notebooks*. In the section "Analysis of Situations. Relations of Force," for example, Gramsci describes the cultural hegemonic phase of state dominance as the moment of "bringing about not only a unison of economic and political aims, but also intellectual and moral unity, posing all the questions around which the struggle rages not on a corporate but on a 'universal' plane, and thus creating the hegemony of a fundamental social group over a series of subordinate groups" (406).

46. Marcuse, "Freedom and Freud's Theory," 11.

47. Marcuse, *Counterrevolution and Revolt*, 62–63.

48. Brecht, "Theatre for Pleasure," 71.

49. Marcuse, *One-Dimensional Man*, 60.

50. Willett, trans., *Brecht on Theatre*, 19.

51. Willett, 99.

52. Shklovsky's essay "Iskusstvo kak priëm" (1917) was also translated into English with the title "Art as Device" (see Erlich, *Russian Formalism*, 76).

53. Philosphical pragmatism was founded by Charles Sanders Peirce, William James, and John Dewey. Peirce later distinguished his position from James and Dewey's by using the term *Pragmaticism*.

54. Peirce, *Collected Papers,* 1.129.

55. There is a strong link between American Pragmatism and the "Protestant work ethic" that puts value on finishing tasks (and perhaps profiting from them) as opposed to questioning norms. See Weber *The Protestant Ethic.* Also see Hamner, *American Pragmatism, 116.*

56. Boyd and Heney, "Peirce on Intuition, Instinct, & Common Sense," 5.

57. Darwin, *On the Origin of the Species*, 185.

58. Peirce, *Collected Papers*, CP 5.400.

59. Darwin, *On the Origin of the Species*, 186.

60. Peirce, *Collected Papers*, CP 7.381.

61. Boyd and Heney, "Peirce on Intuition, Instinct, & Common Sense," 10.

62. The term *life-world* is related to habitualized common sense. The term originally derives from Edmund Husserl (in *The Crisis of European Sciences*) in the sense of "habitually persisting validities" (109) and "the built-up levels of validity acquired by men for the world of their common life" (133). Habermas later applies the term to mean "consisting of individual skills, the intuitive knowledge of *how* one deals with a situation; and from socially acquired practices, the intuitive knowledge of what one can rely on in a situation, not less than, in a trivial sense, the underlying convictions" (Habermas, *Theory of Communicative Action*, 35).

63. Marcuse, *One-Dimensional Man*, 138.

64. Horkheimer, "Traditional and Critical Theory," 201.

65. Marx, "Letter from Marx to Arnold Ruge, September 1843"; italics in original.

66. Marcuse, "Art in the One-Dimensional Society," 28.

67. Marcuse's adherence to *historical materialism* is the most basic evidence to refute any accusation of his blind embrace of abstract utopianism, in which "all the philosophical utopias that followed were also constructed as unchanging and unchangeable—as images of eternity, as expansions of the short periods of individual philosophical contemplation to the whole timeline of human history, as attempts to end history and enter an order that would last forever" (Groys, "Anti-philosophy").

68. Said, "Afterword," *Orientalism*, 332.

69. From the Marxist perspective, on the Darwinian emphasis on the *form* of evolutionary variations rather than their causes, Engels states: "It is true that Darwin, when considering natural selection, leaves out of account the *causes* which have produced the alterations in separate individuals, and deals in the first place with the way in which such individual deviations gradually become the characteristics of a race, variety or species. To Darwin it was of less immediate importance to discover these causes—which up to the present are in part absolutely unknown, and in part can only be stated in quite general terms—than to find a rational form in which their effects become fixed, acquire permanent significance. It is true that in doing this Darwin attributed to his discovery too wide a field of action, made it the sole agent in the alteration of species and neglected the causes of the repeated individual variations, concentrating rather on the form in which these variations become general" (*Anti-Dühring*, 82).

70. Aristotle uses the term "apophantic" in *De Interpretatione* (16a-17a) to speak of the judgment of truth based on the inherent (or "pure") qualities of a phenomenon, as opposed to their *discursive* truth (or falsity). Marcuse's application of the term is derived not only from Aristotle's understanding, but also from its central importance in Husserlian phenomenology in which apophantic logic gives claim to enunciations themselves as judgments. See Husserl, *Formal and Transcendental Logic.*

71. Marcuse, *One-Dimensional Man*, 130.

72. Marcuse, 142.

73. Marcuse, "Apophantic Logos," unpaginated.

74. Marcuse, "Apophantic Logos."

75. Marcuse, *An Essay on Liberation*, 33.

76. Marcuse, "Apophantic Logos."

77. Marcuse, *One-Dimensional Man*, 88.

78. Marcuse, 61.

79. Operationalism is the idea that "a certain way of organizing experience is based on *common* experience shared by the giver and the receiver of the definition" (Rapoport, *Operational Philosophy*, 14. While Marcuse criticizes capitalist operationalism for its "total empiricism in the treatment of concepts . . . [and that] many of the most seriously troublesome concepts are being 'eliminated' by showing that no adequate account of them in terms of operations or behavior can be given" (Marcuse, *One-Dimensional Man*, 14–15), in a dialectical way he sees transformative opportunities, since operationalism also implies potentially radical cohesion around the "belief in the operative value of society's values" (*An Essay on Liberation*, 84) if those values change.

80. Rapoport, *Operational Philosophy*, 205.

81. The shared values of both neoliberalism and neoconservatism converge around "doctrines of competition and entrepreneurship, and posit the rejection of advancing socialist ideas" (Mirowski and Plehwe, *The Road from Mont Pèlerin*, 11). See Brown, "American Nightmare."

82. Darwin, *On the Origin of the Species*, 116.

83. Patrick Tort, *L'Effet Darwin* (Paris: Seuil, 2008), quoted in Dardot and Laval, *The New Way of the World*, 33; italics mine.

84. Dardot and Laval, 33.

85. Hofstadter, *Social Darwinism*, 39.

86. Hofstadter, 31.

87. Spencer, *Study of Sociology*, 401–402.

88. Hofstadter, *Social Darwinism*, 40.

89. Hofstadter, 40.

90. Hofstadter, 41.

91. Spencer, *Study of Sociology*, 346.

92. There are many heinous examples of this toxic hate speech in the English-speaking world undeserving of attention. Steve Bannon, however, warrants a separate mention, since his ambition for a global "populist movement" strategically exploits social sympathies by appealing to "the common man" while reinforcing systemic racism through the myth of equal opportunity—all the while using spurious prophecy based on the pseudo-science of Strauss–Howe generational theory.

93. Marcuse, *One-Dimensional Man*, 15.

94. Marcuse, 142.

95. Marcuse, 142.

96. *Aisthēsis* originally referred to a "living cognition" of sacred texts appealing to both reason *and* bodily sensations of ideals (such as God, Beauty, Freedom) "that can consistently and effectively move the *will* to perform" in a way that promotes (the spirit of) these ideals. See Grote, *The Emergence of Modern Aesthetic Theory, 36.*

97. Grote, *Emergence of Modern Aesthetic Theory*, 14.

98. Marcuse, *Soviet Marxism*, 134.

99. Marcuse, "Art in the One-Dimensional Society," 31.

100. For speculations on the question if nonhuman things can have aesthetic experiences, see Bennet, *Vibrant Matter*; and Barad, *Meeting the Universe Halfway*.

101. Benhabib, *Critique, Norm, and Utopia*, 147.

102. Benhabib, 147.

103. Podro, *Manifold of Perception*, 11. See Kant, *Critique of Judgment*, sections 6 and 7.

104. Miller, "The (Revised) Birth of Negritude," 748.

105. Marcuse demonstrates not only post-Marxist tendencies, but also *post-modern* tendencies avant la lèttre. This is especially evident, I believe, in

Marcuse's paradigmatic difference with Adorno regarding anti-art. See DeKoven, *Utopia Limited*, 26–54.

106. Sim, *Post-Marxism: A Reader*, 5. For other accounts of post-Marxism, see Therborn, *From Marxism to Post-Marxism?*; Keucheyan, *The Left Hemisphere*; and Sim's *Post-Marxism: An Intellectual History*.

107. Feenberg, *Philosophy of Praxis*, 14.

108. See Marcuse, *Counterrevolution and Revolt*, 45–64.

109. Menke, *Sovereignty of Art*, xiii.

110. See the entry for "anamnesis" in Peters, *Greek Philosophical Terms*.

111. In *An Essay on Liberation*, Marcuse refers his reader to the myth of Eros who is "slain by Perseus, and from her truncated body springs the winged horse Pegasus, symbol of poetic imagination" (26–27). On the centrality of "love" in the German Romantic tradition—especially in Friedrich Schlegel's politics founded on the "higher life of the human being that relates to the whole" (21)—see Blechman, "The Revolutionary Dream." On "love" within the Critical Theory tradition, see Feuerbach, "Introduction to *The Essence of Christianity*." The historical materialist response by Engels to Feuerbach as achieving "nothing positive beyond a grandiloquent religion of love and a meagre, impotent system of morals" can be found in Engels, *Ludwig Feuerbach and the Outcome*, 42.

112. The philosopher Theophilus located logos in the heart (*kardia*). See Curry, "The Theogony of Theophilus." Compare to Audre Lorde's emphasis on Eros that challenges mere common-sense efficaciousness. In "Uses of the Erotic," Lorde writes: "Our erotic knowledge empowers us, becomes a lens through which we scrutinize all aspects of our existence . . . projected from within each of us, not to settle for the convenient, the shoddy, the conventionally expected, nor the merely safe" (Lorde, *Sister Outsider*, 57).

113. Marcuse and Popper, *Revolution or Reform*, 77.

114. Prior to Plato's notion, the Pythagoreans believed *anamnesis* to be "the soul's knowledge of earlier forms of embodiment" and "the medium which allows the present *psyche* to train and purify itself, in anticipation of eternal life (Sandywell, *Presocratic Reflexivity*, 217). Sandywell states that the Platonic notion of anamnesis as "recollection" derives directly from its Pythagorean meaning of "rebirth" (218).

115. Shapiro's translator note in Marcuse, "The Concept of Essence," 212.

116. Marcuse, *One-Dimensional Man*, 60.

117. Marcuse, "Art in the One-Dimensional Society," 29.

118. Marcuse, "Freedom and Freud's Theory," 14.

119. Marcuse, *Counterrevolution and Revolt*, 82.

120. Marcuse, 82.

121. Noise, however, can also be used for its sociopolitically dissonant quality that defamiliarizes musical expectations. See Novak's excellent *Japanoise* and the classic Attali, *Noise*.

122. Drafted mainly by René Crevel and signed by André Breton, Paul Eluard, Benjamin Péret, Yves Tanguy, and the Martinican Surrealists Pierre Yoyotte and J. M. Monnerot, the signatories express their revolutionary allegiance not only to "the proletariat and its struggles" but also against colonial racism wherein "the black proletariat whose conditions of life are even more wretched than those of its European equivalent" (Surrealist Group in Paris, "Murderous Humanitarianism," 352). Translated into English by Samuel Beckett as "Murderous Humanitarianism," the original French document is lost.

123. Marcuse, *Soviet Marxism*, 134.

124. Marcuse, *Eros and Civilization*, 163.

125. Aristotle, *De anima*, I, 405a.

126. Ernst Bloch, author of the massive *The Principle of Hope* (1954–1959) was a critic of what he claimed to be Marcuse's use of anamnesis based on its restrictiveness against future knowledge. Bloch preferred to use the term anagnorisis (recognition), which "is linked with reality by only a thin thread" (Landmann, "Talking with Ernst Bloch," 178). Bloch's rejection of anamnesis, therefore, is more akin to Kierkegaard's "leap" (Ferreira, "Faith," 207-215). Marcuse's anamnesis is unlike Bloch's concept of anagnorisis—where "the new is never completely new for us because we bring something with us to measure by it" (Landmann, 178)—since, in Marcuse's opinion, Bloch's anagnorisis measures newness from a one-dimensional viewpoint. Bloch's version of hope is always limited by the possibilities at hand ("wishing"), which places Bloch more firmly within the paradigm of harmonic anti-art.

127. Adorno, *Lectures on Negative Dialectics*, 30.

128. Marcuse, "Nature and Revolution," 242; italics in original.

129. Marx, *Economic and Philosophic Manuscripts, 45.*

130. Marx, 43.

131. Feuerbach, "Towards a Critique," 87.

132. Honneth, *The Idea of Socialism,* 28.

133. Marcuse, *Eros and Civilization*, 91.

134. "Psychic Thermidor" is Marcuse's term named after the month of Thermidor in the French Revolutionary calendar (1794) during which time a right-wing counterrevolutionary coup defeated Robespierre and his followers.

135. Marcuse, "Freedom and Freud's Theory," 38–39.

136. James, *The Principles of Psychology*, 114. For a comprehensive study of attention, see Alford, *Forms of Poetic Attention.*

137. James, 112.

138. James, 105.

139. James, 121.

140. James, 121.

141. Regarding Marcuse's dialectical perspective on operationalism, see note 79 above.

142. It is irresponsible to speak of Heidegger, especially in reference to "authentic Being," without pointing to his now well-known affiliation with Nazism. In Marcuse's letter to Heidegger (dated August 28, 1947), he gives his former teacher the chance to publicly denounce the Nazi regime by invoking *common sense* in this one particular instance: "Common sense (also among intellectuals) . . . refuses to view you as a philosopher, because philosophy and Nazism are irreconcilable. In this conviction common sense is justified." Heidegger's response (January 20, 1948) fails to provide the denunciation Marcuse (and others) sought. Following Marcuse's condemnation in response (May 12, 1948), communication between the two philosophers ceased. See Marcuse and Heidegger, "An Exchange of Letters," 152–164.

143. Heidegger, "The Understanding of Time," 201.

144. Marcuse, *Hegel's Ontology,* 1.

145. Engels, *Ludwig Feuerbach and the End*, 613.

146. Engels, 596.

147. Engels, 613

148. Engels, 613.

149. Engels, 613.

150. Feuerbach, "Hegel's Philosophy," 79.

151. Engels, *Ludwig Feuerbach and the End*, 613–614.

152. Although, if Gadamer is correct, this critique by Feuerbach is a red herring, since it was Hegel's aim from the start to silence self-consciousness *self-consciously*: "In the *Logic* a starting point is firmly established and then a methodological procedure entered upon in which the knowing subject no longer intrudes" (Gadamer, "The Idea of Hegel's *Logic*," 86).

153. Marcuse, *An Essay on Liberation*, 4.

154. Marcuse, 22. Marcuse's own Introduction to *Hegel's Ontology* makes the influence of Heidegger's phenomenological existentialism (*Existenzphilosophie*) indubitable, as he writes: "Any contribution this work may make to the development and clarification of problems is indebted to the philosophical work of Martin Heidegger" (5).

155. Wolin and Abromeit, *Heideggerian Marxism*, xix.

156. See Gillespie, *Hegel, Heidegger, and the Ground of History*, 166–176.

157. Wolin, *Heidegger's Children*, 51.

158. Marcuse, "Art in the One-Dimensional Society," 31.

159. Adorno's critique of Kierkegaard's historicity could in this case be applied to Marcuse: "By rejecting the historical world . . . his dialectics were without a material object and were thus a return to the idealism he claimed to have left behind. By denying real history, he had withdrawn into a pure anthropology based on 'historicity' (*Geschichtlichtkeit*): the abstract possibility of existence in time" (Adorno, *Kierkegaard*, 62).

160. Kellner, "Radical Politics," 2. Also see Ross, *May '68 and Its Afterlives*. In relation to Marcuse and May 1968, Ross challenges the leading role he has been given as a major theoretical influence on protestors by establishing that

"his works were unread in France until after May" (193). However, Ross confirms that *One-Dimensional Man* "began to sell at a rapid pace" (193) soon after the May revolt. Questionably, Ross's claims regarding Marcuse rely in part on the accounts of Daniel Cohn-Bendit with whom Marcuse had a falling out during protests in Italy. See Marcuse's letter to Adorno dated "21 July 1969" in Adorno and Marcuse, "Correspondence."

161. Meaning "with the necessary modifications," using the examples of literature, poetry, and music to speak of the arts in general.

162. See Weiner, "Conversation with Robert C. Morgan," 102.

163. Flynt, " 20 East Broadway, Ben Morea Loft."

164. Marcuse, "Marxism and Feminism," 280.

165. Marcuse, *Counterrevolution and Revolt*, 121–122.

166. Adorno, *Philosophy of New Music*, 82.

167. Marcuse, *Counterrevolution and Revolt*, 122.

168. Isserman, "The Not-So-Dark," 992.

169. Marcuse, "Art in the One-Dimensional Society," 29; italics in original.

170. Schiller, "Kallias," 160.

171. Schiller speaks about artistic technique as the intentional process that leads to the objectification of freedom in artistic form. For Marcuse, in comparison, defamiliarization is the fundamental artistic technique that demonstrates such freedom. See Schiller's statement: "Just as freedom of will can only be thought with the help of causal and material determinations of will, freedom can only be exhibited sensuously with the help of technique. . . . Freedom of appearance may be the ground of freedom, but *technique* is the necessary condition for our representation of freedom" (Kallias, 162; italics in original).

172. Marcuse, "The End of Utopia," 82.

173. "It appears that it was the difficulty connected with the so-called 'problem of induction' which led Whitehead to the disregard of argument displayed in *Process and Reality*" (Popper, *Open Society: Hegel and Marx*, 356, note 9). Popper distrusts inductive reasoning because he claims it is both unfalsifiable and deterministic (i.e., its claims may always be deferred to a future time), which Popper contends is also the case with psychoanalytic and Marxist

theories, the latter especially claiming "the *inevitability* of the transformation of capitalist society into socialism wholly and exclusively" (*Open Society: Hegel and Marx*, 166). Popper was a founding member of the neoliberal, anti-Marxist Mont Pèlerin Society, who on other matters thought the Frankfurt School "vacuous and irresponsible." Popper, "Addendum 1974," 80. Also see Mirowski and Plehwe, *The Road from Mont Pèlerin*.

174. "Provided that communism does not look upon us merely as so many strange animals intended to be exhibited strolling about and gaping suspiciously in its ranks—we shall prove ourselves fully capable of doing our duty as revolutionaries. This, unfortunately, is a commitment that is of no interest to anyone but ourselves: two years ago, for instance, I was personally unable to cross the threshold of the French Communist Party headquarters, freely and unnoticed as I desired, that same threshold where so many undesirable characters, policemen and others, have the right to gambol and frolic at will. In the course of three interrogations, each of which lasted for several hours, I had to defend Surrealism from the puerile accusation that it was essentially a political movement with a strong anticommunist and counterrevolutionary orientation" (Breton, "Second Manifesto of Surrealism," 142).

175. Reiss, "The 'Naturalization' of the Terms 'Ästhetik,'" 646.

176. Baumgarten, *Ästhetik*, 646.

177. Feenberg, *Philosophy of Praxis*, 108.

178. See Beiser, *Schiller as Philosopher*, 215.

179. This conclusion preserves Schiller's overlooked *materialism embedded in his definition of freedom*: "To avoid any misconception I would observe that whenever I speak of freedom I do not mean the sort which necessarily attaches to Man in his capacity as intelligent being, and can neither be given to him nor taken from him, but the sort which is based upon his composite nature. By only acting, in general, in a rational manner, Man displays a freedom of the first kind; by acting rationally within the limits of his material and materially within the laws of actuality, he displays a freedom of the second kind. We might explain the latter simply as a natural possibility of the former" (Schiller, *On the Aesthetic Education*, 90).

180. Schiller, *On the Aesthetic Education*, 99; italics in original.

181. Feenberg, *Philosophy of Praxis*, 108; italics mine.

182. Feenberg, 106.

183. See Herder's "Monument to Baumgarten." For recent commentary on Herder, see Menke, *Force*, 31–33.

184. "Selfishness has established its system in the very bosom of our exquisitely refined society, and we experience all the contagions and all the calamities of community without the accompaniment of a communal spirit. We submit our free judgement to its despotic sanction, our feeling to its fantastic customs, our will to its seductions; only our caprice do we assert against its sacred rights. Proud self-sufficiency contracts, in the worldling, the heart that often still beats sympathetically in the rude natural man, and like fugitives from a burning city everyone seeks only to rescue his own miserable property from the devastation" (Schiller, *On the Aesthetic Education*, 36).

185. Marcuse, "Liberation from the Affluent Society," 178.

186. Jürgen Habermas calls the linking of aesthetics and ethics "overreaching" on the part of Schiller, whose *On the Aesthetic Education of Man* speaks to us of "a utopia reaching beyond art itself" ("Modernity versus Postmodernity,"10).

187. Feenberg, *Philosophy of Praxis*, 106.

188. Feenberg, 106.

189. Feenberg, 106.

190. Feenberg, 111.

191. Reitz, *Art, Alienation, and the Humanities*, 227.

192. Long, *The New Left*, 22.

193. See Hohendahl, *Reappraisals*. In his own defense, Mattick wrote: "But what else is the 'foreseeable future' if not the recognition of some basic trends which affect and alter existing conditions in a definite direction? The emphasis must then be put not on the possibly drawn-out persistency of existing conditions, but on the elements within these conditions which indicate their dissolution" (Mattick, *Critique of Marcuse*, 89.)

194. Marx, "Theses on Feuerbach," 173.

195. "In capitalism, the ordering of society's fundamental requirements regarding production and the proportioning of social labour toward the satisfaction of social needs is largely left to the automatism of the market. Monopolistic

practices disrupt the mechanism, but even without such interferences this form of socio-economic practice can serve only the peculiar 'social' needs of capitalism. The kind of indirect relation between supply and demand established by the market automatism refers to, and is determined by, the profitability of capital and its accumulation. The conscious 'ordering' aspects of the monopolies, concerned as they are with their own special interests only, increase the irrationality of the system as a whole. Even state-capitalistic planning first of all serves the particular needs and the security of its ruling and privileged groups, not the real needs of society" (Mattick, "Spontaneity and Organisation").

196. Jay, *Dialectical Imagination*, xxii. Also see, Jay's "Metapolitics of Utopianism."
197. Jay, "Habermas and Modernism," 137.
198. Beiser, *Schiller as Philosopher*, 110.
199. Marcuse, "The Affirmative Character of Culture," 76.
200. Marcuse, "Repressive Tolerance," 111.

CHAPTER 2

1. Wellmer, "Death of the Sirens."
2. "Reactional countermoves are no more than programmed effects in the opponent's strategy; they play into his hands and thus have no effect on the balance of power" (Lyotard, *The Postmodern Condition*, 16).
3. Marcuse, "The End of Utopia," 71.
4. Marcuse, *The Aesthetic Dimension*, xiii.
5. Marcuse, 50–51.
6. Marcuse, "Art in the One-Dimensional Society," 28.
7. The "Motherfuckers" used for their logo the Zouave smoker on the packets of Zig-Zag cigarettes (see Gitlin, *The Sixties*, 240). Unfortunately, there was no acknowledgment of the colonial significance of this image. Zouave soldiers were elite French infantrymen mainly deployed in North Africa and extensively during the Algerian War (1954–1962).

8. The Living Theatre was founded in 1947 by Judith Malina and Julian Beck. Originally based in New York City, the ensemble toured worldwide in the 1960s and 1970s, returning to New York in the 1980s. The Living Theatre is still active. See Biner, *The Living Theatre*; The Living Theatre, "*Paradise Now*: Notes."

9. Marcuse, *The Aesthetic Dimension*, 9–10; italics in original.

10. Marcuse, 9–10.

11. Beck, *The Life of the Theatre*, section 6.

12. The Living Theatre, "*Paradise Now*: Notes," 99.

13. The Living Theatre, 99.

14. Marcuse, *Counterrevolution and Revolt*, 113.

15. Marcuse, 102.

16. Marcuse, "Art as a Form of Reality," 133–134.

17. Marcuse, 98.

18. Beck, *The Life of the Theatre*, section 40.

19. Marcuse, "Marxism and Feminism," 280.

20. Marcuse, 280.

21. Beck, *The Life of the Theatre*, section 40.

22. Compare to the importance of artworks as afterimages (*Nachbilden*) in Adorno's *Aesthetic Theory* as: "empirical life" (5), "cultic acts" (6), "magic" (18), "enchantment" (58), "the silence that is the single medium through which nature speaks" (74), "the primordial shudder in the age of reification" (79), and "human repression of nature" (288).

23. Marcuse, *An Essay on Liberation*, 24.

24. Marcuse, "Art in the One-Dimensional Society," 28.

25. See Rancière, *Politics of Aesthetics*, 29, and "The Aesthetic Revolution."

26. Marcuse, "Art in the One-Dimensional Society," 31.

27. Marx, *Critique of the Gotha Programme*, 569.

28. Marcuse, "Art in the One-Dimensional Society," 29.

29. Marcuse, 29.

30. Adorno, "Commitment," 91. The original German essay titled "Engagement" is in *Notes zur Literature III* (1962).

31. Sartre, "For Whom Does One Write?," 76. Sartre collaborated with Simone de Beauvoir and Maurice Merleau-Ponty to found *Les Temps Modernes*, a journal devoted to "littérature engagée," for which he served as political editor until 1952. In the face of growing political disagreements with Sartre set in motion by the Korean War, Merleau-Ponty resigned his role as political editor of *Les Temps Modernes* in December 1952 and withdrew from the editorial board altogether in 1953. His critique of Sartre's politics became public in 1955 with *Les Aventures de la dialectique* [*Adventures of the Dialectic*, 1973], in which Merleau-Ponty distanced himself from revolutionary Marxism and sharply criticized Sartre for "ultrabolshevism." Beauvoir's equally biting rebuttal, "Merleau-Ponty and Pseudo-Sartreanism," published the same year in *Les Temps Modernes*, accuses Merleau-Ponty of willfully misrepresenting Sartre's position, opening a rift between the three former friends that would never entirely heal.

32. Adorno, *Aesthetic Theory*, 123.

33. Adorno, "Commitment," 398. Adorno's critique is also relevant to Sartre's commentary on the Négritude movement in his introduction "Orphée noir" to *Anthologie de la nouvelle poésie nègre et malgache* (1948). In this introduction, Sartre reinforces what René Ménil characterizes as Sartre's reproduction of "the black poet" in his own image (Ménil, *Tracées*, 65)—that is, not only "a character without concrete reality who has emerged out of nowhere, exists outside of all social relations, outside the real world and national contexts," but also an undialectically committed character "trapped within its own self-consciousness by its ideological straitjacket" (Richardson, "Introduction," *Refusal of the Shadow*, 9).

34. On the connection of political values and the existential act in the New Left, see Breines, *Community and Organization*; and Isserman, *If I Had a Hammer*.

35. Marcuse, *Counterrevolution and Revolt*, 107; italics in original.

36. Marcuse, *One-Dimensional Man*, 70.

37. Beyond art, it is important to note, Marcuse and Adorno differed greatly on the line separating political commitment and theory. Marcuse chastised Adorno for his famous retreat from engaging in the student protests of the

1960s. In fact, Marcuse found Adorno's unwillingness to commit to any actively *affirmative* refusal to be "intolerable" (see chapter 5) and even, in conversation with his adversary Karl Popper, "disgusting." See the conversations between Adorno and Max Horkheimer in Horkheimer, *Gesammelte Schriften*, 37–71. Also see Marcuse and Popper, *Revolution or Reform?*, 72–73.

38. Marcuse, "Problem of the Dialectic," 80.

39. Adorno, *Negative Dialectics*, 55.

40. See Berger, *Theory of the Avant-Garde*. Originally published in German as *Theorie der Avantgarde* (Frankfurt: Suhrkamp Verlag, 1974). Also see Léger, ed., *The Idea of the Avant Garde*.

41. On Adorno's modernism, see Wellmer "Truth, Semblance, Reconciliation." Republished in Wellmer, *The Persistence of Memory*, 1–35.

42. Wellmer, "Truth, Semblance, Reconciliation," 91–92.

43. Pater, "The School of Giorgione," 106.

44. On the theme of vision in modern European thought, see Jay, *Downcast Eyes*.

45. Reinhardt, "Art-as-Art," 53.

46. See Roman Jakobson, "Co je poesie?/Was ist Poesie (1934)," quoted in Holenstein, "Poetry and Plurifunctionality of Language," 22.

47. Adorno, *Negative Dialectics*, 41.

48. Marcuse, *Counterrevolution and Revolt*, 117.

49. This relates to "Leibniz's concept of *entelechy*, which Goethe formulated as '*geprägte Form, die lebend sich entwickelt*' ['moulded form, which living does unfold']" (Adorno, "Spengler after the Decline," 67).

50. Adorno, "The Actuality of Philosophy," 131.

51. Adorno, *Aesthetic Theory*, 173.

52. Adorno, *Philosophy of New Music*, 41.

53. Leibniz, "Monadology," section 7.

54. Adorno, *Aesthetic Theory*, 179.

55. The Hegelian remnant of "magic" runs throughout Adorno's *Aesthetic Theory*, or at least magic's afterimage (see note 22 above) as does its Marxist variant in the form of the commodity: "The whole mystery of commodities,

all the magic and necromancy that surrounds the products of labour as long as they take the form of commodities, vanishes therefore, so soon as we come to other forms of production" (Marx, *Capital*, 50).

56. Hegel, "The Preface to the *Phenomenology*," 408.

57. Hegel, 408.

58. The monad is distinct from the early modernist symbol, such as that of Stéphane Malarmé, which is only an *image* of the universal in its particulars. Leibniz, on the contrary, understood the monad to *actually* contain the universal in each particular, every particular in the universal: "This connection of all created things with every single one of them and their adaptation to every single one, as well as the connection and adaptation of every single thing to all others, has the result that every single substance stands in relations which express all the others. Whence every single substance is a perpetual living mirror of the universe" (Leibniz, *Monadology*, section 56). See Todorov, *Theories of the Symbol*.

59. Adorno, "Theses upon Art and Religion Today," 296.

60. Gitlin, *The Sixties*, 268.

61. Marcuse, "Art as a Form of Reality," 126.

62. Jay, *Dialectical Imagination*, 183. The same decline of effect could be said of Samuel Beckett's linguistic dissonance that is "the key to contemporary anti-art . . . concretizing this negation, of culling aesthetic meaning from the radical negation of metaphysical meaning" (Adorno, *Aesthetic Theory*, 271).

63. Adorno, "The Dialectical Composer," 205.

64. On Puusemp's transition from "New York Conceptualist working at the socio-metric edge of the genre" to mayor of Rosedale, NY, see Kaprow, "The Real Experiment."

65. Concurrent with *One-Dimensional Man*, we see similar concerns in the writings of Jacques Ellul, Lewis Mumford, and the later Heidegger. See Ellul, *The Technological Society*; Mumford, *Art and Technics*; and Heidegger, *The Question Concerning Technology*, originally published as *Die Technik und die Kehre* (Pfullingen: Günther Neske, 1962).

66. Adorno, "Paralipomena," in *Aesthetic Theory*, 473.

67. See the conversations between Adorno and Max Horkheimer in Horkheimer, *Gesammelte Schriften*, 37–71.

68. Adorno's position on technology exemplifies the "modern" paradigm as described by Jean-François Lyotard in *The Postmodern Condition*. Where this is the case, Marcuse's alternative position implies his "postmodern" quality. Lyotard refers to the modernist dualism between either the embrace or rejection of technological positivism as having its origin in "the theoretical opposition between *Naturwissenschaft* [study of the natural world] and *Geistiswissenschaft* [human studies and the products of the intellect] in the work of Wilhelm Dilthey" (89).

69. Adorno, *Aesthetic Theory*, 168.

70. Higgins, "Synesthesia and Intersenses;" later published as a chapter in Higgins, *Horizons*. Also see Friedman, "FLUXLIST and SILENCE."

71. Compare to Catherine Malabou's notion of "migration," which is "precisely 'multiform' [*vielgestaltig*] and rich in transformations [*reich an Wandlungen*]. So many things pass through it" (Malabou, *Heidegger Change*, 196).

72. Malabou, 196.

73. Kaprow, "Education of the Un-Artist," 105.

74. Kaprow, "Manifesto," 82. Was Marx suggesting a form of intermedia art (which originated in Samuel Coleridge and thus betrays the vestige of Romanticism within Marxism) when he stated: "With a communist organization of society, there disappears a subordination of the artist to local and national narrowness, which arises entirely from division of labour, and also the subordination of the artist to some definite art. . . . In a communist society there are no painters but at most people who engage in painting among other activities" (*The German Ideology* in *Karl Marx: Selected Writings*, 190)?

75. See Higgins, *A Dialectic of Centuries*.

76. Compare to Lawrence Weiner's comment, "I don't want to fuck up somebody's day on their way to work. I want to fuck up their whole life" (Weiner, "Design Matters Live"). Also see "Interview by Patricia Norvell."

77. Handwritten comment in the manuscript version of Marcuse, "Art in the One-Dimensional Society." See Douglas Kellner's editor's note in Marcuse, *Art and Liberation*, 121.

78. Marcuse, 92.

79. Jay, *Dialectical Imagination*, 174. Similarly, Marcuse felt that Georg Lukács's *History and Class Consciousness* was "a contribution to the development of Marxism that is essential and whose importance cannot be overestimated" ("Problem of the Dialectic," 67).

80. For Marcuse's conversational use of the term "debilitating comfort," see Katsiaficas, "Marcuse as an Activist."

81. Marcuse, "Some Social Implications," 63.

82. Marcuse, 258.

83. Marcuse, 225–261.

84. Marcuse, "Art in the One-Dimensional Society," 31.

85. Wellmer "Truth, Semblance, Reconciliation," 103.

86. Wellmer, 103.

87. Wörner, "Stockhausen's Notes," 33.

88. Wörner, 33.

89. Wörner, 38.

90. Wörner, 47.

91. Wörner, 53.

92. Wörner, 54.

93. Wörner, 52.

94. Wörner, 54.

95. Cardew, *Stockhausen Serves Imperialism,* 48.

96. Cardew, 49.

97. Cardew, 53–54.

98. Cardew, 54.

99. To be fair, Adorno's criticism of jazz was against "the standardization, commercialization and rigidification of the medium," causing its canned form to be "deprived of its aesthetic dimension." See Adorno, "Perennial Fashion—Jazz," 131.

100. See Henry Flynt, "Fight Musical Decoration of Fascism!" and "Picket Stockhausen Concert!" flyers, 1964.

101. Flynt flyers.

102. Piekut, *Experimentalism Otherwise*, 65.

103. Indeed, the international network of Fluxus artists included Black artists—namely, the African American artist Ben Patterson (born in Pittsburgh, PA) and the diasporic Dutch artist Stanley Brouwn (born in Paramaribo, Suriname)—but these artists for reasons unknown did not attend the Stockhausen protest. If included in the planning by Maciunus and Flynt, would the protest have taken a radically different form?

104. For Jones's encounters with and resistance to European avant-gardism and the resultant founding of the Black Arts Movement, see chapter 7, "The Black Arts: Politics, Search for a New Life," in his *Autobiography of LeRoi Jones*. In 1965, less than a year after the Stockhausen protest, Jones detached himself from the predominantly white Bohemian scene centered in Manhattan's Lower East Side and moved to Harlem to start the Black Arts Repertory Theatre. "The Revolutionary Theatre should force change, it should be change," wrote Jones in his incendiary manifesto published in the journal *Black Dialogue*. As a preface to the manifesto's reprint in the journal *The Liberator* in July 1965, Jones wrote: "This essay was originally commissioned by the *New York Times* in December 1964, but was refused, with the statement that the editors could not understand it. The *Village Voice* also refused to run this essay. It was first published in *Black Dialogue*" (Jones, "The Revolutionary Theatre," 4). Spurred by the assassination of Malcolm X, Jones coauthored this manifesto under his new name, Amiri Baraka. This marked the beginning of the Black Arts Movement, which Baraka (Jones) would go on to lead for over a decade. See Smethurst, *The Black Arts Movement*.

105. Kelley, "Foreword" in *Black Marxism*, xii.

106. Kelley, 73.

107. Hegel, *The Philosophy of History*, 99.

108. Robinson, *Black Marxism*, 74.

109. Baraka, *Autobiography of LeRoi Jones*, 295.

110. Marcuse, *An Essay on Liberation*, 35.

111. Marcuse, 35.

112. The Surrealist's anti-colonial efforts should be acknowledged here. Two examples stand out most strongly: the 1931 Surrealist counter-exhibition *The Truth about the Colonies* and Breton's public talks in Haiti in December 1945 (including "Surrealism and Haiti") preceding the Haitian Revolution in January 1946. Regarding the influence of Breton's lectures on the radical students associated with the publication *La Ruche*, see Smith, "VIVE 1804!"

113. Quoted in Robinson, *Black Marxism*, 184. Originally quoted by Caute, *Communism and the French Intellectuals*, 211.

114. Baraka, "Technology & Ethos," 155; italics in original.

CHAPTER 3

1. Marcuse, *Eros and Civilization*, 149.

2. Marcuse, "Art in the One-Dimensional Society," 28.

3. Breton, "Surrealist Situation of the Object," 273.

4. Gitlin, *The Sixties*, 238.

5. Gitlin, 31.

6. Marcuse, *The Aesthetic Dimension*, 72; italics mine.

7. First cited by Marcuse in his essay "Über den affirmativen Charakter der Kultur," *Zeitschrift für Sozialforschung* 6, no. 1 (Paris: 1937), the phrase is a shortened version of Stendhal's original in *De L'Amour* (1822): "la beauté n'est que la promesse du bonheur" (beauty is only the promise of happiness). Marcuse's use is also a revision of the original sense, since Stendhal implied that beauty is only the promise of happiness, *not its guarantee*. The shortened phrase "promesse du bonheur" would reappear in many of Marcuse's writings, including *One-Dimensional Man*, 60. Marcuse's 1937 essay appears in English translation as "The Affirmative Character of Culture."

8. Marcuse, "Art in the One-Dimensional Society," 30.

9. Adorno reiterates this thought in "Valéry Proust Museum," 185: "Works of art can fully embody the *promesse du bonheur* only when they have been uprooted from their native soil and have set out along the path to their own destruction."

10. Marcuse, 30.

11. The French translation of "Iskusstvo kak priëm" ("Art as Technique") was published as "L'art comme procédé" in *Théorie de la littérature* (Paris: Éditions du Seuil, 1965).

12. "When Husserl later tried to revive the old philosophical ethos and thematized the act of *epoché*, he understood it to take place in the realm of 'as if.' Thus, the philosophical *epoché* was transposed into the realm of pure imagination—it was no longer a form of life but merely an artistically imagined form" (Groys, "Anti-philosophy).

13. See Erlich, *Russian Formalism*, 61. Husserl explicitly laid out the method of *epoché* in *The Idea of Phenomenology*, which "may be regarded as a radicalization of the methodological constraint, already to be found in *Logical Investigations*" (Beyer, "Edmund Husserl").

14. Marcuse, "Art in the One-Dimensional Society," 29; italics mine.

15. Mukařovský quoted in Holenstein, "Poetry and Plurifunctionality of Language," 22; italics in original. See Mukařovský, "On the Problem of Functions in Architecture." Also see Jakobson and Tynyanov, "Problems of Literary and Linguistic Studies."

16. Marcuse, "Letter to the Chicago Surrealists," 41.

17. "The effect of the congress on the evolution of Soviet art was decisive. The ratification of the socialist realism as the only artistic style acceptable to a Socialist society and, hence, as an international style, together with the several subsequent decrees that attempted to abolish 'formalism' in the arts" (Bowlt, *Russian Art of the Avant-Garde*, 291).

18. Marcuse, *Soviet Marxism*.

19. Breton, "Political Position of Surrealism," 209.

20. Marcuse, *An Essay on Liberation*, 31.

21. Bédouin, *Vingt ans*, 111.

22. Marx, "Letter from Marx to Arnold Ruge, September 1843."

23. Marcuse, "Art in the One-Dimensional Society," 28.

24. Breton, "On the Time When the Surrealists Were Right," 246.

25. Breton, 246.

26. Marcuse, "Letter to the Chicago Surrealists," 42.

27. Compare to Félix Guattari's view of the unconscious as "a rhizome of machinic interactions, a link to power relations that surround us" (Guattari, "Beyond the Psychoanalytic Unconscious," 199).

28. Adorno and Lenk, *Challenge of Surrealism*, 157.

29. Adorno, "The Dialectical Composer," 207.

30. Stephens, *Anti-Disciplinary Protest*, 4.

31. Marcuse, "Art in the One-Dimensional Society," 26.

32. Marcuse, 26.

33. Marcuse, "Some Remarks on Aragon," 202.

34. Marcuse, 202. Compare to Bifo Berardi and Maurizio Lazzarato who attribute this to effects of "semio-capitalism" on the "psychosphere."

35. Marcuse, 14.

36. Marcuse, "Freedom and Freud's Theory," 12.

37. Shklovsky, "Art as Technique," 19.

38. Adorno, "The Dialectical Composer," 207.

39. Marcuse, "Freedom and Freud's Theory," 13.

40. Parsons, "The Life and Work of Emile Durkheim," liv.

41. Breton, "On the Time When the Surrealists Were Right," 246.

42. Kierkegaard, "Ancient Tragedy's Reflection," 118.

43. Aristotle, *Poetics*, 1449b24–28.

44. Regarding "waste," Marcuse may have had in mind Vance Packard's popular *The Waste Makers* (1960), but also waste as "surplus" in all that this suggests. For a contemporary point of view on the importance of waste and surplus to capitalist expansion, see Simon's *Neomaterialism* (especially pages 79–88) and Diederichsen's *On (Surplus)*.

45. Letter from Adorno to Marcuse, "6 August 1969" in "Correspondence on the German Student Movement."

46. Adorno to Marcuse, "6 August 1969," 11.

47. Marcuse, "Freedom and Freud's Theory," 16.

48. Marcuse, *The Aesthetic Dimension*, 10; italics in original.

49. Marcuse, 239. Adorno is quoting the Austrian musicologist Erwin Ratz, member of the Viennese Schönberg circle.

50. Marcuse, 241.

51. Livingstone, "Introduction to 'Presentation IV,'" 148.

52. Smith, "Brecht and the Mothers of Epic Theater," 492.

53. Adorno, *Aesthetic Theory*, 43. On banality in the context of *New Objectivity* (*Neue Sachlichkeit*), see Adorno, "On the Social Situation of Music." In this essay, Adorno also criticizes *Neue Sachlichkeit* music for its "anti-humane triumph of technocracy" (434).

54. There is a distinction between emotion and affect. Emotion is "elicited *by* something, are reactions *to* something, and are generally *about* something, [where] the cognitive appraisal involved in the transaction between person and object is considered a defining element" (Ekkekakis, "Affect, Mood, and Emotion," 322). Affect is "deeper" and less specific than emotion. It is "the name we give to those forces—visceral forces beneath, alongside, or generally other than conscious knowing, vital forces insisting beyond emotion—that can serve to drive us toward movement, toward thought and extension, that can likewise suspend us (as if in neutral) across a barely registering accretion of force-relations" (Seigworth and Gregg, "An Inventory of Shimmers," 1).

55. Wellmer, "Truth, Semblance, Reconciliation," 95.

56. Adorno, *Aesthetic Theory*, 239.

57. An important exception to this claim, although one that remains undeveloped elsewhere, can be found in Jay's observation that "the only kind of negation preserved in mass culture Horkheimer and Adorno allowed was in corporeal rather than intellectual art: for example, the circus performer, whose fully reified body promised to break through the commodity character of mass art by carrying objectification to its extreme, thereby exposing what had hitherto been veiled" (Jay, *Dialectical Imagination*, 217).

58. Adorno, "Trying to Understand *Endgame*," 135.

59. Adorno, 135.

60. Havlock, *A Preface to Plato*.

61. Plato, *Republic*, 599d 2.

62. Plato, *Republic*, 605b, 4–5.

63. Keuls, *Plato and Greek Painting*, 24.

64. Keuls, 26.

65. Compare *catharsis* to *elenchus* in Plato, which is represented as purging one of false beliefs (*Sophist*, 230C–231E).

66. Plato, *Phaedo*, 64c–64d.

67. Plato, *Phaedo*, 64e–66a.

68. On the "soul" and "participation," see Nishitani, "Ontology and Utterance."

69. See Adorno, "Spengler after the Decline," 66: "But the metaphysics of 'souldom' has consequences more far-reaching than the merely tactical. One could call it a latent philosophy of identity."

70. On the cultural significance of the medical metaphor, see Foucault, *The Care of the Self*: "It had long been established that philosophy was closely related to medicine" (99). I have refrained from using Foucault's term "biopolitics" for the same reasons as Jean-Luc Nancy in his response to Giorgio Agamben's statement on COVID-19: "Neither 'biology' nor 'politics' are precisely determined terms today. I would actually say the contrary. That's why I have no use for their assemblage" (Nancy, "Riposte"). For Agamben's original statement, see Agamben, "The Invention of an Epidemic."

71. See Belfiore, *Tragic Pleasures*, 4–39.

72. Fyfe, "Introduction,", xvii; italics mine. Elizabeth Belfiore reiterates this notion of the use-value of a cathartic purge: "It is a commonplace in Greek thought that a certain kind of fear is essential to a well-ordered society. . . . This beneficial fear, which preserves law and custom, prevents civil strife, and averts shameless crimes against kin, is the fear of wrongdoing and the respect of parents, gods, and custom that the Greeks called . . . *aidōs* (shame, respect). Aristotle follows Greek tradition in characterizing aidōs in negative terms as an emotion that restrains people from wrongdoing (EN 1128b18), or as 'avoidance of blame' (EN 1116a29). . . . One function of tragedy was to

provide the kind of beneficial fear that helped prevent strife among friends" (Belfiore, *Tragic Pleasures*, 9–10).

73. Lear, "Katharsis," 310.

74. Adorno, *Aesthetic Theory*, 238.

75. Marcuse, "Freedom and Freud's Theory," 16.

76. Marcuse, 1.

77. Adorno, *Aesthetic Theory*, 246.

78. Marcuse, *Eros and Civilization*, 94.

79. Adorno, *Aesthetic Theory*, 246.

80. I borrow and build upon Fred Moten's evocative use of the ligature æ in the word "æffect": "It would be more precise to say that we are dealing, again, with structure and æffect, doubled and redoubled. But the deep-down love, the bone-deep love, convergence of death and love, memory and narrative (that's what recognition is), that accompanies the miscegenative origin of black/American identity is exceeded by another love: that of/for freedom" (Moten, *In the Break*, 71).

81. Marcuse, "The End of Utopia," 76.

82. Shklovsky, "Art as Technique," 27.

83. Katz, *Herbert Marcuse & the Art of Liberation*, 209.

84. Lenk, "Sense and Sensibility, 188.

85. Marcuse, "Art in the One-Dimensional Society," 29.

86. Higgins, *Fluxus Experience*, xiv.

87. Marcuse, "Letter to the Chicago Surrealists," 41.

88. The notion of the threshold is related to revolution in Marxist dialectics where cumulative *quantitative* changes bring about an abrupt but intense *qualitative* change. This concept may have been influenced by Hegel's discussion of "the measure" (*Maß*), which contains its revolutionary element in each quantitative change until the shift is a qualitative one: "A thing which is an immanent measure relation is self-subsistent . . . its quality is masked in the quantitative element and is thus also indifferent toward the other measure, continuing itself in it and in the newly formed measure" (Hegel, *Science of Logic*, chapter 2, section 749).

89. For instance, Pheng Cheah represents the crossing of a threshold as the "force of dynamism" that "both gives and destabilizes presence, it subjects presence to a strict law of radical contamination" (Cheah, "Non-dialectical Materialism," 74), and William Connolly views this crossing as an event of "real creativity" where human and nonhuman spontaneous energies realize their potential (Connolly, *Fragility of Things*, 156).

90. Marcuse makes a distinction between reification (*Verdinglichkeit*) and objectification (*Versachlichung*). Objectification is the general process of producing things resulting from work. Reification is a specific form of objectification under capitalism in which the producer of things does not own the things produced. Reification and alienation, therefore, go hand in hand. In Marcuse's words: "'Reification' denotes the general condition of 'human reality' resulting from the loss of the object of labour and the alienation of the worker which has found its 'classical' expression in the capitalist world of money and commodities. There is thus a sharp distinction between reification and objectification. Reification is a specific ("estranged," "untrue") *mode* of objectification" (Marcuse, "The Foundation of Historical Materialism," 11).

91. Eng, "Freud and the Changing Present," 466.

92. Kaufmann, *Hegel*, 409.

93. Freud, "Negation," 669.

94. Freud, 669.

95. Marcuse, "Freedom and Freud's Theory," 171.

96. Marcuse, 171.

97. Adorno, *Aesthetic Theory*, 245–246.

98. Marcuse, 115.

99. Marcuse, *Counterrevolution and Revolt*, 112.

100. Marcuse translates *verdinglicht* here as "fixed," but its meaning of "reified" is understood.

101. Marcuse, *Counterrevolution and Revolt*, 115.

102. See Klein, *The Shock Doctrine*. Also see the landmark study by Adorno, Frenkel-Brunswik, Levinson, and Sanford, *The Authoritarian Personality*.

CHAPTER 4

1. Alberro, "Institutions, Critique, and Institutional Critique," 3.
2. Gielen, "Institutional Imagination," 29.
3. Asher, *Writings 1973–1983*, 81.
4. Asher, 81.
5. Buchloh, "Conceptual Art," 135–136; italics in original.
6. Buchloh, 135.
7. Buchloh, 135.
8. Marcuse, *One-Dimensional Man*, 1. Compare to: "A fully-developed bureaucratic mechanism stands in the same relationship to other forms as does the machine to the non-mechanical production of goods. Precision, speed, clarity, documentary ability, continuity, discretion, unity, rigid subordination, reduction of friction and of material and personal expenses are unique to bureaucratic organization" (Adorno, "Culture and Administration," 109).
9. Letter from Adorno to Marcuse, "6 August 1969" in "Correspondence on the German Student Movement."
10. Buchloh, "Conceptual Art," 108.
11. Pincus-Witten, *Postminimalism*, 16.
12. Pincus-Witten, 16.
13. Buchloh, "Conceptual Art," 133.
14. Buchloh, 133.
15. Buchloh, 134.
16. Buchloh, 136.
17. To paraphrase Jacques Derrida, logocentrism is the exposure to—and not a subversion of—the system of speech, consciousness, meaning, presence, truth, etc., of the increasingly powerful historical expansion of a general writing. See Derrida, "Signature Event Context," 20.
18. Buchloh, 124.
19. Buchloh, 140.
20. Asher, *Writings 1973–1983 on Works 1969–1979*, 102.

21. Buchloh, "Conceptual Art," 143.

22. Buchloh, 143.

23. Buchloh, 141.

24. Buchloh, 141.

25. Buchloh, 142.

26. Marcuse, *An Essay on Liberation*, 91.

27. The text on the wall at Gallery Sperone differed slightly from the text on the announcement card. It read:

> A PLACE TO WHICH YOU CAN COME AND FOR A WHILE, "BE FREE TO THINK ABOUT WHAT WE ARE GOING TO DO." (Marcuse)

28. On a defense of "productivism" in art, see Roberts, *Intangibilities of Form*.

29. Alberro, *Conceptual Art*, 151.

30. Lippard and Chandler, "The Dematerialization of Art," 47.

31. Lippard and Chandler, "Dematerialization of Art," 143.

32. Fraser, "From the Critique of Institutions," 414.

33. Lippard and Chandler, "Dematerialization of Art," 47–48.

34. Lippard and Chandler, 49.

35. "The Artist's Reserved Rights Transfer and Sale Agreement," created by Seth Siegelaub and Robert Projansky, 1971. See Siegelaub, *"Better Read Than Dead"*, 111–127.

36. Regarding the relationship between platforms, frameworks, and technique, see chapter 5 in the discussion of the concept of "enframing" (*Ge-stell*).

37. Buchloh, "Conceptual Art," 112.

38. Siegelaub and Kosuth, "Seth Siegelaub and Joseph Kosuth Reply," 157.

39. Siegelaub and Kosuth, 157.

40. Siegelaub, "Preface," 16.

41. In the early and mid-twentieth century, the psychoanalysts Wilhelm Reich, Otto Fenichel, Siegfried Bernfield, Erich Fromm, and others practiced

their own psychopolitical variations of Freudo-Marxism. See Jacoby, *The Repression of Psychoanalysis*. To witness how the different interpretations of Freudo-Marxism often erupted into public rivalry, see Rickert, "The Fromm-Marcuse Debate Revisited"; and Harris and Brock, "Freudian Psychopolitics."

42. Freud, "The Question of *Weltanschauung*," 219.

43. Freud, 221.

44. Freud, 220.

45. Freud, 224.

46. Freud, 224.

47. Freud, 224.

48. Freud, 224.

49. See Negri, "Metamorphoses."

50. Freud, "Anxiety and Instinctual Life," 120.

51. As emotion and affect are interrelated for Marcuse, so too are instinct (*Instinkt*) and drive (*Trieb*). In *Eros and Civilization,* Marcuse explains that "the vicissitudes of the *instincts* are the vicissitudes of the mental apparatus in civilization. The animal *drive* become human instincts under the influence of the external reality" (11–12).

52. Freud did not refer to the "death instinct" as *Thanatos* as is often repeated, but in its plural form (*Todestriebe*)—which Marcuse mainly singularized—first in *Beyond the Pleasure Principle* (1920). Wilhelm Stekel, an early follower of Freud, introduced the term "Thanatos" in relation to anxiety "as a reaction to the advance of the death instinct (Thanatos), caused by a suppression of the sex instinct." As documented by the biographer Paul Roazen, who outlines the psychoanalytic application of the concept, Freud's personal "aversion to Stekel kept him from ever using 'Thanatos' in his writings"; see Roazen, *Freud and His Followers*, 218.

53. Freud, *Outline of Psychoanalysis*, 20.

54. Marcuse, "Art in the One-Dimensional Society," 30.

55. Marcuse, 30.

56. Marcuse, *Counterrevolution and Revolt*, 104; italics in original.

57. Marcuse, *One-Dimensional Man*, 3.

58. For another account of "institutional critique" that further deemphasizes aesthetic experience, see Steiner, "Corruption, Corruptibility."

59. Marcuse, "Freedom and Freud's Theory," 13.

60. Marcuse, 11.

61. Freud, *Civilization and Its Discontents*, 97.

62. Marcuse, *An Essay on Liberation*, 48.

63. Goebel, *Beyond Discontent*, 7.

64. Marcuse, *Counterrevolution and Revolt*, 87–88; italics in original.

65. Marcuse, "Freedom and Freud's Theory," 4.

66. Marcuse, *Eros and Civilization*, ix.

67. Jay, *Dialectical Imagination*, 184.

68. Jay, 193.

69. Marcuse, *One-Dimensional Man*, 75.

70. "No individual and group experiment in liberation can escape this infection by the very system it combats. The infecting agents cannot be pushed aside, they must be combated on their own grounds. This means that, from the beginning, the personal and particular liberation, refusal, withdrawal, must proceed within the political context, defined by the situation in which the radical opposition finds itself, and must continue, in theory and practice, the radical critique of the Establishment within the Establishment" (Marcuse, *Counterrevolution and Revolt*, 49).

71. Marcuse, *An Essay on Liberation*, 48.

72. Marcuse, "Freedom and Freud's Theory," 5.

73. Marcuse, 4.

74. Marcuse, "Beyond One-Dimensional Man," 115–116.

75. Marcuse, *Counterrevolution and Revolt*, 82; italics in original.

76. See Snell's introduction to *On the Aesthetic Education of Man*: "Indeed, Schiller's play impulse is only an elaboration of the view propounded in the Critique of Judgement, where play means all that is not internally or externally contingent, nor yet constrained—the expression of a nature whose

two fundamental tendencies (in the Kantian sense) are fully harmonized and poised, so that the aesthetic-creative impulse cannot develop until the play impulse is in easy and habitual action. But Schiller is nearer Fichte than Kant in his distinction between Subject and Object, and in his view of their necessarily reciprocal operation" (8). Also see Hein, "Play as an Aesthetic Concept."

77. Marcuse, "Freedom and Freud's Theory," 22.
78. Marcuse, "Art in the One-Dimensional Society," 31.
79. Marcuse, 26.
80. Marcuse, 26.

CHAPTER 5

1. See Miller, "The (Revised) Birth of Negritude." Miller acknowledges Christian Filostrat for reproducing in facsimile the section from Césaire's essay in *L'Étudiant noir* 3 (May–June 1935) where the word "Négritude" is used for the first time. See Filostrat, *Negritude Agonistes*.
2. "Légitime défense: Declaration," in Richardson, *Refusal of the Shadow*, 43.
3. The criticism of Marxism from an anti-colonial position is that there is nothing in the writings of Marx and Engels (nor in the agenda or policies of the Communist Party) that clearly concerns *racial* oppression. (Marx's "Outline of a Report on the Irish Question," which comes closest to the question, reverts to nationalism in lieu of racism.) The criticism is based on the fact that orthodox Marxism subordinates all "national problems [which must include language and culture] to the fundamental interests of the proletarian class-struggle" (Schlesinger, *Marx*, 342).
4. A few years prior to Césaire's international group associated with the journal *L'Étudiant noir*—also consisting of Léopold Sédar Senghor (from Senegal) and Léon Gotran Damas (from French Guiana)—a different intellectual circle of Martinican students in Paris overtly embracing Marxism and Surrealism published *Légitime défense* (1932). This circle of Étienne Léro, Thélus Léro, René Ménil, J. M. Monnerot, Michel Pilotin, Maurice-Sabas Quitman, Auguste Thésée, and Pierre Yoyotte offered a scathing anti-colonial critique from within a Marxist-Surrealist framework of "the constraints and restrictions, the extermination of love and confinement of dream, generally

known under the name of Western civilization" (Richardson, *Refusal of the Shadow*, 43). Also see Kelley, *Freedom Dreams*, 165–181.

5. Ménil, "*Tropiques*," 71.

6. Eleven issues of *Tropiques* were published from 1941 to 1945.

7. The enthnographer does exactly the *opposite* of defamiliarization by making "the strange familiar" (see Fields and Fields, *Racecraft*, 221–224). Regarding Surrealist exoticism, I am referring to Breton's ethnographic interest in Haitian Voodou and Hopi ceremony to reinforce his preestablished beliefs in automatism (see Geis, "Myth, History and Repetition"). Marxist essentialism, on the other hand, refers to "the process of abstraction which overlooks the necessary inequalities in capitalist development whilst introducing the delusory expectation of a simultaneous revolution in all" (Schlesinger, *Marx*, 288).

8. See Ménil, "1978 Introduction to *Légitime defense*," in Richardson, *Refusal of the Shadow*, 37–39. Also see Richardson, "Introduction," *Refusal of the Shadow*, 1–33. For a historical analysis of the term, see Miller, "The (Revised) Birth of Negritude." For an early critique of Négritude by a younger generation of artists, see Ischinger, "Negritude."

9. Fanon, *Black Skin, White Masks*, 35.

10. Nielsen, "Frantz Fanon," 343.

11. "Beside phylogeny and ontogeny stands sociogeny," in Fanon, *Black Skin, White Masks*, 11.

12. Gordon, *What Fanon Said*, 22.

13. See Allen, *Invention of the White Race*, vols. 1 and 2.

14. See Horkheimer and Adorno, *Dialectic of Enlightenment*.

15. Wynter and McKittrick, "Unparalleled Catastrophe for Our Species?," 31.

16. Wynter and McKittrick, 35.

17. Gordon, *What Fanon Said*, 24.

18. See Painter, *History of White People*.

19. See Noble, *Algorithms of Oppression*; Browne, *Dark Matters*; and Benjamin, *Race after Technology*. The dialectical aspect of these studies on the relationship between technology, racism, and resistance is captured well in

an excerpt from Katherine McKittrick: "The physicality of the slave ship, then, contributes to the *process* of social concealment and dehumanization but, importantly, black subjectivity is not swallowed up by the ship itself" (*Demonic Grounds*, xii).

20. Adu-Boahen, "The Impact of European Presence," 174.

21. Allen, *Invention of the White Race,* vol. 2, 240. The quote from Allen (quoting Gary B. Nash's "Social Development") relates to Bacon's Rebellion in 1676. See the US Supreme Court decision in *Dred Scott v. Sanford*, March 1857.

22. "In contradistinction to Marx's and Engels's expectations that bourgeois society would rationalize social relations and demystify social consciousness, the obverse occurred. The development, organization, and expansion of capitalist society pursued essentially racial directions, so too did social ideology. As a material force, then, it could be expected that racialism would inevitably permeate the social structures emergent from capitalism" (Robinson, *Black Marxism*, 2).

23. Fields and Fields, *Racecraft*, 17.

24. See Gaertner and Dovidio, "The Aversive Form of Racism."

25. Wynter and McKittrick, "Unparalleled Catastrophe," 85.

26. Du Bois, *Souls of Black Folk*, 7.

27. Hart, "Racing and E-racing Pragmatism," 106.

28. Hart, 107; italics mine.

29. Adorno, "On the Fetish Character of Music," 44.

30. Marcuse, "Repressive Tolerance," 81.

31. "Law and order are always and everywhere the law and order which protect the established hierarchy; it is nonsensical to invoke the absolute authority of this law and this order against those who suffer from it and struggle against it—not for personal advantages and revenge, but for their share of humanity. There is no other judge over them than the constituted authorities, the police, and their own conscience. If they use violence, they do not start a new chain of violence but try to break an established one. Since they will be punished, they know the risk, and when they are willing to take it, no third person, and least of all the educator and intellectual, has the right

to preach them abstention" (Wolff, Moore, and Marcuse, *A Critique of Pure Tolerance*, 137).

32. Marcuse and Popper, *Revolution or Reform?*, 76–77.
33. Butler, *Force of Nonviolence*, 4.
34. Butler, 11.
35. Butler, 11.
36. The Black Lives Matter movement is a powerful example of the defense of self and selfhood.
37. Davis's letter to Marcuse was in regard to her alleged involvement in the Marin County Courthouse Incident, for which she eventually was found not guilty nearly two years later. For comprehensive coverage of Angela Davis's trial, see Davis, *They Come in the Morning*, and Davis, *Angela Davis*.
38. Marcuse, "A Letter to Angela Davis from Herbert Marcuse," *Ramparts Magazine* (February 1971); written on November 18, 1970, and signed "In solidarity." Republished as "Dear Angela" in Marcuse, *The New Left and the 1960s*, 49.
39. Such as the KKK Birmingham bombing of the 16th Street Baptist Church in 1963 and the vicious police brutality at the Selma to Montgomery marches of March 1965.
40. Marcuse, *Eros and Civilization*, xx.
41. Fanon, *Black Skin, White Masks*, 10.
42. The organized resistance of the Black Panthers was fundamentally influenced by Fanon's coruscating writings on structural racism: "We would sit down with *Wretched of the Earth* and talk, go over another section or chapter of Fanon, and Huey would explain it in depth. It was the first time I ever had anybody who could show a clear-cut perception of what was said in one sentence, a paragraph, or chapter, and not have to read it again. He knew it already. He'd get on the streets. We'd be walking down the street and get in some discussion with somebody, and throughout the process of this discussion and argument, Huey would be citing facts, citing that material, and giving perception to it. At that time he was giving the same basic concepts as he's giving now, but now he's in a wider and broader area, because he's had a lot of experience in leadership in the Black Panther Party. His development

now is at the head of the revolutionary struggle. But he always had this vast ability to do things along with a proper perspective, and he could run it down and get things going. Huey was one for implementing things, and I guess this is where the Black Panther Party really started. Because once Huey got hung on that, he started explaining how we had to get something going. Before the Black Panther Party came the Soul Students Advisory Council" (Seale, *Seize the Time, 26).*

43. Fanon, *Wretched of the Earth*, 295. A powerful Fanon-influenced documentary style depiction of counterviolence is Gillo Pontecorvo's film *The Battle of Algiers* (1967). See Said, "The Dictatorship of Truth," 24–25.
44. Wynter and McKittrick, "Unparalleled Catastrophe," 44; italics in original.
45. Wynter and McKittrick, 58.
46. Wynter and McKittrick, 48; italics in original.
47. Wynter and McKittrick, 23; italics in original.
48. Wynter and McKittrick, 23.
49. Wynter and McKittrick, 11.
50. Wynter and McKittrick, 59.
51. Wynter and McKittrick, 55; italics in original.
52. Wynter and McKittrick, 38; italics in original.
53. Butler, *Force of Nonviolence*, 24.
54. Fields and Fields, *Racecraft*, 193–224.
55. Borrowing from Walter Benjamin's "On Some Motifs in Baudelaire," Adorno presents a lengthy analysis of lived experience (Erlebnis) and profound experience (Erfahrung) in *Aesthetic Theory*, 244–246.
56. Adorno, *Aesthetic Theory*, 245.
57. Wynter and McKittrick, "Unparalleled Catastrophe," 38.
58. Wynter and McKittrick, 23.
59. Jack Whitten's sculpture *The Heart of Humanity* (1972–1973) artistically materializes Wynter's position. Karli Wurzelbacher writes: "The interior open spaces that he created are what art historians and artists commonly refer to as 'negative space.' Whitten preferred to call it 'reciprocal space,'

because it has equal bearing on the appearance and the meaning of the sculpture. Suspended in this this reciprocal space, Whitten's sphere represents the locus of our ethics, goodness, and compassion—the true heart of our humanity" (Wurzelbacher, *Odyssey*, 69).

60. Wynter and McKittrick, "Unparalleled Catastrophe," 31.
61. Wynter and McKittrick, 31.
62. Wynter and McKittrick, 30.
63. Marcuse, *One-Dimensional Man*, 154.
64. Marcuse, "Socialism in the Developed Countries," 177.
65. Caputo, *Against Ethics,* 117.
66. Wynter and McKittrick, "Unparalleled Catastrophe," 44; italics in original.
67. Wall, "Phronesis," 317.
68. Marcuse, "History of Dialectics," 133.
69. As mentioned in chapter 1, one cannot associate Heidegger with any real sense of "care" based on his heinous and unapologetic embrace of Nazism.
70. Heidegger, *Being and Time*, 238.
71. Heidegger, 238.
72. See sections 12 and 29 in Heidegger, *Being and Time*, on the differences between "factuality" and "facticity."
73. Heidegger, *Being and Time*, 25.
74. Heidegger, 25.
75. The Heideggerian influence on the artist Joseph Beuys—such as in his statements "The artist gives to society caretaking" (Leonard, *The Halifax Conference*, 120) and "It would be better to speak about mankind in its present cultural situation as *captured*" (Leonard, 140)—is worthy of further examination.
76. Heidegger, *Being and Time*, 365–366.
77. Heidegger, 402.
78. On the relationship of *potentia* and consciousness, see Agamben, "Bartleby," 35–37.

79. Heidegger, *Being and Time*, 238.

80. Marcuse, *One-Dimensional Man*, 16.

81. Marcuse, *An Essay on Liberation*, 3.

82. Marcuse, 24.

83. Félix Guattari developed a comparable ethico-aesthetic materialism. However, outside of shared anti-capitalist concerns and other philosophical overlaps, a central difference between Marcuse's implication of ethico-aesthetics and Guattari's understanding of the same are the paradigms in which they are primarily responding. For Marcuse, it is in dialogue with the tradition of aesthetics; with Guattari it is the history of psychoanalysis. Compare to Guattari, "La Borde."

84. Heidegger, "The Question Concerning Technology," 26.

85. Srnicek, *Platform Capitalism*, 92.

86. Heidegger, "The Question Concerning Technology," 24.

87. Heidegger, 19.

88. Marcuse, "On Concrete Philosophy," 36.

89. Malabou, *Plasticity at the Dusk of Writing*, 196. Also compare Malabou's reference to "serenity" with Robert Barry's *Marcuse Piece* described in chapter 4.

90. Malabou, 70. The crossing of thresholds is relevant to the crossing of disciplines. Leo Löwenthal, the Frankfurt School's practitioner of a hybridized sociology of literature, states that "interdisciplinary work means nothing more than to leave the disciplines as they are while developing certain techniques which foster a kind of acquaintance between them without forcing them to give up their self-sufficiency or individual claims" (Löwenthal, cited in Ludtke, "Utopian Motif Is Suspended," 109). Similarly, Kellner describes the supra-disciplinarity of the Frankfurt School as having an approach that "criticizes the validity claims of the separate disciplines" (Kellner, *Critical Theory*, 7). Meanwhile, Jay describes a "supra-individual subject" who is not "abstractly transcendental . . . but historical instead" (Jay, *Dialectical Imagination*, 177).

91. Malabou, *Heidegger Change*, 70.

92. Marcuse, "Freedom and Freud's Theory," 7. For Freud the quantity of instinctual energy remains constant, but may be converted into another form (or quality), where some work is done on its surroundings. This principle of the effects on and from the body into one's surroundings mirrors the first law of thermodynamics. Compare to the Law of Conservation of Energy as explained by Max Planck in *Treatise on Thermodynamics*: "§66. If no external effects be produced by a change of state of the system, its energy remains constant (conservation of the energy). . . . A system which changes without being acted on by external agents is called a *perfect system*. Strictly speaking, no perfect system can be found in nature, since there is constant interaction between all material bodies of the universe. It is, however, of importance to observe that by an adequate choice of the system which is to undergo the contemplated change, we have it in our power to make the external effect as small as we please, in comparison with the changes of energy of portions of the system itself. Any particular external effect may be eliminated by making the body which produces this effect, as well as the recipient, a part of the system under consideration" (52).

93. James, *Principles of Psychology*, 105.

94. Dewey, *Art as Experience*, 175.

95. Compare the ideas of the familiar, the banal, the everyday, common sense, and life-world to Dewey's description of the humdrum: "The enemies of the esthetic [sic] are neither the practical nor the intellectual. They are the humdrum; slackness of loose ends; submission to convention in practice and intellectual procedure" (Dewey, *Art as Experience*, 42).

96. Dewey, 180.

97. Dewey, "Introductory Word," 1.

98. Hook, 46.

99. Hook, 57.

100. Cornford, *From Religion to Philosophy*, 204.

101. Adorno, *Philosophy of New Music*, 13.

102. Wynter and McKittrick, "Unparalleled Catastrophe," 54.

103. Marcuse, "Ecology," 32.

104. Marcuse, 32.

105. Marcuse, 32.

106. In "Ecology," Marcuse emphasizes that ambivalence can stand in the way of radical sensibility and dialectical consciousness: "The social and political function of this primary, personal radicalization of consciousness is highly ambivalent" (34). Theoretically, this is a contrast between dialectics and ambivalence. Where dialectics produces a reconciliation of contrasting positions through movement (or action), ambivalence recognizes contrasting positions but remains static (or passive). Interestingly, there is an entire field of "ambivalence studies" that refers to perspectives in terms of "one-dimensional," "two dimensional," and "multidimensional." See Deitz and Moruzzi, *Cuts & Clouds*.

107. Marcuse, "Ecology," 34.

108. See Nunes, *Neither Vertical nor Horizontal*, 160–161.

109. Hardt and Negri, *Assembly*, 67.

110. Hardt and Negri, 170.

111. Davis, "An Interview on the Futures of Black Radicalism."

112. Davis, "Angela Davis on fighting injustice." KQED News report featuring a brief excerpt from a press conference with Angela Davis on May 27, 1975, in which she considers an effective means to defend civil liberty and explains the need to "build a mass movement and develop actions through which any and everybody who is opposed to injustice can add their voices to the outcry."

113. Marcuse, *The Aesthetic Dimension*, 45.

114. Marcuse, *Counterrevolution and Revolt*, 82.

115. Marcuse, 121–122.

116. Wynter and McKittrick, "Unparalleled Catastrophe," 45.

117. Marcuse, *The Aesthetic Dimension*, 72.

CODA

1. Marcuse, *Counterrevolution and Revolt*, 122.

2. Reinhardt, "Art vs. History." See Lee, *Chronophobia*, 221–223.

3. Kubler, *The Shape of Time*, 16.

4. Kubler, 16.
5. Kubler, 69.
6. Kubler, 69.
7. Kubler, 68.
8. Kubler, 68.
9. See Breines, "From Guru to Spectre."
10. Meyer, "Eruption of Anti-Art," 126–127.
11. Marcuse, *An Essay on Liberation*, 30.
12. See Burnham's collection of essays from 1969: "Art in the Marcusean Analysis," "Real Time Systems," and "The Aesthetics of Intelligent Systems."
13. Burnham, "Problems of Criticism," 53.
14. Bonin, *Software*.
15. Burnham, "Art and Technology," 201.
16. Marcuse, *One-Dimensional Man*, 235.
17. Rosenberg, "On the De-Definition of Art," 13.
18. Rosenberg, "Set Out for Clayton!," 244.
19. On the "deskilling" of art, see Roberts, *Intangibilities of Form*.
20. Rosenberg, "Set Out for Clayton!" 244.
21. Rosenberg, 244.
22. Rosenberg, 244.
23. Rosenberg, 248.
24. Rosenberg, 246.
25. Rosenberg, 246.
26. Marcuse, *Counterrevolution and Revolt*, 110.
27. Rosenberg, "Set Out for Clayton!," 249.
28. Morris is quoted in Meyer, *Conceptual Art*, xv.
29. Marcuse, *Counterrevolution and Revolt*, 108.

30. "Art as a Form of Reality" (1970) was published after Battcock's series in *Arts Magazine*.

31. Battcock, "Marcuse and Anti-Art," 17.

32. Battcock, 17.

33. See Socrates' speech in Plato's *Symposium*, 209e–212c.

34. Battcock, "Marcuse and Anti-Art," 17.

35. Kellner, *Herbert Marcuse*, 2.

36. Battcock, "Marcuse and Anti-Art," 18.

37. Dewey, *Art as Experience*, 45.

38. Battcock, "Marcuse and Anti-Art," 18.

39. Marcuse, *Counterrevolution and Revolt*, 116.

40. Battcock, "Marcuse and Anti-Art," 18.

41. Marcuse, *An Essay on Liberation*, 45–46; *The Aesthetic Dimension*, 23.

42. Battcock, "Marcuse and Anti-Art," 19.

43. Battcock, 19.

44. Meyer, "Eruption of Anti-Art," 132.

45. Battcock, "Marcuse and Anti-Art," 18.

46. Meyer, "Eruption of Anti-Art," 132.

Bibliography

Adorno, Theodor W. "The Actuality of Philosophy." *Telos*, no. 31 (March 1977): 120–133.

Adorno, Theodor W. *Aesthetic Theory*. Minneapolis: University of Minnesota Press, 1998.

Adorno, Theodor W. "Commitment" (1974). In *Notes to Literature, Volume Two*, 76–94.

Adorno, Theodor W. "Cultural Criticism and Society." In *Prisms*, 17–34.

Adorno, Theodor W. "Culture and Administration." In *The Culture Industry: Selected Essays on Mass Culture*. Edited by J. M. Bernstein. 107–131. London: Routledge, 1991.

Adorno, Theodor W. "The Dialectical Composer" (1934). In *Essays on Music*, 203–212.

Adorno, Theodor W. *Essays on Music*. Edited by Richard Leppert. Translated by Susan H. Gillespie. Berkeley: University of California Press, 2002.

Adorno, Theodor W. "Is Art Lighthearted?" (1967). In *Notes to Literature, Volume Two*, 247–256.

Adorno, Theodor W. *The Jargon of Authenticity*. Translated by Knut Tarnowski and Frederic Will. London: Routledge & Kegan Paul, [1964] 1973.

Adorno, Theodor W. *Kierkegaard: Construction of the Aesthetic*. Translated by Robert Hullot-Kentor. Minneapolis: University of Minnesota Press, [1933] 1989.

Adorno, Theodor W. *Lectures on Negative Dialectics*. Edited by Rolf Tiedemann. Translated by Rodney Livingstone. London: Polity Press, 2008.

Adorno, Theodor W. *Negative Dialectics*. Translated by E. B. Ashton. London: Routledge & Kegan Paul, [1966] 1973.

Adorno, Theodor W. "Notes on Kafka." In *Prisms*, 243–271.

Adorno, Theodor W. *Notes to Literature, Volume 2*. Translated by Shierry Weber Nicholsen. New York: Columbia University Press, 1992.

Adorno, Theodor W. "On Jazz" (1936). In *Essays on Music*, 470–495.

Adorno, Theodor W. "On the Fetish Character of Music and the Regression of Listening" (1938). In *Essays on Music*, 288–317.

Adorno, Theodor W. "On the Social Situation of Music" (1932). In *Essays on Music*, 391–436.

Adorno, Theodor W. "Paralipomena." In *Aesthetic Theory*. Minneapolis: University of Minnesota Press, 1998.

Adorno, Theodor W. "Perennial Fashion—Jazz." In *Prisms*, 119–132.

Adorno, Theodor W. *Philosophy of New Music*. Translated by Robert Hullot-Kentor. Minneapolis: University of Minnesota Press, [1946] 2007.

Adorno, Theodor W. *Prisms*. Translated by Sam and Shierry Weber. Cambridge, MA: MIT Press, [1967] 1981.

Adorno, Theodor W. "Spengler after the Decline." In *Prisms*, 51–72.

Adorno, Theodor W. "Theses upon Art and Religion Today." In *Notes to Literature, Volume Two*, 292–298.

Adorno, Theodor W. "Trying to Understand *Endgame*." *New German Critique*, no. 26, Critical Theory and Modernity (Spring–Summer 1982): 119–150.

Adorno, Theodor W. "Why Is the New Art So Hard to Understand?" (1931). In *Essays on Music*, 127–134.

Adorno, Theodor W., and Elisabeth Lenk. *The Challenge of Surrealism: The Correspondence of Theodor W. Adorno and Elisabeth Lenk*. Translated and edited by Susan H. Gillespie. Minneapolis: University of Minnesota Press, 2015.

Adorno, Theodor W., and Herbert Marcuse. "Correspondence on the German Student Movement." *New Left Review* I/233 (January–February 1999): 123–136.

Adorno, Theodor W., Else Frenkel-Brunswik, Daniel J. Levinson, and R. Nevitt Sanford. *The Authoritarian Personality*. London: Verso, [1950] 2019.

Adorno, Theodor W., Walter Benjamin, Ernst Bloch, Bertolt Brecht, and Georg Lukács. *Aesthetics and Politics*. London: Verso, [1977] 2007.

Adu-Boahen, Kwabena. "The Impact of European Presence on Slavery in the Sixteenth to Eighteenth-Century Gold Coast." *Transactions of the Historical Society of Ghana*, New Series, no. 14 (2012): 165–199.

Agamben, Giorgio. "Bartleby." In *The Coming Community*, translated by Michael Hardt, 35–37. Minneapolis: University of Minnesota Press, [1990] 2009.

Agamben, Giorgio. "The Invention of an Epidemic: 26/02/2020." *European Journal of Psychoanalysis*. https://www.journal-psychoanalysis.eu/coronavirus-and-philosophers.

Aiken, Scott F. "Pragmatism, Naturalism, and Phenomenology." *Human Studies* 29, no. 3 (September 2006): 317–340.

Alberro, Alexander. *Conceptual Art and the Politics of Publicity*. Cambridge, MA: MIT Press, 2003.

Alberro, Alexander. "Institutions, Critique, and Institutional Critique." In *Institutional Critique*, 2–19.

Alberro, Alexander, and Blake Stimson, eds. *Conceptual Art: A Critical Anthology*. Cambridge, MA: MIT Press, 1999.

Alberro, Alexander, and Blake Stimson, eds. *Institutional Critique: An Anthology of Artists' Writings*. Cambridge, MA: MIT Press, 2009.

Alford, Lucy. *Forms of Poetic Attention*. New York: Columbia University Press, 2021.

Allen, Theodore W. *The Invention of the White Race: Volume 1, Racial Oppression and Social Control*. London: Verso, 2012.

Allen, Theodore W. *The Invention of the White Race: Volume 2, The Origin of Racial Oppression in Anglo-America*. London: Verso, 2012.

Aristotle. *The Complete Works: The Revised Oxford Translation, Volume One*. Edited by Jonathan Barnes. Princeton, NJ: Princeton University Press, 1984.

Aristotle. *The Complete Works: The Revised Oxford Translation, Volume Two*. Edited by Jonathan Barnes. Princeton, NJ: Princeton University Press, 1984.

Aristotle, *On the Soul*. In *The Complete Works, Volume One*, 641–692.

Aristotle *De Interpretatione*. In *The Complete Works, Volume One*, 25–38.

Aristotle. *The Nichomachean Ethics*. In *The Complete Works, Volume Two*, 1729–1867.

Aristotle. *Poetics*. In *The Complete Works, Volume Two*, 2316–2340.

Aristotle. *Politics*. In *The Complete Works, Volume Two*, 1986–2129.

Aristotle, *Rhetoric*. In *The Complete Works, Volume Two*, 2152–2269.

Artaud, Antonin. *The Theater and Its Double*. New York: Grove Press, Inc, 1958.

Asher, Michael. *Writings 1973–1983 on Works 1969–1979*. Edited by Benjamin H. D. Buchloh. Halifax, NS: Press of the Nova Scotia College of Art and Design; Los Angeles: The Museum of Contemporary Art Los Angeles, 1983.

Attali, Jacques. *Noise: The Political Economy of Music*. Translated by Brian Massumi. Minneapolis: University of Minnesota Press, 2006.

Barad, Karen. *Meeting the Universe Halfway: Quantum Physics and the Entanglement of Matter and Meaning*. Durham, NC: Duke University Press, 2007.

Baraka, Amiri. *The Autobiography of LeRoi Jones*. Chicago: Lawrence Hill Books, 1997.

Baraka, Imamu Amiri. “Technology & Ethos: Vol. 2 Book of Life.” In *Raise Race Rays Raze: Essays Since 1965*, 155–157. New York: Random House. 1969.

Battcock, Gregory, ed. *Idea Art: A Critical Anthology*. New York: Dutton, 1973.

Battcock, Gregory. “Marcuse and Anti-Art.” *Arts Magazine* 43, no. 8 (Summer 1969): 17–19.

Battcock, Gregory. “Marcuse and Anti-Art II” *Arts Magazine* 44, no. 2 (November 1969): 20–22.

Baumgarten, Alexander Gottlieb. *Ästhetik*. Trajectis cis viadrum [Frankfurt on Oder], 1750.

Beck, Julian. *The Life of the Theatre: The Relation of the Artist to the Struggle of the People*. San Francisco: City Lights, 1972.

Bédouin, Jean-Louis. *Vingt ans de surréalisme: 1939–1959*. Aubin: Denoël Ligugé, 1961.

Beiser, Frederick. *Schiller as Philosopher: A Re-examination*. Oxford: Oxford University Press, 2005.

Belfiore, Elizabeth S. *Tragic Pleasures: Aristotle on Plot and Emotion*. Princeton, NJ: Princeton University Press, 1992.

Beller, Jonathan. *The Message Is Murder: Substrates of Computational Capital*. London: Pluto Press, 2018.

Benhabib, Seyla. *Critique, Norm, and Utopia*. New York: Columbia University Press, 1986.

Benjamin, Ruha. *Race after Technology*. Cambridge, UK: Polity Press, 2019.

Benjamin, Walter. "Surrealism: The Last Snapshot of the European Intelligentsia." In *Reflections: Essays, Aphorisms, Autobiographical Writings*. New York: Schocken Books, [1929] 1978.

Bennet, Jane. *Vibrant Matter: A Political Ecology of Things*. Durham, NC: Duke University Press, 2010.

Berardi, Franco "Bifo." *The Soul at Work: From Alienation to Autonomy*. Translated by Francesca Cadel and Giuseppina Mecchia. South Pasadena, CA: Semiotext(e), 2009.

Berger, Peter. *Theory of the Avant-Garde*. Translated by Michael Shaw. Minneapolis: University of Minnesota Press, [1974] 1984.

Berlina, Alexandra, ed. *Victor Shklovsky: A Reader*. Translated by Alexandra Berlina. New York: Bloomsbury, 2017.

Bernstein, Jay. *Beyond the Aesthetic and Anti-Aesthetic*. Edited by James Elkins and Harper Montgomery. University Park: Pennsylvania State University Press, 2013.

Bernstein, Richard J. *The Pragmatic Turn*. Cambridge, UK: Polity, 2010.

Bernstein, Richard J. *Praxis and Action*. Philadelphia: University of Pennsylvania Press, 1971.

Bernstein, Richard J. "The Varieties of Pluralism." *American Journal of Education* 95, no. 4 (August 1987): 509–525.

Beyer, Christian, "Edmund Husserl." In *The Stanford Encyclopedia of Philosophy* (Winter 2020 Edition). https://plato.stanford.edu/archives/win2020/entries/husserl.

Biner, Pierre. *The Living Theatre*. New York: Horizon Press, 1972.

Black, David. *The Philosophical Roots of Anti-Capitalism: Essays on History, Culture, and Dialectical Thought*. Lanham, MD: Lexington Books, 2013.

Blackman, Lisa. *Immaterial Bodies: Affect, Embodiment, Mediation*. London: Sage Publications, Ltd., 2012.

Blechman, Max. "The Revolutionary Dream of Early German Romanticism." In *Revolutionary Romanticism*, 1–34.

Blechman, Max, ed. *Revolutionary Romanticism*. San Francisco: City Lights Books, 1999.

Boggs, Carl. "Revolutionary Process, Political Strategy, and the Dilemma of Power." *Theory and Society* 4, no. 3 (Autumn 1977): 353–393.

Bologh, Roslyn Wallach. *Dialectical Phenomenology: Marx's Method*. London: Routledge & Kegan Paul Ltd., 1979.

Bonin, Vincent. *Software: Information Technology: Its New Meaning for Art*. Montreal: Daniel Langlois Foundation, 2004. https://www.fondation-langlois.org/html/e/page.php?NumPage=541.

Booker, M. Keith. *The Post-Utopian Imagination*. Westport, CT: Greenwood Press, 2002.

Bowlt, John E., ed. *Russian Art of the Avant-Garde: Theory and Criticism*. London: Thames and Hudson, 1988.

Boyd, Kenneth, and Diana Heney. "Peirce on Intuition, Instinct, and Common Sense." *European Journal of Pragmatism and American Philosophy* 9, no. 2 (2017): 1–24.

Brazill, William J. *The Young Hegelians*. New Haven, CT: Yale University Press, 1970.

Brecht, Bertolt. "Theatre for Pleasure or Theatre for Instruction." In *Brecht on Theatre*. London: Methuen, 1986.

Breines, Paul. "From Guru to Spectre Marcuse and the Implosion of the Movement." In *Critical Interruptions: New Left Perspectives on Herbert Marcuse*. New York: Herder and Herder, 1970.

Breines, Wini. *Community and Organization in the New Left, 1962–1968: The Great Refusal*. New York: Praeger, 1982.

Breton, André. "A Great Black Poet (1943)." In Césaire, *Notebook of a Return to the Native Land*, ix–xix.

Breton, André. *Manifestoes of Surrealism*. Translated by Richard Seaver and Helen R. Lane. Ann Arbor: University of Michigan Press, 1969.

Breton, André. "Political Position of Surrealism: Preface." In *Manifestoes of Surrealism*, 207–211.

Breton, André. "Second Manifesto of Surrealism." In *Manifestoes of Surrealism*, 117–187.

Breton, André. "Surrealist Situation of the Object." In *Manifestoes of Surrealism*, 255–278.

Breton, André. "On the Time When the Surrealists Were Right." In *Manifestoes of Surrealism* 243–254.

Bronner, Stephen Eric. *Modernism at the Barricades: Aesthetics, Politics, Utopia.* New York: Columbia University Press, 2012.

Bronner, Stephen Eric. "Reconstructing the Experiment." *Social Text*, no. 8 (Winter 1983–1984): 127–141.

Brown, Wendy. "American Nightmare: Neoliberalism, Neoconservatism, and De-Democratization." *Political Theory* 34, no. 6 (Dec. 2006): 690–714.

Brown, Wendy. *Undoing the Demos: Neoliberalism's Stealth Revolution.* Brooklyn, NY: Zone Books, 2015.

Browne, Simone. *Dark Matters*. Durham, NC: Duke University Press, 2015.

Bryan-Wilson, Julia. *Art Workers: Radical Practice in the Vietnam War Era*. Berkeley: University of California Press, 2009.

Buchloh, Benjamin H. D. "Benjamin Buchloh Replies to Joseph Kosuth and Seth Siegelaub." *October* 57 (Summer 1991): 158–161.

Buchloh, Benjamin H. D. "Conceptual Art 1962–1969: From the Aesthetic of Administration to the Critique of Institutions." *October* 55 (Winter 1990): 105–143.

Buchloh, Benjamin H. D. "The Press of NSCAD: A Brief Incomplete History and Its Future Books." In *NSCAD: The Nova Scotia College of Art & Design*, 64–75. Halifax, NS: Press of the Nova Scotia College of Art and Design, 1982.

Burnham, Jack. "The Aesthetics of Intelligent Systems" (1969). In *On the Future of Art*, edited by Edward Fry, 95–122. New York: Viking Press, 1970.

Burnham, Jack. "Art and Technology: The Panacea That Failed." In *The Myths of Information: Technology and Postindustrial Culture*, edited by Kathleen Woodward, 200–215. Madison, WI: Coda Press, 1980.

Burnham, Jack. "Art in the Marcusean Analysis." In *Penn State Papers in Art Education*, vol. 6, edited by Paul Edmonston, 1–22. Philadelphia: Pennsylvania State University, 1969.

Burnham, Jack. "Problems of Criticism, IX: Art and Technology." *Artforum* 9, no. 5 (January 1971): 40–45.

Burnham, Jack. "Real Time Systems." *Artforum* 8, no. 1 (September 1969): 49–55.

Butler, Judith. *The Force of Nonviolence: An Ethico-Political Bind*. London: Verso, 2020.

Butler, Judith. *Subjects of Desire: Hegelian Reflections in Twentieth-Century France*. New York: Columbia University Press, 1987.

Campbell, Timothy, and Adam Sitze, eds. *Biopolitics: A Reader*. Durham, NC: Duke University Press, 2013.

Caputo, John D. *Against Ethics: Contribution to a Poetics of Obligation with Constant Reference to Deconstruction*. Bloomington: Indiana University Press, 1993.

Caputo, John D. *The Mystical Element in Heidegger's Thought*. Athens: Ohio University Press, 1978.

Cardew, Cornelius. *Stockhausen Serves Imperialism*. London: Latimer New Directions Ltd., 1974.

Caute, David. *Communism and the French Intellectuals, 1914–1960*. New York: Macmillan, 1964.

Césaire, Aimé. *Notebook of a Return to the Native Land*. Middletown, CT: Wesleyan University Press, 2001.

Cheah, Pheng. "Non-dialectical Materialism." In *New Materialisms: Ontology, Agency, and Politics*, edited by Diane Coole and Samantha Frost, 70–91. Durham, NC: Duke University Press, 2010.

Connolly, William E. *The Fragility of Things: Self-Organizing Processes, Neoliberal Fantasies, and Democratic Activism*. Durham, NC: Duke University Press, 2013.

Cornell, Drucilla. "Derrida's Negotiations as a Technique of Liberation." *Discourse* 39, no. 2 (Spring 2017): 195–215.

Cornell, Drucilla, and Stephen D. Seely. *The Spirit of Revolution: Beyond the Dead Ends of Man*. Cambridge, UK: Polity Press, 2016.

Cornford, F. M. *From Religion to Philosophy: A Study in the Origins of Western Speculation*. Princeton, NJ: Princeton University Press, 1991.

Curry, Carl. "The Theogony of Theophilus." *Vigiliae Christianae* 42, no. 4 (December 1988): 318–326.

Dardot, Pierre, and Christian Laval. *The New Way of the World: On Neo-Liberal Society*. Translated by Gregory Elliott. London: Verso, [2009] 2013.

Darwin, Charles. *The Descent of Man, and Selection in Relation to Sex*. London: John Murray, 1871.

Darwin, Charles. *On the Origin of the Species by Means of Natural Selection*. New York: D. Appleton and Company, 1861.

Davis, Angela Y. *Angela Davis: An Autobiography*. New York: International Publishers, [1974] 1988.

Davis, Angela Y. "Angela Davis on Fighting Injustice." KQED News. Bay Area TV Archive. May 27, 1975. https://diva.sfsu.edu/collections/sfbatv/bundles/189466.

Davis, Angela Y. "An Interview on the Futures of Black Radicalism." *Verso* (blog), June 23, 2020. https://www.versobooks.com/blogs/3421-angela-davis-an-interview-on-the-futures-of-black-radicalism.

Davis, Angela Y. *They Come in the Morning . . . Voices of Resistance*. Edited by Angela Y. Davis. London: Verso, [1971] 2016.

Davis, Mike and Jon Wiener, *Set the Night on Fire: L.A. in the Sixties*. Brooklyn, NY: Verso, 2020.

de Boer, Karin. *On Hegel: The Sway of the Negative*. London: Palgrave MacMillan, 2010.

Decety, Jean, and Thalia Wheatley, eds. *Moral Brain*. Cambridge, MA: MIT Press, 2015.

Deitz, Richard, and Sebastiano Moruzzi, eds. *Cuts & Clouds: Vagueness, Its Nature, and Its Logic*. Oxford: Oxford University Press, 2010.

DeKoven, Marianne. *Utopia Limited: The Sixties and the Emergence of the Postmodern*. Durham, NC: Duke University Press, 2004.

Derrida, Jacques. "Signature Event Context." In *Limited Inc.*, 1–24. Evanston, IL: Northwestern University Press, 1988.

de Waal, Frans. *Primates and Philosophers*. Princeton, NJ: Princeton University Press, 2006.

Dewey, John. *Art as Experience*. New York: Perigree, 1934.

Dewey, John. "Introductory Word." In Hook, *The Metaphysics of Pragmatism*, 1–5.

Diederichsen, Diedrich. *On (Surplus) Value in Art*. Berlin: Sternberg Press, 2008.

Du Bois, W. E. B. *The Souls of Black Folk: Essays and Sketches*. Chicago: A. C. McClurg & Co, 1903.

Ekkekakis, Panteleimon. "Affect, Mood, and Emotion." In *Measurement in Sport and Exercise Psychology*, edited by G. Tenenbaum, R. C. Eklund, and A. Kamata, 321–332. Champaign, IL: Human Kinetics, 2012.

Elbaum, Max. *Revolution in the Air: Sixties Radicals Turn to Lenin, Mao and Che*. London: Verso, 2002.

Ellul, Jacques. *The Technological Society*. New York: Vintage Books, [1954] 1964.

Eng, Erling. "Freud and the Changing Present." *The Antioch Review* 16, no. 4 (Winter 1956): 459–468.

Engels, Frederick. *Anti-Dühring: Herr Eugen Dühring's Revolution in Science*. Edited by C. P. Dutt. Translated by Emile Burns. New York: International Publishers, 1966.

Engels, Frederick. *Feuerbach: The Roots of the Socialist Philosophy*. Translated by Austin Lewis. Chicago: Charles H. Kerr & Co., 1908.

Engels, Frederick. *Ludwig Feuerbach and the End of Classical German Philosophy*. Moscow: Foreign Languages Publishing House, 1950.

Engels, Frederick. *Ludwig Feuerbach and the Outcome of Classical German Philosophy*. New York: International Publishers, 1967.

Erlich, Viktor. *Russian Formalism: History - Doctrine*. The Hague: Mouton Publishers, 1980.

Fanon, Frantz. *Black Skin, White Masks*. Translated by Charles Lamm Markman. New York: Grove Press, [1952] 2008.

Fanon, Frantz. *The Wretched of the Earth*. Translated by Richard Philcox. New York: Grove Press, [1961] 2004.

Feenberg, Andrew. *Heidegger and Marcuse: The Catastrophe and Redemption of History*. New York: Routledge, 2005.

Feenberg, Andrew. *The Philosophy of Praxis: Marx, Lukács and the Frankfurt School*. London: Verso, [1981] 2014.

Feenberg, Andrew and William Leiss, eds. *The Essential Marcuse*. Boston: Beacon Press, 2007.

Fenichel, Otto. "The Drive to Amass Wealth." *Psychoanalytic Quarterly* 7, no. 1 (1938): 69–95.

Fenichel, Otto. "Psychoanalysis as the Nucleus of a Future Dialectical-Materialistic Psychology." *American Imago* 24, no. 4 (Winter 1967): 290–311.

Fenichel, Otto. *The Psychoanalytic Theory of Neuroses*. London: Routledge, [1946] 2005.

Ferreira, M. Jamie. "Faith and the Kierkegaardian leap." In *The Cambridge Companion to Kierkegaard*, edited by Alastair Hannay and Gordon D. Marino, 207–234. Cambridge, UK: Cambridge University Press, 1998.

Feuerbach, Ludwig. *The Fiery Brook: Selected Writings*. Translated by Zawar Hanfi. London: Verso, 2012.

Feuerbach, Ludwig. "Introduction to *The Essence of Christianity*." In *The Fiery Brook*, 97–134.

Feuerbach, Ludwig. "Towards a Critique of Hegel's Philosophy." In *The Fiery Brook*, 53–96.

Fields, Karen E., and Barbara J. Fields. *Racecraft: The Soul of Inequality in American Life*. London: Verso, 2012.

Filostrat, Christian. *Negritude Agonistes, Assimilation Against Nationalism in the French-Speaking Caribbean and Guyane*. Cherry Hill, NJ: Africana Homestead Literary Publishers, 2008.

Flynt, Henry. "20 East Broadway, Ben Morea Loft, 1 of 2." Part of *Henry Flynt in New York*, interview by Benjamin Piekut, 2008. https://youtu.be/ONsoVep5x1s.

Foucault, Michel. *The Birth of Biopolitics: Lectures at the Collège de France, 1978–79*. Translated by Graham Burchell. New York: Picador, 2008.

Foucault, Michel. *The History of Sexuality, Volume 3: The Care of the Self*. Translated by Robert Hurley. New York: Vintage Books, 1988.

Fraser, Andrea. "From the Critique of Institutions to an Institution of Critique." In Alberro and Stimson, *Institutional Critique*, 408–421.

Freud, Sigmund. "Anxiety and Instinctual Life." In *New Introductory Lectures on Psycho-Analysis*, 113–123.

Freud, Sigmund. *Civilization and Its Discontents*. Standard edition, vol. 24. London: Hogarth, 1956–1974.

Freud, Sigmund. "Negation." In *The Freud Reader*, edited by Peter Gay, 666–669. New York: W. W. Norton, 1989.

Freud, Sigmund. *New Introductory Lectures on Psycho-analysis*. Translated by James Strachey. New York: W. W. Norton, [1933] 1989.

Freud, Sigmund. *An Outline of Psychoanalysis*. New York: W. W. Norton, 1949.

Freud, Sigmund. "The Question of *Weltanschauung*." In *New Introductory Lectures on Psycho-Analysis*, 219–224.

Friedman, Ken. "FLUXLIST and SILENCE Celebrate Dick Higgins." *Umbrella* 21, no. 3–4 (December 1998): 106–109.

Fyfe, W. Hamilton. "Introduction." In *Aristotle: The Poetics*, vol. 199, i–xvii. Cambridge, MA: Harvard University Press; London: W. Heinemann, 1932.

Gablik, Suzi. "Connective Aesthetics: Art after Individualism." In *Mapping the Terrain: New Genre Public Art*, edited by Suzanne Lacy, 74–87. Seattle, WA: Bay Press, 1995.

Gadamer, Hans. *Dialogue and Dialectic: Eight Hermeneutical Studies on Plato*. Translated by P. Christopher Smith. New Haven, CT: Yale University Press, 1980.

Gadamer, Hans. "The Idea of Hegel's Logic." In *Hegel's Dialectic: Five Hermeutical Studies*, translated by P. Christopher Smith, 75–99. New Haven: Yale University Press, 1976.

Gadamer, Hans. *Truth and Method*. London: Continuum, [1960] 1975.

Gaertner, Samuel L. and John F. Dovidio. "The Aversive Form of Racism." In *Prejudice, Discrimination and Racism*, edited by J. F. Dovidio and S. L. Gaertner, 61–89. Orlando, FL: Academic Press, 1986.

Geis, Terri. "Myth, History and Repetition: André Breton and Vodou in Haiti." *South Central Review* 32, no. 1, Dada, Surrealism, and Colonialism (Spring 2015): 56–75.

Gershman, Herbert S. *The Surrealist Revolution in France*. Ann Arbor: University of Michigan Press, 1969.

Gielen, Pascal. "Institutional Imagination: Instituting Contemporary Art Minus the 'Contemporary.'" In *Institutional Attitudes*, edited by Pascal Gielen, 11–32. Amsterdam: Valiz, 2013.

Gillespie, Michael Allen. *Hegel, Heidegger, and the Ground of History*. Chicago: University of Chicago Press, 1984.

Gitlin, Todd. *The Sixties: Years of Hope, Days of Rage*. New York: Bantam Books, 1987.

Goebel, Eckart. *Beyond Discontent: Sublimation from Goethe to Lacan*. Translated by James C. Wagner. London: Bloomsbury, 2012.

Gordon, Lewis R. *What Fanon Said: A Philosophical Introduction to His Life and Thought*. New York: Fordham University Press, 2015.

Gramsci, Antonio. *The Prison Notebooks*. London: Lawrence & Wishart, 1971.

Gregg, Melissa, and Gregory J. Seigworth, eds. *The Affect Theory Reader*. Durham, NC: Duke University Press, 2010.

Grote, Simon. *The Emergence of Modern Aesthetic Theory: Religion and Morality in Enlightenment Germany and Scotland*. Cambridge, UK: Cambridge University Press, 2017.

Groys, Boris. "Anti-philosophy and the Politics of Recognition" *e-flux journal* no. 108 (April 2020). https://www.e-flux.com/journal/108/325614/anti-philosophy-and-the-politics-of-recognition.

Guattari, Félix. "Beyond the Psychoanalytic Unconscious." In *Chaosophy*, 195–205.

Guattari, Félix. *Chaosophy: Texts and Interviews 1972–1977*. Los Angeles: Semiotext(e), 2009.

Guattari, Félix. "La Borde: A Clinic Unlike Any Other." In *Chaosophy*, 176–194.

Guattari, Félix. *Schizoanalytic Cartographies*. Translated by Andrew Goffey. London: Bloomsbury Academic, 2012.

Habermas, Jürgen. "Excursus on Schiller." In *The Philosophical Discourse of Modernity*, 45–50. Cambridge, UK: Polity, 1987.

Habermas, Jürgen. "Modernity versus Postmodernity." *New German Critique*, no. 22 (Winter 1981): 3–14.

Habermas, Jürgen. "Psychic Thermidor and the Rebirth of Rebellious Subjectivity." *Berkeley Journal of Sociology* 25 (1980): 1–12.

Habermas, Jürgen. "Questions and Counter Questions." In *Habermas and Modernity*, edited by Richard J. Bernstein, 192–216. Cambridge, MA: MIT Press, 1985.

Habermas, Jürgen. "A Reply to My Critics." In *Habermas: Critical Debates*, edited by John B. Thompson and David Held, 219–283. Cambridge, MA: MIT Press, 1982.

Habermas, Jürgen. *The Theory of Communicative Action*, vol. 2. Boston: Beacon Press, 1984.

Haldar, Hiralal. "Leibniz and German Idealism." *Philosophical Review* 26, no. 4 (July 1917): 378–394.

Hammermeister, Kai. *The German Aesthetic Tradition*. Cambridge, UK: Cambridge University Press, 2002.

Hamner, M. Gail. *American Pragmatism: A Religious Genealogy*. Oxford: Oxford University Press, 2003.

Hanfi, Zawar. "Introduction." In Feuerbach, *The Fiery Brook*, 1–49.

Hardt, Michael, and Antonio Negri. *Assembly*. Oxford: Oxford University Press, 2017.

Harris, Benjamin and Adrian Brock. "Freudian Psychopolitics: The Rivalry of Wilhelm Reich and Otto Fenichel, 1930–1935." *Bulletin of the History of Medicine* 66, no. 4 (Winter 1992): 578–612.

Hart, William David. "Racing and E-racing Pragmatism." *American Journal of Theology & Philosophy* 33, no. 2 (May 2012): 97–116.

Haskins, Ekaterina V. "Mimesis between *Poetics* and *Rhetoric*." *Rhetoric Society Quarterly* 30, no. 3 (Summer 2000): 7–33.

Havlock, Eric. *A Preface to Plato*. New York: Grosset and Dunlap, 1963.

Hegel, Georg Wilhelm Friedrich. *Encyclopedia of the Philosophical Sciences in Basic Outline, Part I: Science of Logic*. Translated by Klaus Brinkmann and Daniel O. Dahlstrom. London: Cambridge University Press, 2015.

Hegel, Georg Wilhelm Friedrich. *The Philosophy of History*. Edited by C. J. Friedrich. New York: Dover, 1956.

Hegel, Georg Wilhelm Friedrich. "The Preface to the *Phenomenology*." In *Hegel: Reinterpretation. Texts and Commentary*, translated and edited by Walter Kaufmann, 9–20. Garden City, NY: Doubleday & Co., 1965.

Hegel, Georg Wilhelm Friedrich. *Science of Logic*. Translated by A. V. Miller. London: Allen and Unwin, 1969.

Heidegger, Martin. *Being and Time*. Translated by John Macquarrie and Edward Robinson. New York: Harper & Row, 1962.

Heidegger, Martin. *The Question Concerning Technology and Other Essays*. New York: Garland Publishing, [1962] 1977.

Heidegger, Martin. "The Turning." In *The Question Concerning Technology*, 39–42.

Heidegger, Martin. "The Understanding of Time in Phenomenology and in the Thinking of the Being-Question." Translated by Thomas Sheehan and Frederick Elliston. *The Southwestern Journal of Philosophy* 10, no. 2 (Summer 1979): 199–201.

Hein, Hilde. "Play as an Aesthetic Concept." *The Journal of Aesthetics and Art Criticism* 27, no. 1 (Autumn 1968): 67–71.

Held, David. *Introduction to Critical Theory: Horkheimer to Habermas*. Berkeley: University of California Press, 1980.

Hendricks, John, and Jean Toche. *GAAG: The Guerrilla Art Action Group*. New York: Printed Matter, Inc., 1978.

Herder, Johann Gottfried. "A Monument to Baumgarten." In *Selected Writings on Aesthetics*, edited and translated by Gregory Moore, 41–50. Princeton, NJ: Princeton University Press, 2006.

Higgins, Dick. "Synesthesia and Intersenses: Intermedia." *Something Else Newsletter* 1, no. 1. (February 1966): 1–3.

Higgins, Dick. *A Dialectic of Centuries: Notes towards a Theory of the New Arts*. New York: Printed Editions, 1978.

Higgins, Dick. *Horizons: The Poetics and Theory of the Intermedia*. Carbondale: Southern Illinois University Press, 1984.

Higgins, Hannah. *Fluxus Experience*. Berkeley: University of California Press, 2002.

Hofstadter, Richard. *Social Darwinism in American Thought*. New York: George Braziller, Inc., 1969.

Hohendahl, Peter. *Reappraisals: Shifting Alignments in Postwar Critical Theory*. New York: Cornell University Press, 1991.

Holenstein, Elmar. "On the Poetry and Plurifunctionality of Language." In *Structure and Gestalt: Philosophy and Literature in Austria-Hungary and Her Successor States*, edited by Barry Smith, 1–44. Amsterdam: John Benjamins, 1981.

Honneth, Axel. *The Idea of Socialism: Towards a Renewal*. Cambridge, UK: Polity Press, 2017.

Honneth, Axel. *Reification: A New Look at an Old Idea*. Oxford: Oxford University Press, 2008.

Hook, Sidney. *The Metaphysics of Pragmatism*. Chicago: Open Court Publishing, 1927.

Horkheimer, Max. *Gesammelte Schriften*, vol. 19: Nachträge, Verzeichnisse und Register. Frankfurt: Fischer Verlag, 1996.

Horkheimer, Max. "Traditional and Critical Theory." In *Critical Theory: Selected Essays*, translated by Matthew J. O'Connell, 188–243. New York: Continuum, 2002.

Horkheimer, Max and Theodor W. Adorno. *Dialectic of Enlightenment*. Translated by Edmund Jephcott. Stanford, CA: Stanford University Press, 2002.

Huhn, Tom, and Lambert Zuidervaart, eds. *The Semblance of Subjectivity: Essays in Adorno's Aesthetic Theory*. Cambridge, MA: MIT Press, 1997.

Hunt, R. N. Carew. *The Theory and Practice of Communism*. London: Penguin, [1950] 1973.

Husserl, Edmund. *The Crisis of European Sciences and Transcendental Phenomenology*. Translated by David Carr. Evanston: Northwestern University Press, [1954] 1970.

Husserl, Edmund. *Formal and Transcendental Logic*. Translated by Dorion Cairns. The Hague: Martinus Nihoff, 1969.

Husserl, Edmund. *The Idea of Phenomenology*. Translated by Lee Hardy. Dordrecht: Kluwer Academic Publishers, 1999.

Husserl, Edmund. *Logical Investigations, Volume 1*. Translated by J. N. Findlay. London: Routledge & Kegan Paul Ltd., 1970.

Ischinger, Barbara. "Negritude: Some Dissident Voices." *Issue: A Journal of Opinion* 4, no. 4 (Winter 1974): 23–25.

Isserman, Maurice. *If I Had a Hammer: The Death of the Old Left and the Birth of the New Left*. New York: Basic Books, 1987.

Isserman, Maurice. "The Not-So-Dark and Bloody Ground: New Works on the 1960s." *The American Historical Review* 94, no. 4 (October 1989): 990–1010.

Jakobson, Roman and Yuri Tynyanov. "Problems of Literary and Linguistic Studies." In *Poetics Today* 2, no. 1a, "Roman Jakobson: Language and Poetry." (Autumn 1980): 29–31.

Jacoby, Russell. *The Repression of Psychoanalysis: Otto Fenichel and the Political Freudians*. New York: Basic Books, 1983.

James, William. *A Pluralistic Universe*. Cambridge, MA: Harvard University Press, [1909] 1977.

James, William. *Pragmatism*. Cambridge, MA: Harvard University Press, 1975.

James, William. *The Principles of Psychology*. New York: Holt, 1890.

Jameson, Frederic. "'End of Art' or 'End of History.'" In *The Cultural Turn: Selected Writings on the Postmodern, 1983–1998*, 73–92. London: Verso, 1998.

Jameson, Frederic. "Foreword: A Monument to Radical Instants." In *The Aesthetics of Resistance*, vol. 1, by Peter Weiss, translated by Joachim Neugroschel , vii–xlix. Durham, NC: Duke University Press, 2005.

Jameson, Frederic. *Marxism and Form: 20th Century Dialectical Theories of Literature*. Princeton, NJ: Princeton University Press, 1974.

Jameson, Frederic. *The Political Unconscious: Narrative as a Socially Symbolic Act*. Ithaca, NY: Cornell University Press. 1981.

Jameson, Frederic. *Postmodernism; or, the Cultural Logic of Late Capitalism*. Durham, NC: Duke University Press, 1991.

Jameson, Frederic. *Valences of the Dialectic*. Brooklyn, NY: Verso, 2009.

Jauss, Hans Robert. *Toward an Aesthetic of Reception*. Translated by Timothy Bahti. Minneapolis: University of Minnesota Press, 1982.

Jay, Martin. "Anamnestic Totalization: Reflections on Marcuse's Theory of Remembrance." *Theory and Society* 11, no. 1 (January 1982): 1–15.

Jay, Martin. *The Dialectical Imagination: A History of the Frankfurt School and Institute of Social Research, 1923–1950*. Berkeley: University of California Press, 1973.

Jay, Martin. *Downcast Eyes: The Denigration of Vision in Twentieth-Century French Thought*. Oakland: University of California Press, 1993.

Jay, Martin. "Habermas and Modernism." In *Habermas and Modernity*, edited by Richard J. Bernstein, 125–139. Cambridge, MA: MIT Press, 1985.

Jay, Martin. "The Metapolitics of Utopianism." In *Permanent Exiles: Essays on the Intellectual Migration from Germany to America*, 3–13. New York: Columbia University Press, 1986.

Johnson, Pauline. "An Aesthetics of Negativity/An Aesthetics of Reception: Jauss's Dispute with Adorno." *New German Critique* 42 (Autumn 1987): 51–70.

Jones, LeRoi (Amiri Baraka), "The Revolutionary Theatre." *The Liberator* (July 1965): 4–6.

Kant, Immanuel. *Critique of Judgment*. Translated by Werner S. Pluhar. Indianapolis, IN: Hackett Publishing Company, 1987.

Kant, Immanuel. *Critique of Pure Reason*. Translated by Max Müller. Garden City, NY: Doubleday, Anchor Books, 1966.

Kaprow, Alan. "The Education of the Un-Artist, Part I (1971)." In *Essays on the Blurring of Art and Life*, 97–109.

Kaprow, Alan. *Essays on the Blurring of Art and Life*. Edited by Jeff Kelley. Berkeley: University of California Press, 1993.

Kaprow, Alan. "Manifesto (1966)." In *Essays on the Blurring of Art and Life*, 81–83.

Kaprow, Alan. "The Real Experiment (1983)." In *Essays on the Blurring of Art and Life*, 201–218.

Katsiaficas, George. *The Global Imagination of 1968: Revolution and Counterrevolution*. Oakland, CA: PM Press, 2018.

Katsiaficas, George. "Marcuse as an Activist: Reminiscences of His Theory and Practice." *New Political Science* (Summer/Fall 1996): 36–37.

Katz, Barry. *Herbert Marcuse & the Art of Liberation*. London: Verso, 1982.

Kaufmann, Walter. *Hegel: A Reinterpretation*. Notre Dame, IN: University of Notre Dame Press, 1977.

Kelley, Robin D. G. *Freedom Dreams: The Black Radical Imagination*. Boston: Beacon Press: 2002.

Kellner, Douglas. *Critical Theory, Marxism and Modernity*. Baltimore: Johns Hopkins University Press, 1989.

Kellner, Douglas. "From 1984 to One-Dimensional Man: Reflections on Orwell and Marcuse." *Current Perspectives in Social Theory*, 223–252. Greenwich, CT: JAI Press, 1990.

Kellner, Douglas. *Herbert Marcuse and the Crisis of Marxism*. Berkeley: University of California Press, 1984.

Kellner, Douglas. "Radical Politics, Marcuse and the New Left." In *The New Left and the 1960s: Collected Papers of Herbert Marcuse, Volume Three*, edited by Douglas Kellner, 1–37. London: Routledge, 2005.

Keucheyan, Razmig. *The Left Hemisphere*. London: Verso, 2010.

Keuls, Eva C. *Plato and Greek Painting*. Leiden: E. J. Brill, 1978.

Kierkegaard, Søren. "Ancient Tragedy's Reflection in the Modern." In *Either/Or: A Fragment of Life*, edited by Victor Eremita, translated by Alastair Hannay, 110–130. New York: Penguin Classics, 1992.

Királyfalvi, Béla. *The Aesthetics of György Lukács*. Princeton, NJ: Princeton University Press, 1975.

Klein, Naomi. *The Shock Doctrine*. New York: Henry Holt and Company, 2008.

Koopman, Colin. *Pragmatism as Transition: Historicity and Hope in James, Dewey, and Rorty*. New York: Columbia University Press, 2009.

Kotz, Liz. "Post-Cagean Aesthetics and the 'Event' Score." *October* 95 (Winter 2001): 55–89.

Kotz, Liz. *Words to Be Looked At: Language in 1960s Art*. Cambridge, MA: MIT Press, 2007.

Kubler, George. *The Shape of Time*. New Haven, CT: Yale University Press, 1962.

Kubler, George. "Style and the Representation of Historical Time." In "The Minimalism Issue," edited by Brian O'Doherty, *Aspen*, no. 5+6 (1967): section 3.

Landmann, Michael. "Talking with Ernst Bloch: Korcula, 1968." *Telos* 25 (Fall 1975): 165–185.

Lear, Jonathan. "Katharsis." *Phronesis* 33, no. 3 (1988): 297–326.

Lee, Pamela M. *Chronophobia: On Time in the Art of the 1960s*. Cambridge, MA: MIT Press, 2004.

Léger, Marc James, ed. *The Idea of the Avant Garde—And What It Means Today*. Manchester and New York: Manchester University Press; Oakland: Left Curve, 2014.

Leibniz, Gottfried Wilhelm. "Monadology." In *Monadology and Other Philosophical Essays*, translated by Anne Martin Schrecker and Paul Schrecker, edited by Paul Schrecker, 148–163. New York: Bobbs-Merrill Company, 1965.

Leiss, William. "Critical Theory and Its Future." *Political Theory* 2, no. 3 (August 1974): 330–349.

Leiss, William. "Herbert Marcuse: Lectures on Marxian Theory and Communism (Politics 171b), History of Ideas Program, Brandeis University Spring 1963, Handwritten Course Notes." Transcribed by Michael G. Tyshenko. Ottawa: University of Ottawa, February 2017.

Lenk, Elisabeth. "Sense and Sensibility: Afterword to Louis Aragon's *Paris Peasant*." In Adorno and Lenk, *The Challenge of Surrealism*, 187–196.

Leonard, Craig. *The Halifax Conference*. Los Angeles: New Documents, 2019.

Lippard, Lucy R. *Six Years: The Dematerialization of the Art Object*. New York: Praeger, 1973.

Lippard, Lucy R., and John Chandler. "The Dematerialization of Art." In Alberro and Stimson, *Conceptual Art*, 47.

Livingstone, Rodney. "Introduction to 'Presentation IV'." In Adorno, *Aesthetics and Politics*, 9–15.

Living Theatre, The. "*Paradise Now*: Notes." *The Drama Review* 13, no. 3 (Spring 1969): 90–107.

Long, Priscilla, ed. *The New Left: A Collection of Essays*. Boston: Beacon Press, 1969.

Lorde, Audre. "Uses of the Erotic: The Erotic as Power." In *Sister Outsider: Essays and Speeches*, 53–59. Berkeley, CA: Crossing Press, 1984.

Lowenthal, Leo. *Literature, Popular Culture, and Society*. Englewood Cliffs, NJ: Prentice-Hall, Inc., 1961.

Ludtke, Martin. "The Utopian Motif Is Suspended: Conversation with Leo Löwenthal." *New German Critique* 38 (Spring–Summer 1986): 105–111.

Lukács, Georg. "Reification and the Consciousness of the Proletariat." In *History and Class Consciousness: Studies in Marxist Dialectics*, translated by Rodney Livingston, 83–222. Cambridge, MA: MIT Press, [1923] 1971.

Lukács, Georg. *The Theory of the Novel*. Cambridge, MA: MIT Press, [1920] 1971.

Luxemburg, Rosa. "The Mass Strike, The Party and the Trade Unions." In *The Rosa Luxemburg Reader*, edited by Peter Hudis and Kevin B. Anderson, 168–199. New York: Monthly Review Press, [1906] 2004.

Lyotard, Jean-François. *The Postmodern Condition: A Report on Knowledge*. Minneapolis: University of Minnesota Press, 1974.

Malabou, Catherine. *The Heidegger Change: On the Fantastic in Philosophy*. Albany: SUNY Press, 2011.

Malabou, Catherine. *Plasticity at the Dusk of Writing: Dialectic, Destruction, Deconstruction*. Translated by Carolyn Shread. New York: Columbia University Press, 2010.

Malabou, Catherine. *What Should We Do with Our Brain?* Translated by Sebastian Rand. New York: Fordham University Press, 2008.

Malina, Judith, and Julian Beck. *Paradise Now*. New York: Random House, 1971.

Mandel, Ernest. *Late Capitalism*. Brooklyn, NY: Verso, [1975] 1999.

Marcuse, Herbert. *The Aesthetic Dimension: Towards a Critique of Marxist Aesthetics*. Boston: Beacon Press, 1978.

Marcuse, Herbert. "The Affirmative Character of Culture." In *Negations*, 65–98.

Marcuse, Herbert. "Apophantic Logos. Poetic Language: Language of Negation, Absence, Silence." Manuscript. Marcuse Archive, Archivzentrum, Universitätsbibliothek, Frankfurt am Main. Undated and unpaginated.

Marcuse, Herbert. *Art and Liberation. Collected Papers of Herbert Marcuse: Volume Four*. Edited by Douglas Kellner. Oxford and New York: Routledge, 2007.

Marcuse, Herbert. "Art as a Form of Reality." In *On the Future of Art*, edited by Edward Fry, 123–134. New York: Viking Press, 1970.

Marcuse, Herbert. "Art in the One-Dimensional Society." *Arts Magazine* (May 1967): 26–31.

Marcuse, Herbert. "Art in the One-Dimensional Society: Manuscript." Marcuse Archive, Archivzentrum, Universitätsbibliothek, Frankfurt am Main. Undated and unpaginated.

Marcuse, Herbert. "Beyond One-Dimensional Man." In *Towards a Critical Theory of Society: Collected Papers of Herbert Marcuse, Volume Two*, edited by Douglas Kellner, 107–120. London: Routledge, 2001.

Marcuse, Herbert. "The Concept of Essence." In *Negations*, 31–64.

Marcuse, Herbert. "Contributions to a Phenomenology of Historical Materialism." *Telos* 4 (Fall 1969): 3–34.

Marcuse, Herbert. *Counterrevolution and Revolt*. Boston: Beacon Press, 1972.

Marcuse, Herbert. "Dear Angela." In *The New Left and the 1960s: Collected Papers of Herbert Marcuse, Volume Three*, edited by Douglas Kellner, 49. London: Routledge, 2005.

Marcuse, Herbert. "Ecology and the Critique of Modern Society." In *Capitalism, Nature, Socialism: A Journal of Socialist Ecology* 3, no. 3 (1992): 29–38.

Marcuse, Herbert. "The End of Utopia." In *Five Lectures*, 62–82.

Marcuse, Herbert. *Eros and Civilization: A Philosophical Inquiry into Freud*. Boston: Beacon Press, [1955] 1966.

Marcuse, Herbert. *An Essay on Liberation*. Boston: Beacon Press, 1969.

Marcuse, Herbert. "Failure of the New Left?" *New German Critique*, no. 18 (Autumn 1979): 3–11.

Marcuse, Herbert. *Five Lectures: Psychoanalysis, Politics, and Utopia*. Translated by Jeremy J. Shapiro and Shierry M. Weber. Boston: Beacon Press, 1970.

Marcuse, Herbert. "The Foundation of Historical Materialism" (1932). In *Studies in Critical Philosophy*, translated by Joris de Bres, 1–48. Boston: Beacon Press, 1972.

Marcuse, Herbert. "Freedom and Freud's Theory of Instincts." In *Five Lectures*, 1–27.

Marcuse, Herbert. *Hegel's Ontology and the Theory of Historicity*. Translated by Seyla Benhabib. Cambridge, MA: MIT Press, [1932] 1987.

Marcuse, Herbert. "The History of Dialectics." In *Marxism, Revolution and Utopia*, 132–152.

Marcuse, Herbert. "Karl Popper and the Problem of Historical Laws" (1959). In *Studies in Critical Philosophy*, translated by Joris de Bres, 191–208. Boston: Beacon Press, 1972.

Marcuse, Herbert. "Letters to the Chicago Surrealists (March 6, 1973)." In *Arsenal: Surrealist Subversion* 4 (1989): 43–44.

Marcuse, Herbert. "Liberation from the Affluent Society." In *The Dialectics of Liberation*, edited by David Cooper, 175–192. Harmondsworth/Baltimore: Penguin, 1968.

Marcuse, Herbert. "Marxism and Feminism." *Women's Studies* 2 (1974): 279–288.

Marcuse, Herbert. *Marxism, Revolution and Utopia: Collected Papers of Herbert Marcuse, Volume Six*. Edited by Douglas Kellner and Clayton Pierce. London: Routledge, 2014.

Marcuse, Herbert. "Nature and Revolution." In *The Essential Marcuse*, edited by Andrew Feenberg and William Leiss, 233–247. Boston: Beacon Press, 2007.

Marcuse, Herbert. *Negations: Essays in Critical Theory*. Translated by Jeremy J. Shapiro. London: MayFlyBooks, 2009.

Marcuse, Herbert. "On Concrete Philosophy." In *Heideggerian Marxism*, edited by Richard Wolin and John Abromeit, 34–52. Lincoln: University of Nebraska Press, 2005.

Marcuse, Herbert. "On the Problem of the Dialectic." *Telos*, no. 29 (March 20, 1976): 12–39.

Marcuse, Herbert. *One-Dimensional Man*. Boston: Beacon Press, 1964.

Marcuse, Herbert. "Problem of Violence and the Radical Opposition." In *Five Lectures*, 83–108.

Marcuse, Herbert. "Repressive Tolerance" (1965). In Wolff, Moore, and Marcuse, *A Critique of Pure Tolerance*, 95–137.

Marcuse, Herbert. "Sartre's Existentialism." In *Studies in Critical Philosophy*, translated by Joris de Bres, 157–190. Boston: Beacon Press, 1972.

Marcuse, Herbert. "Socialism in the Developed Countries" (1965). In *Marxism, Revolution and Utopia*, 169–179.

Marcuse, Herbert. "Some Remarks on Aragon: Art in Politics in the Totalitarian Era." In *Technology, War and Fascism*, 199–214.

Marcuse, Herbert. "Some Social Implications of Modern Technology." In *Technology, War and Fascism*, 39–66.

Marcuse, Herbert. *Soviet Marxism: A Critical Analysis*. New York: Vintage Books, 1961.

Marcuse, Herbert. *Technology, War and Fascism: Collected Papers of Herbert Marcuse, Volume 1*. Edited by Douglas Kellner. London: Routledge, 1998.

Marcuse, Herbert, and Martin Heidegger. "An Exchange of Letters." In *The Heidegger Controversy: A Critical Reader*, edited by Richard Wolin, 152–164. Cambridge, MA: MIT Press, 1993.

Marcuse, Herbert, and Karl Popper. *Revolution or Reform? A Confrontation*. Chicago: New University Press, 1976.

Marinetti, F. T., Emilio Settimelli, and Bruno Corra, "The Futurist Synthetic Theatre." In *Futurism: An Anthology*, edited by Lawrence Rainey, Christine Poggi, and Laura Wittman, 204–208. New Haven, CT: Yale University Press, 2009.

Marx, Karl. *Capital: A Critique of Political Economy. Volume I: The Process of Capitalist Production*. Translated by Samuel Moore and Edward Aveling. Moscow: Progress Publishers, 1887.

Marx, Karl. *Critique of the Gotha Programme*. In *Karl Marx, Selected Writings*, 610–616.

Marx, Karl. *Economic and Philosophic Manuscripts of 1844*. Translated by Martin Milligan. Mineola, NY: Dover Publications, Inc., 2007.

Marx, Karl. *Grundrisse: Foundations of the Critique of Political Economy*. Translated by Martin Nicolaus. London: Penguin, 1973.

Marx, Karl. *Karl Marx: Selected Writings*, edited by David McLellan. Oxford: Oxford University Press, 1977.

Marx, Karl. "Letter from Marx to Arnold Ruge, September 1843." Marx & Engels Internet Archive. https://www.marxists.org/archive/marx/works/1843/letters/43_09-alt.htm.

Marx, Karl. "Outline of a Report on the Irish Question to the Communist Educational Association of German Workers in London." In *Marx and Engels on Ireland and the Irish Question*, 126–139. Moscow: Progress Publishers, 1971.

Marx, Karl. "Preface to *Capital*." In *Karl Marx: Selected Writings*, 452–458.

Marx, Karl. "Theses on Feuerbach." In *Karl Marx: Selected Writings*, 171–174.

Mattick, Paul. *Critique of Marcuse: One-Dimensional Man in Class Society.* London: The Merlin Press, 1972.

Mattick, Paul. "Spontaneity and Organisation" (1949). Marxist Internet Archive. https://www.marxists.org/archive/mattick-paul/1949/spontaneity.htm.

McEvilley, Thomas. *The Triumph of Anti-Art: Conceptual and Performance Art in the Formation of Post-Modernism.* Kingston, NY: McPherson & Company, 2005.

McKittrick, Katherine. *Demonic Grounds.* Minneapolis: University of Minnesota Press, 2006.

McMillan, John and Paul Buhle, eds. *The New Left Revisited.* Philadelphia: Temple University Press, 2003.

Ménil, René. "1978 Introduction to *Légitime défense.*" In Richardson, *Refusal of the Shadow*, 37–40.

Ménil, René. *Tracées: Identité, négritude, esthétiques aux Antilles.* Paris: Éditions Robert Laffont, 1981.

Ménil, René. "For a Critical Reading of *Tropiques.*" In Richardson, *Refusal of the Shadow*, 69–78.

Menke, Christoph. *Force: A Fundamental Concept of Aesthetic Anthropology.* Translated by Gerrit Jackson. New York: Fordham University Press, 2012.

Menke, Christoph. *The Sovereignty of Art.* Translated by Neil Solomon. Cambridge, MA: MIT Press, [1988] 1998.

Meyer, James. *Minimalism: Art and Polemics in the Sixties.* New Haven, CT: Yale University Press, 2001.

Meyer, Ursula. *Conceptual Art.* New York: E. P. Dutton & Co., 1972.

Meyer, Ursula. "Eruption of Anti-Art." In Battcock, *Idea Art*, 116–133.

Miller, Christopher L. "The (Revised) Birth of Negritude and 'the Immanent Negro' in 1935." *PMLA* 125 (May 2010): 743–749.

Miller, James. *Democracy in the Streets: From Port Huron to the Siege of Chicago.* Cambridge, MA: Harvard University Press, 1994.

Mirowski, Philip, and Dieter Plehwe, eds. *The Road from Mont Pèlerin: The Making of the Neoliberal Thought Collective.* Cambridge, MA: Harvard University Press, 2009.

Misak, Cheryl. *The American Pragmatists*. Oxford: Oxford University Press, 2013.

Moore, Alan W. *Art Gangs: Protest & Counterculture in New York City*. New York: Autonomedia, 2011.

Moore, Duston. "Whitehead and Marcuse: The Great Refusal, Universals and Rational Critical Theories." *Journal of Classical Sociology* 7 (2007): 109–126.

Morea, Ben, and Ron Hahne. "Black Mask, No. 1—November 1966." In *Black Mask & Up Against the Wall Motherfucker: The Incomplete Works of Ron Hahne, Ben Morea, and the Black Mask Group*, 4–10. New York: PM Press, 2011.

Moten, Fred. *In the Break: The Aesthetics of the Black Radical Tradition*. Minneapolis: University of Minnesota Press, 2003.

Mukařovský, Jan. "On the Problem of Functions in Architecture." In *Structure, Sign, and Function. Selected Essays by Jan Mukařovský*, translated and edited by John Burbank and Peter Steiner, 236–250. New Haven, CT: Yale University Press, 1978.

Mumford, Lewis. *Art and Technics*. New York: Columbia University Press, 1952.

Nadeau, Maurice. *The History of Surrealism*. Translated by Richard Howard. New York: Collier Books, 1965.

Nancy, Jean-Luc. "Riposte by Jean-Luc Nancy to Roberto Esposito: 28/02/2020." *European Journal of Psychoanalysis*. https://www.journal-psychoanalysis.eu/on-pandemics-nancy-esposito-nancy.

Nash, Gary B. "The Social Development of Colonial America." In *Colonial British America: Essays in the New History of the Early Modern Era*, edited by Jack P. Greene and J. R. Pole, 233–261. Baltimore, MD: Johns Hopkins University Press, 1984.

Negri, Antonio. "Metamorphoses: Art and Immaterial Labour." In *Art & Multitude*, translated by Ed Emery, 101–122. Cambridge, UK: Polity, [2009] 2011.

Neumann, Osha. *Up Against the Wall Motherf**cker: A Memoir of the '60s, with Notes for Next Time*. New York: Seven Stories Press, 2008.

Nielsen, Cynthia R. "Frantz Fanon and the Négritude Movement: How Strategic Essentialism Subverts Manichean Binaries." *Callaloo* 36, no. 2 (Spring 2013): 342–352.

Nishitani, Keiji. "Ontology and Utterance." *Philosophy East and West* 31, no. 1 (January 1981): 29–43.

Nkrumah, Kwame. *Neo-Colonialism, the Last Stage of Imperialism*. London: Thomas Nelson & Sons, Ltd., 1965.

Noble, Safiya Umoja. *Algorithms of Oppression: How Search Engines Reinforce Racism*. New York: NYU Press, 2018.

Novak, David. *Japanoise: Music at the Edge of Circulation*. Durham, NC: Duke University Press, 2013.

Nunes, Rodrigo. *Neither Vertical nor Horizontal: A Theory of Political Organization*. London: Verso, 2021.

O'Doherty, Brian. *Inside the White Cube: The Ideology of the Gallery Space*. San Francisco: Lapis Press, 1976.

Oren, Michel. "Anti-Art as the End of Cultural History." *Performing Arts Journal* 15, no. 2 (May 1993): 1–30.

Owens, Craig. "The Allegorical Impulse: Toward a Theory of Postmodernism." *October* 12 (Spring 1980): 67–86.

Painter, Nell Irvin. *The History of White People*. New York: W. W. Norton & Company, 2010.

Parsons, Talcott. "The Life and Work of Emile Durkheim." In Emile Durkheim, *Sociology and Philosophy*, xliii–lxx. New York: Free Press, 1974.

Pater, Walter. "The School of Giorgione." In *The Renaissance: Studies in Art and Poetry*, edited by Donald L. Hill, 102–122. Berkeley, CA: University of California Press, 1980.

Peirce, Charles Sanders. *The Collected Papers of Charles Sanders Peirce: Volume 1: Principles of Philosophy*. Edited by Charles Hartshorne and Paul Weiss. Cambridge: Harvard University Press, 1931.

Peltomäki, Kirsi. *Situation Aesthetics: The Work of Michael Asher*. Cambridge, MA: MIT Press, 2010.

Peters, F. E. *Greek Philosophical Terms: A Historical Lexicon*. New York: NYU Press, 1967.

Phelan, Shane. "Interpretation & Domination: Adorno and the Habermas-Lyotard Debate." *Polity* 25, no. 4 (Summer 1993): 597–616.

Piekut, Benjamin. *Experimentalism Otherwise: The New York Avant-Garde and Its Limits*. Berkeley: University of California Press, 2011.

Pincus-Witten, Robert. *Postminimalism*. New York: Out of London Press, Inc., 1977.

Planck, Max. *Treatise on Thermodynamics*. Third English edition. Translated by A. Ogg. London: Longmans, Green & Co., 1903.

Plato. *Phaedo*, Translated by R. S. Buck. London: Routledge, 2001.

Plato. *Sophist*. Translated by Seth Benardete. Chicago: University of Chicago Press, 1986.

Podro, Michael. *The Manifold of Perception*. Oxford: Clarendon Press, 1972.

Popper, Karl. "Addendum 1974: The Frankfurt School." In *The Myth of the Framework*, edited by M. A. Notturno, 78–81. London: Routledge, 1994.

Popper, Karl. *The Open Society and Its Enemies: The High Tide of Prophecy: Hegel, Marx, and The Aftermath, Volume 2*. Princeton, NJ: Princeton University Press, 1962.

Rancière, Jacques. "The Aesthetic Revolution and Its Outcomes: Emplotments of Autonomy and Heteronomy." *New Left Review* 14 (2002): 133–151.

Rancière, Jacques. *The Politics of Aesthetics: The Distribution of the Sensible*. Translated by Gabriel Rockhill. London: Continuum, 2004.

Rapoport, Anatol. *Operational Philosophy: Integrating Knowledge and Action*. San Francisco: International Society for General Semantics, [1953] 1969.

Raunig, Gerald, and Gene Ray, eds. *Art and Contemporary Critical Practice: Reinventing Institutional Critique*. London: Mayfly, 2009.

Rebentisch, Juliane. *Aesthetics of Installation Art*. Berlin: Sternberg Press, [2003] 2012.

Rebentisch, Juliane. "Realism Today." In *Thinking—Resisting—Reading the Political*, translated by Gerrit Jackson and Stephen Packard, 245–261. Chicago: University of Chicago Press, [2010] 2013.

Reinhardt, Ad. "Art-as-Art." In *Art-as-Art: The Selected Writings of Ad Reinhardt*, edited by Barbara Rose, 53–56. New York: Viking Press, 1975.

Reinhardt, Ad. "Art vs. History." *Art News* 64, no. 19 (January 1966): 19–21.

Reiss, Hans. "The 'Naturalization' of the Terms 'Ästhetik' in Eighteenth-Century German: Alexander Gottlieb Baumgarten and His Impact." *The Modern Language Review* 89, no. 3 (July 1994): 645–658.

Reitz, Charles. *Art, Alienation, and the Humanities: A Critical Engagement with Herbert Marcuse.* Albany: State University of New York Press, 2000.

Reitz, Charles. *Celebrating Herbert Marcuse's One-Dimensional Man: Deprovincialization and the Recovery of Philosophy.* Self-published, 2014.

Reitz, Charles. "Liberating the Critical in Critical Theory: Transcending Marcuse on Alienation, Art and the Humanities." Paper presented at the Twentieth World Congress of Philosophy. Boston, Massachusetts, August 1998.

Richardson, Joan. *Pragmatism and American Experience: An Introduction.* Cambridge, UK: Cambridge University Press, 2014.

Richardson, Michael, ed. *Refusal of the Shadow: Surrealism and the Caribbean.* London: Verso, 1996.

Richter, Gerhard. "Aesthetic Theory and Nonpropositional Truth Content in Adorno." *New German Critique*, no. 97, Adorno and Ethics (Winter 2006): 119–135.

Richter, Hans. *Dada: Art and Anti-Art.* New York: McGraw-Hill, 1965.

Rickert, John. "The Fromm-Marcuse Debate Revisited." *Theory and Society* 15, no. 3 (May 1986): 351–400.

Roazen, Paul. *Freud and His Followers.* New York: De Capo Press, 1992.

Roberts, John. *The Intangibilities of Form: Skill and Deskilling after the Readymade.* London: Verso, 2007.

Robinson, Cedric. J. *Black Marxism: The Making of the Black Radical Tradition.* Chapel Hill: University of North Carolina Press, [1983] 2000.

Rose, Margaret A. *Marx's Lost Aesthetic: Karl Marx and the Visual Arts.* Cambridge, UK: Cambridge University Press, 1984.

Rosemont, Franklin, Penelope Rosement, and Paul Garon, eds. *The Forecast Is Hot! Tracts & Other Collective Declarations of the Surrealist Movement in the United States: 1966–1976.* Chicago: Black Swan Press, 1997.

Rosen, Charles. *Arnold Schoenberg.* Chicago: University of Chicago Press, 1975.

Rosenberg, Harold. *The Anxious Object.* New York: Horizon Press, 1964.

Rosenberg, Harold. "On the De-Definition of Art." In *The De-Definition of Art*, 11–16. New York: Horizon Press, 1972.

Rosenberg, Harold. "Set Out for Clayton!" In *The De-Definition of Art*, 243–249.

Ross, Kristin. *May '68 and Its Afterlives*. Chicago: University of Chicago Press, 2002.

Said, Edward W. "The Dictatorship of Truth: An Interview with Gillo Pontecorvo." *Cinéaste* 25, no. 2 (2000): 24–25.

Said, Edward W. *Orientalism*. New York: Vintage Books, 1994.

Sandywell, Barry. *Presocratic Reflexivity: The Construction of Philosophical Discourse c. 600–450 B.C.* London: Routledge, 1996.

Sartre, Jean-Paul. *What Is Literature?* Translated by Bernard Frechtman. New York: Washington Square Press, Inc., [1947] 1966.

Schiller, Friedrich. "Kallias or Concerning Beauty: Letters to Gottfried Körner." In *Classic and Romantic German Aesthetics*, edited by J. M. Bernstein, 145–184. Cambridge, UK: Cambridge University Press, 2003.

Schiller, Friedrich. *On the Aesthetic Education of Man*. Translated and introduction by Reginald Snell. New Haven, CT: Yale University Press, 1954.

Schirmacher, Wolfgang, ed. *German 20th Century Philosophy: The Frankfurt School*. New York: Continuum, 2000.

Schlesinger, Rudolf. *Marx: His Time and Ours*. London: Routledge, [1950] 2002.

Scott, David. "The Re-enchantment of Humanism: An Interview with Sylvia Wynter." *Small Axe*, no. 8 (2000): 119–207.

Seale, Bobby. *Seize the Time: The Story of the Black Panther Party*. New York: Random House, 1970.

Seifermann, Ellen, and Beat Wismer. *Some Places to Which We Can Come: Robert Barry Works 1963 to 1975*. Bielefeld, Germany: Kerber Verlag, 2003.

Seigworth, Gregory J. and Melissa Gregg, "An Inventory of Shimmers." In Gregg and Seigworth, *The Affect Theory Reader*, 1–28.

Shaviro, Steven. *The Universe of Things: On Speculative Realism*. Minneapolis: University of Minnesota Press, 2014.

Shklovsky, Viktor. "Art as Technique." In *Modern Criticism and Theory: A Reader*, edited by David Lodge, 15–30. London: Longman, 1988.

Siegelaub, Seth. *"Better Read Than Dead": Writings and Interviews, 1964–2013*. London: Koenig Books Ltd., 2020.

Siegelaub, Seth. "Preface: Working Notes on Social Relations in Communication and Culture." In *Communication and Class Struggle: 2. Liberation and Socialism*, 11–16. New York: International General, 1983.

Siegelaub, Seth. *Untitled (Xerox Book)*. New York: John W. Wendler, 1968.

Siegelaub, Seth, and Joseph Kosuth. "Seth Siegelaub and Joseph Kosuth Reply to Benjamin Buchloh on Conceptual Art." *October* 57 (Summer 1991): 152–157.

Sim, Stuart. *Post-Marxism: An Intellectual History*. New York: Routledge, 2013.

Sim, Stuart, ed. *Post-Marxism: A Reader*. Edinburgh: Edinburgh University Press, 1998.

Simon, Joshua. *Neomaterialism*. Berlin: Sternberg Press, 2013.

Singer, Peter. *The Expanding Circle: Ethics, Evolution and Moral Progress*. Princeton, NJ: Princeton University Press, 1981.

Sithole, Tendayi. *The Black Register*. Cambridge: Polity Press, 2020.

Smethurst, James Edward. *The Black Arts Movement: Literary Nationalism in the 1960s and 1970s*. Chapel Hill: University of North Carolina Press, 2005.

Smith, Iris. "Brecht and the Mothers of Epic Theater." *Theatre Journal* 43, no. 4 (December 1991): 491–505.

Smith, Matthew J. "VIVE 1804!: The Haitian Revolution and the Revolutionary Generation of 1946." *Caribbean Quarterly* 50, no. 4 (December 2004): 25–41.

Smith, Owen F. *Fluxus: The History of an Attitude*. San Diego: San Diego State University Press, 1998.

Snell, Reginald. "Introduction." *On the Aesthetic Education of Man*. Mineola, NY: Dover, 2004, 1–20.

Spencer, Herbert. *The Study of Sociology*. New York: D. Appleton & Co., 1874.

Srnicek, Nick. *Platform Capitalism*. Cambridge, UK: Polity Press, 2017.

Steiner, Barbara. "Corruption, Corruptibility and Complicity." In *Meaning Liam Gillick*, edited by Monika Szewczyk, 71–90. Cambridge, MA: MIT Press, 2009.

Stephens, Julie. *Anti-Disciplinary Protest: Sixties Radicalism and Postmodernism*. Cambridge, UK: Cambridge University Press, 1998.

Strickland, Edward. *Minimalism: Origins*. Bloomington: Indiana University Press, 1993.

Surrealist Group in Paris. "Murderous Humanitarianism." In *Negro: An Anthology*, edited by Nancy Cunard, 352. Translated by Samuel Beckett. London: Bloomsbury, [1934] 1996.

Szeemann, Harald. *Live in Your Head. When Attitudes Become Form: Works, Processes, Concepts, Situations, Information*. Bern: Kunsthalle Bern, 1969.

Taggart, Geoff. "Whitehead and Marcuse: Teaching the 'Art of Life.'" *Process Papers* 8 (2004): 53–67.

Therborn, Göran. *From Marxism to Post-Marxism?* London: Verso, 2008.

Todorov, Tzvetan. *Theories of the Symbol*. Ithaca, NY: Cornell University Press, 1984.

Touraine, Alain. *Beyond Neoliberalism*. Translated by David Macey. Cambridge, UK: Polity, [1998] 2001.

Tytell, John. *The Living Theatre: Art, Exile, and Outrage*. New York: Grove Press, 1995.

Ursprung, Philip. *Allan Kaprow, Robert Smithson, and the Limits to Art*. Translated by Fiona Elliot. Berkeley: University of California Press, 2013.

Wall, John. "Phronesis, Poetics and Moral Creativity." *Ethical Theory and Moral Practice* 6, no. 3 (September 2003): 317–341.

Weber, Max. *The Protestant Ethic and the Spirit of Capitalism*. Translated by Peter Baehr and Gordon C. Wells. New York, Penguin, [1905] 2002.

Weiner, Lawrence. "A Conversation with Robert C. Morgan." In *Having Been Said*, 100–104.

Weiner, Lawrence. *Having Been Said: Writings and Interviews of Lawrence Weiner, 1968–2003*. Edited by Gerti Fietzek and Gregor Stemmrich. Ostfildern-Ruit, Germany: Hatje Cantz Verlag, 2004.

Weiner, Lawrence. "Design Matters Live with Lawrence Weiner." Filmed interview with Debbie Millman at Weiner's New York studio. Directed and coproduced by Hillman Curtis, 2008.

Weiner, Lawrence. "Interview by Patricia Norvell (June 3, 1969)." In *Recording Conceptual Art*, edited by Alexander Alberro and Patricia Norvell, 101–111. Berkeley and Los Angeles: University of California Press, 2001.

Wellmer, Albrecht. "The Death of the Sirens and the Origin of the Work of Art." *New German Critique* 81, Dialectic of Enlightenment (Autumn 2000): 15–19.

Wellmer, Albrecht. *The Persistence of Memory*. Cambridge, MA: MIT Press, 1991.

Wellmer, Albrecht. "Truth, Semblance, Reconciliation: Adorno's Aesthetic Redemption of Modernity." *Telos* 17, no. 62 (1984): 89–115.

Whitehead, Alfred North. *Adventures in Ideas*. London: Cambridge University Press, 1933.

Whitehead, Alfred North. *Process and Reality: An Essay in Cosmology*. New York: The Free Press, [1929] 1978.

Whitehead, Alfred North. *Science and the Modern World*. Cambridge, UK: Cambridge University Press, 1929.

Willett, John, trans. *Brecht on Theatre*. By Bertolt Brecht. London: Methuen, 1986.

Wolin, Richard. *Heidegger's Children: Hannah Arendt, Karl Löwith, Hans Jonas, and Herbert Marcuse*. Princeton, NJ: Princeton University Press, 2001.

Wolin, Richard, and John Abromeit, eds. *Heideggerian Marxism*. Lincoln, Nebraska: University of Nebraska Press, 2005.

Wolff, Robert Paul, Barrington Moore Jr., and Herbert Marcuse. *A Critique of Pure Tolerance* Boston: Beacon Press, [1965] 1969.

Wörner, Karl H. "Stockhausen's Notes on the Works." In *Stockhausen: Life and Work*, translated and edited by Bill Hopkins, 30–77. Berkeley, CA: University of California Press, 1973.

Wurzelbacher, Karli. *Odyssey: Jack Whitten Sculpture, 1963–2017*. Baltimore, MD: Baltimore Museum of Art; New York: Gregory R. Miller and Co., 2018.

Wynter, Sylvia. "1492: A New World View." In *Race, Discourse, and the Origin of the Americas*, edited by Vera Lawrence Hyatt and Rex Nettleford, 5–57. Washington, DC: Smithsonian Institution Press, 1995.

Wynter, Sylvia. "Towards the Sociogenic Principle: Fanon, Identity, the Puzzle of Conscious Experience, and What It Is Like to Be 'Black.'" In *National Identity and Sociopolitical Change: Latin America Between Marginizalization and Integration*, edited by Mercedes Durán-Cogan and Antonio Gómez-Moriana, 30–36. Minneapolis: University of Minnesota Press, 1999.

Wynter, Sylvia, and Katherine McKittrick. "Unparallelled Catastrophe for our Species? Or, to Give Humanness a Different Future: Conversations." In *Sylvia Wynter: On Being Human as Praxis*, edited by Katherine McKittrick, 9–89. Durham, NC: Duke University Press, 2015.

Index